MURDER OR MUTINY

MURDER OR MUTINY

Mystery, Piracy and Adventure in the Spice Islands

PAMELA STEPHENSON

Foreword by Billy Connolly

WEIDENFELD & NICOLSON

CONTENTS

It is, it is, a glorious thing
To be a pirate king

Pirates of Penzance, W. S. Gilbert and Sir Arthur Sullivan

To Bill-Bill
The Partick Pirate
Thank you

FOREWORD

Some time ago I was idly reading a book review in a newspaper. I don't remember much about the book, but the reviewer had used a term to describe the urgency of the text: 'a real page-turner,' he wrote. At the time, I thought it was a particularly stupid thing to say about the book. How else are you supposed to read it but by turning the pages? It is almost on a par with the galactically inane 'thumping good read' which has always conjured up to me a gruff type of idiot punching a book while making grunting noises.

Recently I've been re-thinking my position, particularly over the former. I've come to think that my role, when it comes to Pamela's writings, is that of a page turner, a bit like the person who stands at the elbow of the man who is performing one of Beethoven's sonatas and dutifully whips over the manuscript mid-bar. Like him, I've become a sort of creative enabler, agreeing to her arcane demands in the hope of a pleasant outcome for us both. In the case of this book – and the last one, come to think of it – I am reminded of Masefield's lines:

> *I must go down to the sea again, to the lonely sea in the sky*
> *And all I ask is a tall ship, and a star to steer her by…*

I can't help but see myself as that same, constant, guiding light. If there is a rank in the Navy of Maritime and Literary Enabler, I would like to apply for the post. I'd do my best, though, to keep my mind off boys standing on burning decks.

Billy Connolly

INTRODUCTION

APRIL 29, BALI

Some people have their lives well sorted. You see them everywhere: satisfied, complacent folks sitting on porches, popping into butchers' shops or mowing the lawn. They know where they come from, they know where they're going; they're punctual, predictable, and confident in their family history.

Not me. I'm the restless, shifting type, the one whose eyes are always following the horizon, the one on whom you can never fully depend. People like me know what it's like trying to reconstitute their universe once a chink has appeared; that a crack in a once solid body of self-knowledge can be so disturbing that they might risk everything to patch it up.

A new little hole appeared in my world last summer. At the time it wasn't that shocking. And when I think about it, there have been other rips and fractures in my background that I managed to ignore for many years. Like Hira. Hira Moewaka, my great-grandmother. No one ever told me, until I was in my twenties, that she was a New Zealand Maori. When I learned about her, clandestinely, from a cousin, I thought, "That's nice. Exotic, really, for a fair-skinned blonde like me." It wasn't until a year or two later that the question came screaming through: "Why the hell was that kept a secret?"

But last summer, late one evening, I happened to be walking into a bar, already two gin and tonics closer to feeling no pain at all, when a sun-beaten Englishwoman I'd never met before punctured my existence with one throaty statement. She has since passed away, poor Trudy, but her single mystifying sentence launched me and my sailboat, along with a sixteen-strong band of fellow voyagers, into a crazy expedition that began on Australia's Queensland coast and has yet to end only God knows where.

Upon hitting the high seas we were immediately chased across the Gulf of Carpentaria by Hurricanes Larry, Kate, Glenda, Uncle Tom Cobley and all. We have so far managed to survive at least nine liquid beasts: the Arafura Sea, the Sawu Sea, the Banda Sea, the Ceram Sea, the Malaku Sea and the Makassar Straits, the Indian Ocean, the Java Sea, and the Badung ('naughty') Straits of Bali … and there's worse ahead.

I both thank and curse Trudy at every treacherous step. God rest her, I bet she sleeps more peacefully than my ancestor Salty Sam, whose violent and mysterious demise has inspired our quest. I swear on my own confused life, I will discover the truth; I will put him, and a part of me, to rest.

So here I am in Benoa Harbour, Bali, preparing to depart for Surabaya; to recreate Salty Sam's final voyage eastwards to the Straits of Alas. We face all kinds of danger, from both the elements and humankind. My crew is unsettled, and pirates lurk… However, I'm in no mind to let my great-great-grandfather's tragic history repeat itself.

But let me take you back a few months. To just before last Christmas, when I was still dreaming up what my husband called 'a nutter's nautical mystery tour'.

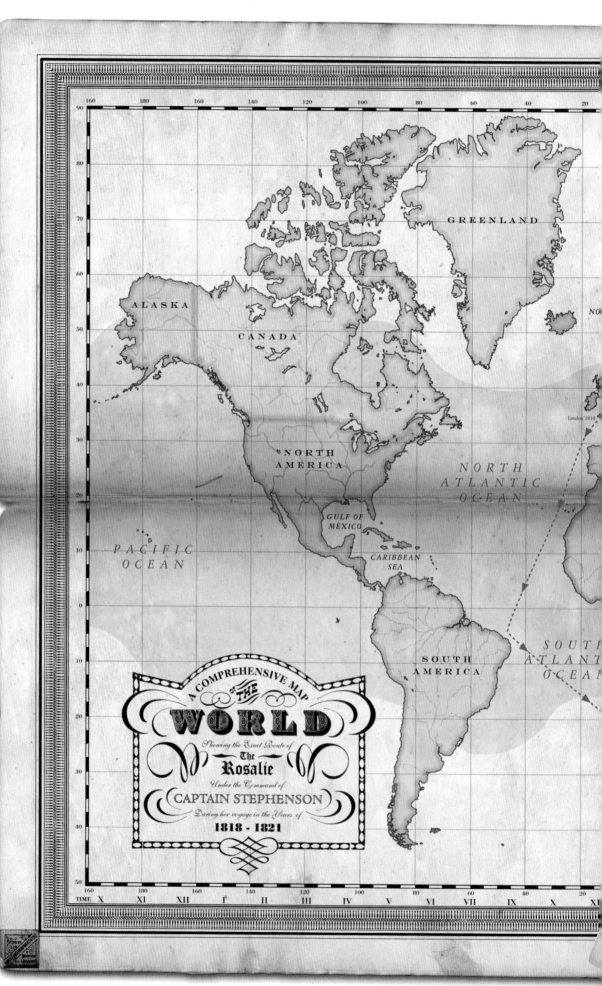

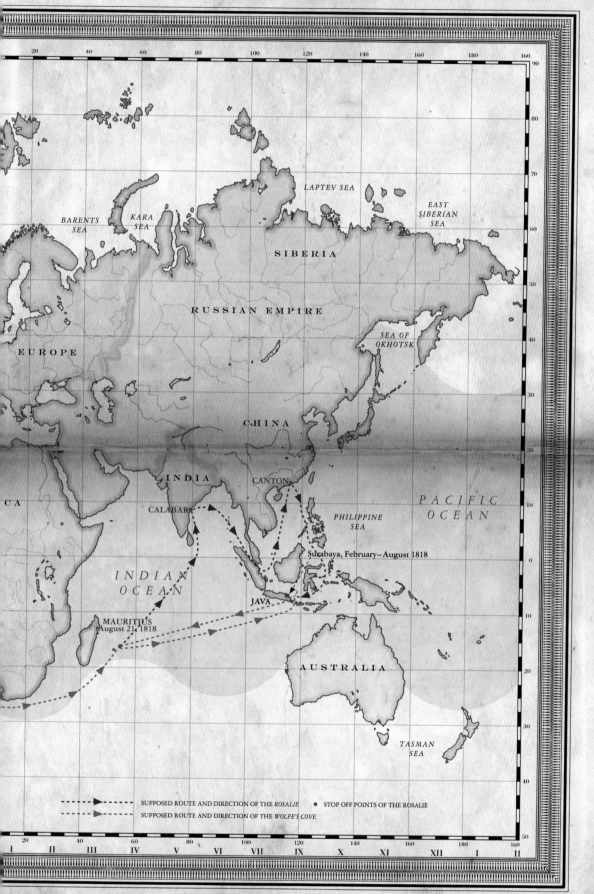

SUPPOSED ROUTE AND DIRECTION OF THE *ROSALIE*   • STOP OFF POINTS OF THE ROSALIE

SUPPOSED ROUTE AND DIRECTION OF THE *WOLFE'S COVE*

Engraved by Mr W. SALAD esq.

PHILIPPINE

SOUTH CHINA
SEA

SULU
SEA

BRUNEI   SABAH

CELEBES SEA

SARAWAK

MANADO
AMARANG
TERNATE

SINDA
ISLANDS

MOLUCCA
SEA

BORNEO

CELEBES

BANDA
SEA

MAKASSAR

JAVA

FLORES SEA

INDIAN OCEAN

TIMOR

KUPANG

TIMOR
SEA

A MAP OF
INDONESIA
SHOWING THE ROUTE OF
THE **TAKAPUNA**
ON HER 2006 VOYAGE

- - - ▶ ROUTE AND DIRECTION OF TAKAPUNA
○ STOP OFF POINT OF TAKAPUNA

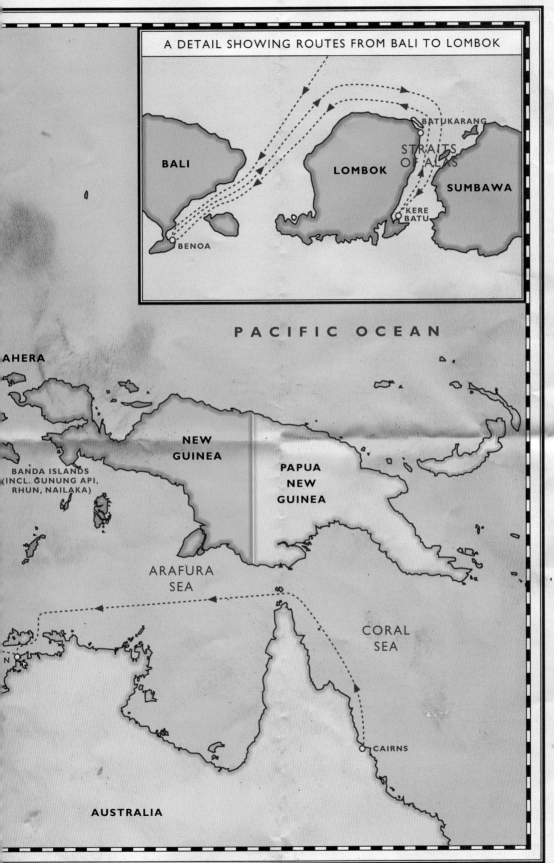

A DETAIL SHOWING ROUTES FROM BALI TO LOMBOK

BALI

LOMBOK

SUMBAWA

STRAITS OF ALAS

BATUKARANG

KERE BATU

BENOA

PACIFIC OCEAN

AHERA

NEW GUINEA

PAPUA NEW GUINEA

BANDA ISLANDS
(INCL. GUNUNG API,
RHUN, NAILAKA)

ARAFURA SEA

CORAL SEA

N

CAIRNS

AUSTRALIA

printed by W.SALAD & Sons

The line of descent from Salty Sam to Pamela: five generations of Stephensons

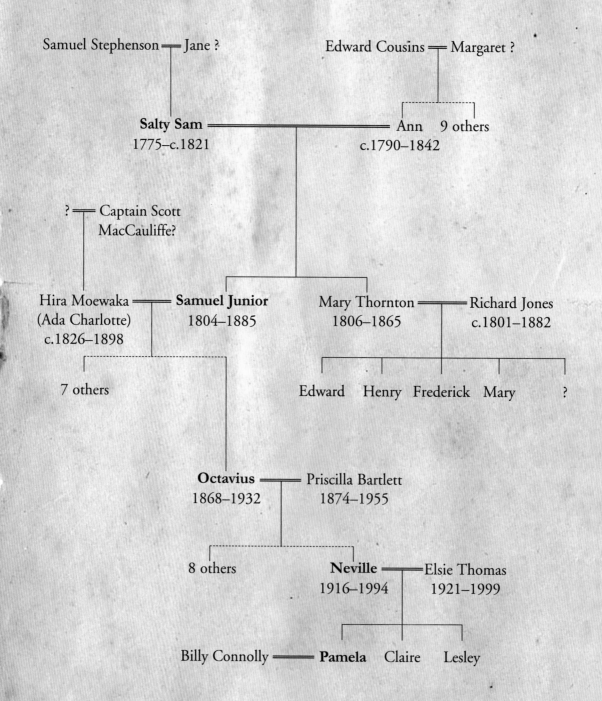

Samuel Stephenson ═ Jane ?

Edward Cousins ═ Margaret ?

Salty Sam
1775–c.1821

Ann
c.1790–1842   9 others

? ═ Captain Scott
MacCauliffe?

Hira Moewaka   ═   **Samuel Junior**
(Ada Charlotte)   1804–1885
c.1826–1898

Mary Thornton ═ Richard Jones
1806–1865   c.1801–1882

7 others

Edward   Henry   Frederick   Mary   ?

Octavius ═══ Priscilla Bartlett
1868–1932   1874–1955

8 others

Neville ═══ Elsie Thomas
1916–1994   1921–1999

Billy Connolly ═══ **Pamela**   Claire   Lesley

Chapter **I** Voices From The Deep

5 MONTHS EARLIER

NOVEMBER 15, LONDON

The expedition taking me and my little band of fellow-adventurers across perilous waters was inspired by an ancient family riddle. It concerns my ancestor Samuel Stephenson – otherwise known as Salty Sam, an entrepreneurial master mariner from Rotherhithe, London. In 1821 he set off from Java aboard his trading ship, the *Rosalie*. His plan was presumably to trade along the old spice route in the Indonesian archipelago, a well-beaten but nevertheless hazardous sea trail established by the British and Dutch East India Trading Companies. But he never made it back.

Some of Sam's crew mutinied and seized control of the *Rosalie* with all its cargo. My great-great-grandfather was apparently thrown overboard and never seen again. After a sole survivor had returned to Java to tell the story, three years passed before Sam's only son – Samuel Junior – came of age and was able to set off for the Far East to try to recover the ship and assets. He failed, however; and still smarting from the loss of his inheritance, Samuel Jr eventually took passage for New Zealand. There he established a trading post at Russell in the Bay of Islands, married my great-grandmother Hira Moewaka and settled down to a harsh but ultimately rewarding life in the Colony.

All of the above I accepted as family history, until last summer, when I happened to be visiting the Maltese island of Gozo during *festa* time. I'd stopped by for a drink one evening at Rosina's Bar in the village of Sannat. From the shadowy depths of the smoky, cave-like salon, a complete stranger suddenly addressed me.

"It wasn't a mutiny!" she barked. I stopped dead and blinked in the candlelight at her intense, sun-touched face.

"One of my ancestors was aboard the *Rosalie*," she continued. The hairs on my neck became erect.

"I'm sorry … ?" I managed. But the Englishwoman was on a roll.

"They were pirated," she insisted. "In the Sunda Straits."

I fell into a seat beside her. "What makes you think that?"

She looked at me intently. "I inherited a tapestry of the ship."

Now, I had recently written a biography of my husband, Billy, in which I'd briefly mentioned the loss of the *Rosalie*, so it wasn't impossible that a stranger might recognize me and refer to it. But here I was, in the same bar, at the same time, with a woman bearing this two-hundred-year-old secret. I ask you, what are the chances of that? And if this woman's story was true, the veracity of my entire Stephenson family history was in question.

"Show me the tapestry," I challenged. We hurried down the street to her house, where this woman, whose name was Trudy Prior (née Adam), unveiled a faded, wooden-framed sampler dated 1861. It had been sewn in red, blue, yellow, brown and green thread on a beige background by Elizabeth Valentine Adam, a sixteen-year-old from the Scottish port of Stonehaven. The girl had depicted the *Rosalie* as a three-masted wooden trading ship lying in harbour and flanked by two Chinese junks. The ship's name was embroidered above (spelled Rosele), and below in large letters were the portentous words: 'HOMEWARD BOUND'.

"I believe that was wishful thinking," said Trudy. "She'd probably lost her grandfather in that pirate attack, and the family had suffered ever since."

Across the top was the sad little comment 'My Parents Dear Paid For This That

New threads from old – Trudy Prior's inherited 1861 sampler that, despite incorrect spelling of 'Rosalie', established her connection to Salty Sam.

I Have Got. When Friends are Gone, and Funds are Done, Learning is Still Most Excellent'. The sampler was decorated in fine, fancy stitching with baskets of English red and white roses, several birds, rabbits, dogs, and trees. There were other symbols that I could not interpret, and anyway, my head was spinning. From that moment I was caught up in a fascinating, two-centuries-old intrigue.

You see, this new chink in my universe is too big to be explained by forgetfulness, prejudice or some other human foible. If Trudy's story is true, there has been a sizable cover-up. Did Salty Sam die by Captain Hook or by onboard crook? Either way, my great-great-grandfather was the victim of a foul deed, in the days when no crime-scene investigator was going to leap into the fray with a DNA sample kit. It's as if Salty Sam had reached out to me over the years, from the bottom of the spice-tinged sea and, through Trudy, channelled his dead-man's wish: that I uncover the truth and lay him finally to rest. And why me? It's obvious. Because I'm the wild one. The one who two years ago set out to roam the seas. The one with the sailboat and the means to travel. The tenacious, do-or-die adventurer – just like Salty Sam himself.

Here's my plan: to trace Samuel Stephenson's voyage along the Spice Route, so that I can try to solve the mystery. Moreover, I'm drawn to know more about the character of my great-great-grandfather, along with the thrilling story of his time in history. What kind of man was he? Brave, reckless, or a total bastard? Was he pragmatist, poet, lout or lover? Eventually, don't we all long to understand our generational past, because it tells us more about who *we* are?

No matter what we encounter from now on, I hope at least to learn the truth about some aspects of Salty Sam's life, his struggles, successes and disappointments. And perhaps at the end of it all, I will have a plausible answer to the question: "Murder by pirates? Or mutiny?"

NOVEMBER 16

I woke early with my brain racing. Drinking Lapsang Souchong tea and languishing in a chic hotel bed in the dull winter light, it occurred to me that it's an absurd idea, launching an expedition into the pirate-infested Far Eastern waters to find out what happened to a man who's been dead two hundred years. "But I *am* absurd," I told myself. "My teenage children will vouch for that. And anyway there can be no logic to a striving of passion."

Urgently, questions went on presenting themselves: Was it piracy? Was it murder, or mutiny? Who survived? Did my great-great-grandfather ever set foot on land after being thrown overboard? Then again, was he thrown overboard? What happened to the *Rosalie* and her cargo? What happened to the rest of the crew?

By the time I had showered, dressed and inhaled a double espresso, my powers of critical thinking had kicked in. How shall I go about this? First I must gather as many documented facts as possible: archival information about the history and background of seafaring and trading in the 1820s. I began to make a list: British Library, Maritime Museum, National Archives. Also, shortly before he died, my father collaborated with my cousin Brett on a book about Salty Sam's son. Is there a copy of that at home in Scotland?

By teatime I'd figured it out. My husband and I are lucky enough to own a wonderful sailboat, the *Takapuna*, which is waiting in Australia for me, in Brisbane, already seaworthy and crewed up. I had planned to sail her to the Mediterranean for a spot of easy cruising – but that will have to wait; instead she must be fully prepared, with provisions, spare parts and the relevant nautical charts, ready to enter the tricky Java Sea.

The notorious waters of the Indonesian Archipelago are still known as one of the worst places in the world for pirate attacks. It would be prudent, therefore, to engage a security team, kit out the boat with protective devices, and provide piracy training for everyone on board. After searching for clues in the old Spice Islands (once the Moluccas, now Moluku), we will head for the Javan capital, Jakarta, formerly Batavia – and from there, anywhere our research leads us.

By bedtime I was even visualizing the *Takapuna*'s triumphant return to my great-great-grandfather's old stomping ground, the River Thames. Yes, by the time we reach Rotherhithe, then we should have some answers about the fate of Salty Sam.

NOVEMBER 18, CANDACRAIG, SCOTLAND

A bracing walk in the Scottish highlands prepared me for today's task. First, I located my father's booklet about Samuel Stephenson Jr. There's not much in it about Salty Sam, and of course my father had never heard of the piracy story, but at least it provides some dates, places and company names that I can follow up.

From my father's book:

> Captain Samuel Stephenson was a Master Mariner. In 1821 he sailed on a voyage from the island of Java in a ship called the *Rosalie*, going to the Molucca Islands and intending to return to Batavia [now Jakarta]. In the course of this voyage, a part of the crew rose up against the rest, killing several and taking possession of the ship and cargo, which were afterwards never recovered. One

of the crew succeeded in getting back to Batavia, where he gave the foregoing account. He furthermore related that "when confined below they heard a scuffle upon deck and a noise as if someone had been thrown overboard, which they believed to have been Captain Stephenson, as he was never afterwards seen or heard of". Unlike Captain Bligh who, in the case of the mutiny of the Bounty, was given a sporting chance by being cast off in an open boat, Captain Stephenson was apparently just thrown overboard. Whether he was first killed, or knocked senseless, or very much in possession of his faculties at the time, is anyone's guess.

When news of the 1821 mutiny reached England, there were some obvious difficulties for [his wife] Ann Stephenson and the two children, although they seem, at least initially, to have been well provided for financially. At the time, Samuel Jr was 17 years of age and Mary 15, and therefore unable for some years to take an active role in the legal complications that followed. Captain Samuel Stephenson had actually made a Will in England on December 23, 1815, and shortly after the news of his fate reached England, his executors ... applied to the Consistory Court of the Archbishop of Canterbury to have the Will proved... Power of Attorney was granted to the English Executors...

On behalf of the English Executors, Mr Henry Gardner then wrote to Miln, Haswell & Co., who were Captain Stephenson's agents in Batavia. The English Executors then learned, no doubt to their horror, that Captain Stephenson had made another Will, witnessed by seven people, in the offices of J. Jessen & Co., his agents in Surabaya, before finally leaving the island of Java. He furthermore gave Messrs Jessen & Co. Power of Attorney over his affairs as well as instructions. He apparently walked away from the Surabaya offices with the Will, according to Messrs Jessen & Co., and this Will was never found. Complications immediately arose, with English Law being pitted against Dutch Law, and various legal opinions being sought in England and Java.

Captain Samuel Stephenson was a well established ship-owner ... and at least for a number of years prior to his death he had been involved in the shipping trade between London, Java and the Isle de France [Mauritius]. Moreover, the *Rosalie* was owned by him and, after the mutiny in 1821, his agents in Batavia and Surabaya reported that they were between them holding a total of close to 80,000 Java florins of his money. No wonder the son, Samuel, who turned 21 on June 21, 1825, and became legally eligible for his share of the Estate, made tracks for Batavia. He was not looking for his father, who was widely presumed dead, but trying to get the frozen assets of the Estate released... However, he was not successful in expediting the release of assets. The Javan agents wanted security in the form of a Bond of Indemnity before they would be willing to remit funds to England. After all, there was no body,

A family-authored booklet about Salty Sam's son who, when denied a large part of his inheritance, ran off to New Zealand and became a pioneer merchant.

Samuel Stephenson

Pioneer Merchant of Russell
1 8 0 4 - 1 8 8 5

and they were concerned about what their position would be if Captain Stephenson were to turn up on their doorsteps one day. It seems that a very long period of time would need to elapse before the courts in Java would presume a person under these circumstances to be dead.

Good old Dad. So that confirmed what I had remembered from my childhood story – that Salty Sam was trading out of Batavia on the *Rosalie*, and had been

The first page of Salty Sam's British Will. Claims of a second Will sworn in Surabaya led to a legal row that was never resolved.

thrown overboard by mutineers, after which all hell broke loose over the question of 'Which Will?' and a huge sum of money he'd left with his shipping agents in Surabaya. Dad did not indicate whether the family had ever managed to get their hands on the money – which begs a few questions. Perhaps there were crooked agents who conspired to top Sam in order to keep the then enormous sum of 80,000 Java florins. And what about the supposed seven witnesses to a second will that was never found? Distinct smell of rotting fish.

My conspiracy theories are running amok. How, I'm thinking, does all this fit in with Trudy's piracy story? Not at all, I suppose – although if you survive a mutiny and want to show your face in Batavia, you're probably not going to try the old 'There was a mutiny on board, but it was nothing to do with me, mate!' No, with pirate attacks so common it would be smarter, and easy enough, to come up with something far less likely to get you hanged.

NOVEMBER 19

Today I concentrated on my family tree, all the way back to Salty Sam. Letters and documents in the Alexander Turnbull Library in Wellington, New Zealand, show that, in the early 1800s, the Stephenson family resided in Ipswich, then later moved to Rotherhithe. On September 13, 1803, at St Leonard's Church, Shoreditch, Salty Sam married twenty-three-year-old Ann Cousins, one of nine children of Edward and Margaret Cousins.

Being a sea captain who undertook long voyages, Salty Sam wasn't around enough to provide Ann with more than two children – Samuel Jr and Mary Thornton. But subsequent generations made up for that deficit, starting with Samuel Jr and his Maori wife Hira Moewaka. And Samuel begat Ted, Henry, Arthur, Carrie, Theodore, Fanny; then kept going. In fact, he begat fourteen children, who later did a great deal of begetting themselves, in a time when a nuclear family comprised a dozen sprogs and a two-buggie barn. His eighth-born son was my grandfather Octavius, known as Octie. My grandfather let down the side a bit by having only nine children. But the youngest, Neville, was my father; so without him Billy Connolly might have married Annie Lennox, had twins called Yin and Yang, and become an Aberdeen supporter.

Below left: This damaged photo is thought to be the only surviving image of Hira Moewaka, Salty Sam's daughter-in-law. Her chin bears a traditional Maori 'moko' tattoo.

Below right: A 1916 photo of my father as a baby with his brothers and sisters. The longest-survivor, Uncle Bill (bottom left), died in Takapuna on August 19, 2006, aged 93.

21

Chinese junks hover
by a European opium
runner, preparing to
smuggle contraband
ashore.

NOVEMBER 20

One slice of peppercorn cheese at lunchtime, and now I'm racing down a different avenue of investigation: the spice trade. Evidently a bag of pepper was once worth more than its own weight in gold! I'm thrilled by stories of the London East India Company, and now rather fancy my great-great-grandfather as a posh gentleman mariner who stood to reap vast rewards from just one voyage. He may have set sail for Batavia with a cargo of chintz and silks from Bengal or Surat, steered his ship in search of the highly desirable spices – pepper, cloves and nutmeg – from the Moluccas, or Spice Islands, then back to England and a big mark-up.

Or Salty Sam may have been carrying a cargo of opium. At that time the British participated, in a clandestine way, in the opium trade. The drug was produced in India then shipped to Indonesia, where it was bought by the Chinese. As the trade grew, addiction became a major social problem in China. The Chinese authorities outlawed trading in opium, but the East India Company illegally sent ships direct to China, knowing the Chinese could not oppose British naval power, and that eventually led to the Opium Wars.

In the 1820s opium was the most profitable cargo for British captains in the Far East. In Penang, then known as Prince of Wales Island, on April 3, 1820, when the market price for a pair of elephant's tusks was listed at 70 silver dollars, the same weight in rabbit skins was 55 and shark fins 35, you could sell your opium for 1,200 dollars per chest, while the Canton price was even higher. The route to China took the opium runners through Indonesian waters, and ships returning from China brought back porcelain and tea. It is conceivable that when Sam encountered either mutiny or piracy he may have been on his way back from China. Perhaps that's why Trudy's 'tapestry' places the *Rosalie* among Chinese junks. Was the sum of 80,000 Java florins Sam's booty from an opium run? How else would he have got so much cash? Let's face it: my great-great-grandfather was probably a drug smuggler.

Chapter 2 To Do Or Die

NOVEMBER 21, CANDACRAIG, SCOTLAND

My husband's not enthralled by the idea of my going off for months on end. He's heard about the current problems with both terrorism and pirates in Indonesia, and thinks I'm 'off my fucking head'. And he means that in the nicest possible way.

NOVEMBER 22

Today I began to consider just how little I really know about Salty Sam and his ship. I'm feeling quite overwhelmed by all the missing pieces, and I'm not even sure where to start. For example, where was the *Rosalie* built and registered? Probably either London or Plymouth, so I suppose I should begin by searching records in those two ports. It would be useful to know the ship's exact design and construction materials. Was she really a three-masted ship, as the sampler depicts her?

After she was launched, where did she go next? Presumably to Batavia, but she would have had to stop somewhere on the way. My father's book mentions Mauritius, so might there be some information there? I've gleaned that the newspapers of the day sometimes reported shipping movements between ports. Perhaps some carried articles about the ship's disappearance. Where could I find those early publications, and would they be in English?

There might be records of insurance premiums paid by Sam on his ship and cargo. Aha! I could check Lloyd's register. And I wonder if I could trace those shipping agents in Surabaya and Batavia. Wouldn't it be miraculous if they were still operating? According to Dad's booklet the Turnbull Library in Wellington holds full legal records of the fight over Samuel's Will, and other relevant documents. I'd better get there as soon as possible and scour the whole file.

There must be hundreds of people alive today, aside from Trudy, whose great-great-something-or-others were on board the *Rosalie* – I wonder if they are traceable. Perhaps there is a crew list somewhere? I also need to look into Trudy's family history and track down the descendants of Sam's daughter Mary. See if they know anything more.

I imagine that general historical research may throw up further clues, but more specifically I'm keen to know about any wrecked ships from the period, especially those lying in waters between Batavia and the Spice Islands. Since Batavia belonged to the Dutch in 1821, I hope all that information is not locked away in massive, impenetrable archives in The Hague.

In any case, I don't think I will be able to trace the *Rosalie* – or is it spelled Rosele? – on the web. Lots of resources list ships from the 1800s, but I've now been through hundreds of sites without finding any variation of that name. I'm going to have to do some leg work and search the physical archives. That's scary. I'm used to carrying out professional psychological research, but this type of historical scavenging seems particularly daunting for a genealogy virgin like me.

NOVEMBER 23

I love shopping online, although it apparently leaves me open to identity theft. But who would want to be me right now? A mad woman in the grips of an incomprehensible passion to placate a man who's been dead 200 years.

My girlfriends have been taking me to task: "Why don't you just have an affair like everybody else?"

Today I ordered a copy of Van Linschoten's *Itinerario*. This was written by a Dutchman who worked in India in the 17th century, came home the long way, and created an incredibly impressive account of the Far East, together with beautiful charts, and detailed illustrations of the region's people, flora and fauna. I can't wait to see it – apparently it's huge, and has to be shipped in a crate.

After doing my sums I have figured out that this expedition will be expensive so I shall have to find funding and sponsorship. I wonder if it's worthy of being visually recorded as a TV documentary?

I have also realized that there is a weather window for sailing safely around Indonesia – to avoid the cyclone season we must arrive there by March. But then, in order to be in Europe that same year, the boat must start crossing the Indian Ocean by June at the latest. That leaves only three months' travelling time, preceded by less than three months' development and research (given that Christmas is in the way), to solve the riddle of Salty Sam.

Yes, to do this thing properly and expect results, it will have to be a grand-scale enterprise – and put together extremely fast. Can I do it in time? I need help.

Dutchman Van Linschoten's lavishly illustrated 17th century travel guide, *Itinerario*.

NOVEMBER 24, LONDON

A very frustrating day in Kew. The archives had only part of Lloyd's Register of Shipping, from 1835 onwards. It did mention Samuel Jr's ship *Fortitude*, but not the *Rosalie*. HM Customs kept a similar merchant shipping record to Lloyd's, the indexes of which are available on microfilm. There was only one semi-legible entry for a ship beginning with 'R' with a master called Stephenson, but he was not a Samuel. In the books for 1820 and 1821 there was only a Robert Stephenson, of a different ship. There were some muster rolls, or lists of all crew members, plus their brief career histories and ship details, for British registered merchant ships dating from 1747. Unfortunately they listed only Dartmouth vessels, and almost every master and hand hailed from the west of England.

I had high hopes that the Shipping Registers made by every British port might yield something, but for the period I'm interested in, only the plantations ports (i.e. the West Indies, Canada etc) survive. Finally, an online index of more than 6,000 ships in the service of the British East India Company, showed nothing like 'Rosalie, Rosele' etc.

NOVEMBER 25

The National Maritime Museum in Greenwich did have the complete Lloyd's record. Two ships with the name 'Rosalie' were listed in the period 1808–1830, and neither of them had a master named Stephenson. In any case, both were still recorded until at least 1824, so I concluded that neither was the one. One of the assistants suggested trying Lloyd's List, a daily report of all incidents affecting shipping worldwide, i.e. if a ship ran aground or was damaged, sunk, boarded by pirates etc. The older lists (1820s) are not indexed, so it was a case of going through page by page and looking for the ship's name at the start of each paragraph. This was an arduous and thankless task; nothing turned up.

I'm not sure where to try next. As a matter of fact, I'm beginning to wonder if Samuel Stephenson, Master Mariner – and his ship, the *Rosalie* – aren't just a figment of my father's imagination.

NOVEMBER 27

Today I met Russ Malkin, the charismatic man who produced the award-winning TV show 'Long Way Round' about a challenging bike ride across the northern part of the globe. I told him about wanting to find out what happened to my great-great-grandfather.

"It will be a thrilling, historic journey, and it should be recorded. But I need financial backing or it's not going to happen. Will you help me?"

Of all people, Russ is one who can make harebrained projects happen. He listened as I told him the story, seeming reserved at first. It wasn't until I began to talk about the dangers and apparent impossibilities of the trip that his eyes really began to sparkle. As we chatted, an 'Event' began to evolve, a multi-faceted expedition linked to a TV show, book, DVD, lecture tour, website, T-Shirt, lollipop and key-chain. Brilliant.

"How long would it take to set up such an event?" I asked

"A year," he replied.

"How about three months?" I challenged him. "There's a weather issue. We'd have to be finished by June."

"Right then," he said, betraying only minimal panic. "Three months it is."

Displaying a touching level of trust, Russ has given me the resources of his 'Long Way Round' production team – Lucy will co-ordinate the filming, personnel and logistical elements, Lisa will make a marketing and promotional DVD, and Robin will film everything, starting in January.

Russ is a man after my own heart: a brave voyager who hates to hear the word 'can't'. Just like Salty Sam, he's another 'do-or-die' character. I think we'll get along excellently, and I am relieved to have a worthy co-conspirator.

DECEMBER 4, CANDACRAIG, SCOTLAND

I'm becoming anxious about the lack of new information. Our British archival search has so far turned up a big fat zero, so I'm trying to come up with less orthodox ways of gathering information. Perhaps I'll learn more about Sam and his final destination by discovering what kind of cargo he might have been carrying, and his exact route.

More importantly, by actually sailing in the area we will have a far better idea of the navigational challenges he faced: the sea, currents, weather, beaches, anchorages and ports. Likewise, by finding an approximate place where this murder by pirates, or mutiny, may have occurred, and gauging the winds, currents and marine environment, I might get a sense of whether or not Sam may have survived. Could he have drifted to a nearby island and ended his days there without rescue? I should examine nearby islands for people with Caucasian blood or for any local history, written or oral, that may afford some clues.

Was it mutiny? If so, what could have been the reasons for mutiny aboard the *Rosalie*? By examing the life aboard other merchant ships in those days, and investigating historical accounts of known mutinies, we'll be able to build a picture of the types of grudges, dissatisfactions, frustrations or greed that might have led to such a crisis.

Was it piracy? By looking at the history of sea-robbery in the relevant waters we'll be able to assess the likelihood of someone boarding the *Rosalie* with evil intent. I'd like to find some early examples of various types of piratical crimes. I gather in those days the line between piracy and mutiny was sometimes very thin.

Where is the *Rosalie* now? I am keen to dive in likely locations to try and find her. Not only that, but I should check for any similar ships that could have been repainted and renamed to disguise the crime. And what happened to the crew? If only we could find the muster roll we could search the genealogy of all those family names.

With everything closing down for the holidays the only quarry I'm hunting now is a tired old box of tree decorations. I wish I were not so seasonally inconvenienced.

JANUARY 7

With the holiday season out of the way, I can now attack this research unhindered. Tomorrow I'm taking the train down to Portsmouth to meet Captain Chris Page and his staff at the Naval Historical Branch of the Ministry of Defence. When it comes to British maritime history they are, I hear, the experts of all experts. Not only might they have records of Salty Sam but they should be able to provide background information about what it was like to sail from Rotherhithe to Batavia in the early 19th century. I'm thrilled that they have granted me access to their library.

I have spoken to the captain of my sailboat *Takapuna*, and informed him and the crew about my expedition. I'm sure he thinks I'm a lunatic. But he's looking at charts and weather and beginning to plan the trip. A gruff Miami resident with a formidable sailing record, he isn't too keen to go to Indonesia. I guess he's noticed Americans are prime targets in most Muslim countries these days, so he'd probably prefer to stay in the South Pacific.

Rolle, our Swedish engineer, will have to prepare for the trip. Spare parts will need to be ordered, fuel requirements will have to be gauged, and every piece of equipment on board must be checked. Fortunately the boat is in good shape, having just had an extensive refit in Brisbane. As soon as the weather's right I shall meet the whole crew in Cairns, on Queensland's north coast, and set off for the Spice Islands.

Iain MacKenzie, of the Naval Historical Branch of the Ministry of Defence, makes the case for Salty Sam as a 'get-rich-or-die-trying' type.

JANUARY 8, PORTSMOUTH

Sam wasn't on a naval vessel of course, as a trader. He would have had more of a fighting chance – at least against pirates – if he'd had a ship like HMS *Warrior*. I glimpsed the dark-hulled beauty, docked in Portsmouth, on my way to the well-protected Royal naval yard.

"She was the first major ironclad, built in 1860 to frighten the French," said Captain Page, a bright, friendly man whom I instantly liked. "She made every ship before her obsolete." By contrast, he explained, the *Rosalie* would have been a much smaller wooden ship, built to merchant specifications – not as solidly built, and not carrying quite as many guns.

We went into the impressive library, home of the Navy's written history from 1508, where I met librarian Jenny Wraight, and her colleague Iain

MacKenzie. A number of enticing books had been laid out for me but I cut to the chase, and asked if anyone had come across any reference to my great-great-grandfather or his ship.

"I haven't been able to find one," said Iain. "But we're not best placed here for merchant-ship history." I had thought the Royal Navy would have records of all shipping movements in the various harbours, but it turns out that the Navy had absolutely no interest in what the merchant ships were doing in peace time. "The Navy rises above that sort of thing," said Iain. But the Navy did protect merchant ships against piracy in those days, when officers were mainly kept busy surveying the seas and coastlines. Otherwise, there was a bit of a slump in the shipping trade at just about that time, compared to the peak spice trading era of the 17th and 18th centuries.

"Your ancestor's East India voyage was a kind of 'get-rich-or-die-trying' enterprise," said Iain. "It was a pretty marginal area to be trading in then."

I let this sink in. My romantic notion of Sam as a swashbuckling nutmeg trader right in the thick of things was fast evaporating. Might he have been one of the East India men? But Iain had already searched lists of officers of the East India Company and Samuel Stephenson does not appear there. He might have been in what they called the 'Country Trade', the ships owned and manned in India, but in the opinion of these experts my great-great-grandfather was probably a rung below even them – some sort of independent trader; an 'interloper', as such men were regarded by the pukka East India traders.

Low tide at London's dockland in Salty Sam's day.

"So they were an annoyance?" I was quite pleased to hear Salty Sam was a rebel.

"Well," smiled Iain, "they were snatching the bread out of the mouths of the very, very rich men of the East India Company."

So there it was. I used to think Salty Sam was a rather posh fellow, belonging to all the right gentlemen mariners' clubs … but it turns out he was nothing of the sort. Nor was he a glamorous Russell-Crowe-in-Master-and-Commander type. He lived in Rotherhithe, in the Thames dockland area, around 200 years before it became a trendy warren of designer city-lofts. Salty Sam was the maritime equivalent of an East End barrow boy. And good on him.

Rotherhithe was the centre for the East India trade. There weren't any licences or certification required for being a master mariner, but you needed to be able to navigate, to deal with the cargoes, agents and investors. You could start as an apprentice and work your way through the various degrees of mate until you became a master, captaining your own ship. It was not all that common for a master and owner to be one and the same. You first of all had to acquire the capital to buy a ship. I wonder how he managed that. She must have been a substantial vessel.

"And what about the *Rosalie*?" I asked. "How big would she have been? You reckon she was a three master as the sampler shows?"

"What's the basis of the sampler?"

"Mid–1800s, and it was done by a sixteen-year-old girl who was a descendant of somebody on board."

"Hmm. If somebody was leaning over her shoulder I'm sure she'd have got it right."

I shoved a photograph of it under his nose.

"Well, it's a ship, for sure, three masted, square rigged in all three masts. Probably around 110 feet. A Dutch flag there and…"

"Which is the Dutch flag?" I asked, surprised. He pointed to the red, white and gold tricolour on the left. I had never even noticed it before. "I think that all of our family resources were sunk into that ship," I mused.

"Probably," nodded Iain. "By the time he'd bought the ship, fitted it, equipped it, stored it and got the cargo for it … but if he did get rich, he'd get seriously rich. If he was the owner and the master of the ship, it'd be his cargo. He'd stand to gain, or lose, everything."

Iain rejected the idea that Salty Sam was trading in opium.

"There'd be no real need to go into the opium trade if he had that much capital sunk into his ship," he reasoned. "It was too much of a risk. Just being a straightforward trader he'd have found it difficult enough dealing with the Dutch, let alone the Chinese. Especially as an independent type…"

I was keen to find out everything I could about life on board a ship like the *Rosalie*. It seems there would have been around 30 crew, a figure Iain arrived at by guestimating the ship was 300 tons and dividing by 10 (he based this on one man per ten tons). If the crew were Indian or Asian, and therefore less familiar with the ship, there would probably have been more.

"Any women on board, do you think?"

Chris sighed. "I'm afraid women get everywhere."

"Would they have been sex workers?"

"No," said Jenny. "Prostitutes would certainly visit the ship when it was in port but the women who stayed on board were often wives of the master or senior members of the crew."

"Wasn't it bad luck to have women at sea?"

"No," said Jenny, while simultaneously Chris joked, "Yeah, it's terrible."

"It's not unlucky," Iain joined in the fun. "It's just really, really annoying."

"Some captain's wives became such good navigators," said Jenny, ignoring them, "that if their husband happened to die they could take over the management of the ship."

"Would the *Rosalie* have had lots of guns on board?" I asked.

"I think Sam would have been an absolute fool if he didn't have any guns on board, going to that part of the world."

I took a deep breath. "So what do you think happened to him?"

"I think it's almost certain he was just knocked on the head and thrown overboard," said Iain.

"See," said Chris, "they wouldn't have put him in an open boat. That was the mistake with Bligh. But even if they did, being cast adrift in an open boat in those waters is bad news. Apart from finding your way to land safely, you have still got to deal with any unfriendly pirates that you might bump into on the way."

"Piracy or mutiny," rejoined Iain, "either way, the penalty was death. If it's piracy there's no premium in keeping the captain alive. If it's mutiny, then they definitely don't want to keep the captain alive, so I'm afraid he probably went over the stern, either unconscious or dead. And no one would ever be able to trace what happened to the ship."

"But," I asked, "how would you hide a large ship?"

"All that water there," smiled Iain, "that's only the top of it you can see. They'd have stripped it, burnt it, sunk it, ran it up a creek somewhere…"

"Or else sold both cargo and ship," added Chris.

"Given it a paint job," said Iain.

I brought up the intrigue of the two Wills.

"Well," said Chris, "he's got 80,000 Dutch florins which aren't covered by his first Will, and he's about to set off on another lucrative voyage, so he's obviously thinking, well, what I'll do now is produce another Will to make sure if anything happens to me that this 80,000 Dutch florins doesn't go adrift. So he'd make a copy, wouldn't he, and leave it with his agent?"

"Ah," I said, "but they claimed he didn't leave them a copy. It was their word against his Executors'. And anyway, why exactly did Salty Sam have these agents?"

"There had to be an agent in each port to trade on his behalf in a limited way until he returned," explained Iain. "But there's another possible reason for mutiny. He's got a slip of paper in his pocket saying 80,000 florins, and by the time that gets around the crew it's a big chest of 80,000 florins under the Captain's bunk."

Now *there's* a motive!

Chapter 3 Sex, Drugs
and Pirates

JANUARY 9, LONDON

I woke up with one question on my mind. Where did Sam get those 80,000 Java florins? If he wasn't trading in opium, what other cargo would have fetched such a massive amount of money? I tend to think he *was* smuggling. In a book of 1798 sailing directions for Batavia and Samarang written by a James Horsburgh, I'd found a brilliant set of 'how to' instructions on smuggling opium into Batavia:

> *Immediately on your arrival your first visit should be made to the Shabunder, to whom you should give a true invoice of your goods (opium excepted) … which shall be … offered for sale to the Company. As this article is a monopoly of the Company's, care should be taken how you proceed… The Council will perhaps take all your opium at 500 rix dollars per chest, or may perhaps order you out of the roads; in this case recourse must be had to smuggling … you must sign a certificate for the behaviour of your officers and people, at the forfeit of your life, that you, nor none of your crew, will smuggle opium or spices … for which reason you are to follow these rules: viz, you must first find out whether the Fiscal or Shabander have any opium of their own on their hands; if they have you can do no business, as they will keep too good a look out, and have armed cruisers near you; but if they have none, you may succeed by offering to deliver any quantity to any of the islands for them…*
>
> *If the Company take your opium they will offer you paper in payment; but … you must endeavour to make them pay you in cash…*

This morning I went on board the HQS *Wellington*, a beige-funnelled beauty moored in the Thames by Temple Stairs on Victoria Embankment, to see Commander Rod Craig, Clerk to the Honourable Company of Master Mariners. In 1932 King George V gave this company the singular honour of being called Honourable – because of the huge contribution that the merchant service played in the First World War.

Commander Craig is a lanky, genial man whose office made me very jealous. "I want portholes in mine too!"

The ceremonial outfit worn by the Master of the Company also inspired my envy, especially the gorgeous heavy Master's chain of office – really a necklace –

Packing and weighing chests of opium.

Left: "Don't go anywhere near these places!" Commander Rod Craig of HQS *Wellington* is starting to sound rather like my husband.

Below: The 'Red Rover Cup' was awarded as a reward for superior opium-running skills.

of 22-carat gold and enamel, with seven diamonds and twelve rubies ornately fashioned into a sea-theme, complete with mermaids, fish, seaweed and shells.

"What, no matching earrings?" I cried.

To make matters worse, the blessed man immediately dashed my hopes that Sam's name might be contained among the lists of master mariners stored in his archives.

"I'm afraid the Company only started in 1926," he said, beginning to share his considerable knowledge about the trading days of Sam's time, when the East India Company ran fleets of fast, professionally-sailed clippers.

"Getting cargoes back to Britain and manufactured goods out to the rest of the world," said Rod, "was very much what created the prosperity of this country."

But the trading business was a big gamble for outsiders like Sam. They bought or built their own ships and made or lost fortunes, depending on whether they sold their cargoes on time, if they brought back valuable goods, and provided they weren't wrecked.

"An awful lot of opium was traded," said Rod, "even though it was illegal. Ships would sail to China with their legal cargoes, but hidden inside them was opium. Of course, this commanded a very good price, particularly at the end of the monsoon, when the square-rigged clippers found it difficult to sail; so because of the price the race was on to be the first ship into Canton. There was one very fast ship based on an American design, called the Red Rover, that could always sail a bit closer to the wind than the British-designed ships. It was invariably the first into Canton and got the highest price for its opium – and in fact, there was a trophy awarded to its master, and in subsequent years to whichever ship got there first. We have that cup on board, and its unofficial title is the 'Red Rover Cup'."

He led me to the dining room and showed it to me. Within a glass case sat the coveted trophy: a huge, ornate silver filigree cup, with grapevine design and a fninial representing Neptune.

"Ostensibly it was awarded in recognition of superb seamanship skills," smiled Rod. "But it was really a trophy for drug running."

"Do you think Sam was actually pushing opium?"

"It's highly likely, if he was looking to make a big profit on one voyage.

Besides, everyone else was doing it, including the East India Company."

"But secretly?"

Rod cleared his throat. "Not officially. It was, I suppose, a tolerated policy. I mean, the Royal Navy was sent to defend British merchant ships, so everyone knew it was going on."

After leaving Britain trading ships invariably would have headed for Brazil then turned left and rounded the bottom of Africa. If they were engaged in the opium trade they would have had to stop off to acquire it somewhere in the Indian subcontinent, then pick up the trade winds again, and sail for what is now northern Malaysia, round the north of Sumatra, and down the Malacca Straits. That's still the most direct course to the Far East, and a world shipping route even today.

"So," I asked Rod, "what's your hunch? Murder or mutiny?"

"Mutiny could be for many reasons but, generally speaking, it's because the crew is very unhappy about the way the ship is being run or how they are being treated. It might be inadequate rations, it might be overly harsh punishments, or perhaps the feeling that they weren't going to get paid eventually – or even that someone else in the crew knows better than the captain. It's not inconceivable that the crew took command of the *Rosalie*. They could have renamed her and then traded around that region themselves. Then again, they may indeed have been attacked by pirates, all murdered, then the ship burnt. Lots of ships were lost for natural reasons too but mariners often had the problem of pirates, particularly in areas like the Malacca Straits. These get narrower and narrower, so it was easy for ships to be spotted from the shore. Somebody sent a signal to a friend, by mirrors or something, that a ship was approaching and then a little boat would come out and attack it, much as some pirate attacks happen today."

I had to ask. "Tell me about the pirate attacks today."

"Well, there's a lot of concern about it now. Some of the armed forces and police forces are not terribly well paid and so they literally moonlight, carrying out acts of piracy."

"You mean it's … government-sponsored?"

"Not exactly. But there have been instances where members of the Indonesian armed forces have actually conducted acts of piracy. The Indonesian government

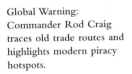

Global Warning: Commander Rod Craig traces old trade routes and highlights modern piracy hotspots.

doesn't sanction this, of course, but it is known to be a problem. There are many others, fisherman by day, pirates by night…"

"What do they do?"

"Generally speaking they have small, fast boats, and they wait to see what type of ship is passing. Lots of merchant ships are very low in the water when fully laden. The pirates come alongside, put grappling irons on, and climb on board. Merchant ships have very small crews these days, so you've probably got one person on the bridge and perhaps a few other people elsewhere. Typically the pirates hold a gun to the watch officer's head or they knock the windows out with a burst of gunfire and take the crew hostage. They either rob them, hold them for ransom – which is quite a popular thing – and in some instances they steal the ship and cargo."

"What do you think the potential piracy danger might be to a private yacht like mine?"

"Well, it's not without risk. Private yachts, to the people who carry out these attacks, represent rich people – which means watches, cash, jewellery – and are an easy target for robbery. The problem is that if an attack takes place in someone's national waters, it is that country's responsibility to do something about it. Other countries can't send warships into that country's territorial waters without permission. The pirates know this, so even if they attack on the high seas they can then take off into their own territorial waters and law enforcement agencies from other countries can't follow."

"So no one's gonna save me?" I thrust out my lower lip.

"I'm sure someone will come…" He didn't look too confident. I asked what kind of weapons modern pirates carried.

"Generally, what's called small arms. Pistols and automatic weapons. AK47s…"

"You call that small arms?"

"Yes. Occasionally, rocket-propelled grenades. These people are pretty ruthless. They are there to get whatever they want and if people get in their way they invariably kill them. There have been some terrible cases of merchant ship crews murdered, chucked over the side and, in one instance, marooned on an island. To put it into perspective, this sort of thing doesn't happen as often as the more sensational headlines would have you believe. But it does happen, not just in the Malacca Straits, but further east in the seas between the Indonesian islands and the Philippines. In fact, the whole area has a piracy problem."

I brought up my intention to go to Maluku, the original Spice Islands, which is known to be quite dangerous in places, especially Ambon.

"Pamela, the whole of the Indonesian archipelago is tailor-made for acts of piracy," said Rod. "There are a myriad of small islands or creeks, where people can hide. Very often attacks are opportunistic. They'll be fishing and see something come along, and they'll try it on. So I hope you're taking guards."

"How many do you think I should take?"

"Well the obvious answer is, don't go anywhere near these places."

"Now you're sounding like my husband!"

"Well that would be my professional advice. Some countries aren't particularly happy about private vessels with lots of firearms, but you should definitely have a couple of ex-military people on board, and if you can legally carry firearms I think you should have those as well. The problem is that once you start an exchange of fire, it gets extremely nasty. Some people would advise that if you don't have firearms the worst you can expect is that the pirates would just rob you, but you must go to experts in this area for personal protection and ask their advice." There was a pause. "I hope I haven't put you off?"

JANUARY 11

After some uncomfortable telephone conversations with my captain on the subject of piracy in Indonesia, I met with Chris, the ex-SAS man who advises me about on-board security.

"What do you think about Indonesia?" I asked.

"Lovely place," he replied, "Hope you're not taking the *Takapuna* there."

"'Fraid so."

"You're insane," he said. "You've got a slow boat with a low stern, and there's a good chance you'll be attacked. Indonesia has the highest instance of piracy in the world." He brought out a map showing recent incidents and sure enough, Indonesia topped the poll.

"Chris, I have to go there. What do I need to do?"

He sighed. "First of all, when you enter each port you'll need to declare your weapons. It would be a big risk not to. You could end up in jail, or the boat could be impounded. "The catch is, there's a good chance that once you declare the weapons they'll be taken away from you and you'll never see them again."

"Great. And what about personnel?"

"I'll put a couple of good chaps aboard for you. A Hereford guy, or an ex-Royal Marine Commando. And a couple of Gurkhas."

"Gurkhas?"

"They'd be brilliant," he said. "They're used to the Malacca Straits run. Incredibly loyal, and hard workers. Help out on deck, and they're solid fighters. Make a great curry, too."

"OK, then." It was getting more and more bizarre.

"And that pilot house of yours is very open. You might want to get a couple of ballistic blankets for cover, in case you get into a gun battle. And you'll need some body armour. I might be able to get you a deal."

"That bad, huh?" I was feeling rather shaky.

"I'll plot the places on your charts where pirates are most prevalent," he said. "Try to avoid those clusters. And if anything happens, especially if someone gets … 'hurt', the expedition's over. Get out of the region as fast as you can. You hear me? Expedition's over!"

Chapter 4 Murder Most Foul?

JANUARY 25, LONDON

It was about time I got a break after all my disappointments to date. Having conferred with Far East expert Dr Andrew Cook, who is in charge of the British Library's Asia and Africa map collections, and received tip-offs from Penny Brooke and a few other kindly curators at the British Library, I began to pore through microfilm of early newspapers. After only a few hours, I got lucky. In the *Asiatic Journal and Miscellany*, December 1821, I found a snippet that set my heart racing:

> The Rosalie, *a Mauritius-built ship, is said to have been lost, which account is ascribed to one of the mates and a seaman, arrived at Sumanup (to the eastward), and it is supposed that Capt. Stephenson has been murdered. She was from Somabaya, bound to the Moluccas.*

I sat back in my chair and tried to stop myself screaming "Yes!" Here at last was a new, written-down version of what might have happened to Salty Sam. Murder most foul. It was shocking, though, to see my ancestor's name in print like this. Whatever the details of his demise, it was becoming more certain that he did suffer a horrible, violent death.

I called Russ. "So you weren't making it all up!" he teased. "I was beginning to think you were leading us on a wild goose chase."

"So was I," I confessed, "but listen – it says the ship was lost. That could mean anything, including shipwreck. And it says Salty Sam was murdered, but not by whom."

Moreover, the article says the *Rosalie* was built in Mauritius. So that's why I've had such a hard time finding records of her in the UK! And it even indicates Salty Sam's exact final route – from Surabaya (I suppose that is what's meant by 'Somabaya') to the Spice Islands. Now I have several new leads that should send lots more details tumbling into place. This is thrilling!

Good things come to those who wait ... and wait ... and wait. An hour or so later, in the November 28 edition of the *Prince of Wales Island Gazette* (a Penang publication that covered shipping and other reports of colonial trading) I was stunned to read this front page article:

'ROTHERHITHE MAN IN FAR EAST TRAGEDY.' My research in the British Library uncovers a microfilm of an 1821 newspaper account of the death of Salty Sam.

By this occasion we have received the melancholy account of the loss of the ship Rozella, *Capt Stevens, belonging to the Port of Mauritius, in the Straits of Alass, off Carabatoo Island, and the subsequent murder of the Captain and his wife, and officers and crew, by the crew of a Malayan Prow which it pretended was affording them protection and conveyance to the Port of Beemah.*

The St Antonio fell in with a Prow, off Bally Hill, having on board the Gunner and six Lascars of this ill-fated vessel, who reported that after the ship had got aground and no hopes entertained of getting her off, the Captain and all on board took to the boats and landed on Carabatoo Island, where the Rajah received them with seeming hospitality and gave them a Prow to convey them to the Port of Beemah, and on which they embarked in perfect confidence with the exception of the Gunner and six Lascars, who fortunately proceeded in the ship's cutter, the Prow not being sufficiently capacious to accommodate the whole. They had, however, scarcely got out of sight of the island when they beheld with horror the bodies of their late Commander, his wife, and several others floating past them, and immediately after they were hailed by the Malays to go alongside of the Prow; but the cutter being a superior sailor made the best of her way to Beemah where the Resident with great humanity afforded them assistance and provided a prow to convey them to Surabaya.

I was frozen in my chair. I re-read the article time and time again until I could begin to take it in. There were several confusing elements here, not least of which was the mention of a 'wife', when good old Ann was presumably sitting by the hearth in Rotherhithe. Then, 'Rosalie' was misspelled 'Rozella', and 'Stephenson' had become 'Stevens'. But this must surely be about my great-great-grandfather. The mistakes were probably made by whoever scribbled down the eyewitnesses' accounts, in fact the inaccurate spellings of 'Rosalie' and Sam's name possibly pointed to the nationality of the apparent survivors. For example, gunners in those days were often Portuguese.

So, according to the Gazette, the Rosalie ran aground off this island of Carabatoo, whereupon they were received by some local chief who offered Sam and his crew transport to the Port of Beemah. On the way, the crew of the prow killed Sam, his 'wife' and officers. This was according to the Rosalie's gunner and Lascars following in the cutter who had seen the bodies in the water and nearly became victims themselves.

Where exactly was all this supposed to have taken place? Half an hour later I'd identified Beemah as Bima, now a large port on the north-east corner of Sumbawa. In Sam's day it was a well-established colonial outpost. An 1827 sailing directory says, "Bima Bay stretches deeply inland, and forms a safe harbour, where ships lie quite landlocked and sheltered." The same sailing manual warns of the dangers in the region. "Great caution is requisite in small ships, if not well armed, when passing through any of the eastern straits," and quotes one Dutch resident as saying that "pirates, who have often … plundered the different villages, had … driven the inhabitants all away, and taken possession themselves" and that he understood there were upwards of 100 sail of *prahus* "marauding around these coasts." *Prahu*, yet another variable spelling, is the name for a local type of sailing boat, also referred to as a 'prow' or 'proa'.

I consulted a modern atlas to try to find the other places mentioned in the newspaper articles, but none were there except the Straits of Alas, which were shown to be a slice of water lying between the islands of Lombok and Sumbawa, just east of Bali. I quickly emailed the captain of the *Takapuna* and asked him to take a look on the charts and see if he can figure out the exact location of the island where Sam was supposed to have disappeared.

Why was the local chief called a 'Raja' so far from India? An explanation for the use of the term 'Raja' turned up in one account of Java in the 19th century. A Major William Thorn wrote:

> *It is remarkable that the title of Rajah, which in India is exclusively confined to Hindoos, is in this instance adopted by Mussulmans, or at least by Chiefs possessing themselves of that faith. This is a circumstance which serves to prove that the Aborigines of all these islands were Hindoos.*

This evening I took stock. Exciting as today has been, the truth is that I still don't know for sure if any of this is accurate. The article in the *Prince of Wales Island Gazette* is quite detailed, but it is just one newspaper account.

Actually seeing Salty Sam's name in print, though, was a real shock. It was also encouraging, because if I could find those two articles in one day, I should be able to find out a lot more over time. Of course, today's findings have thrown up even more questions. The kind of treachery supposedly practised by the Raja who 'befriended' Sam is a type of piracy that still goes on today. But it might have been some other kind of foul play, perhaps arranged by someone who wanted to rob Sam of assets that were either aboard the boat or at his agent's office in Surabaya – and the piracy tale might therefore be a cover story.

And then there's the 'wife'. How do we know there really was somebody on board who fitted the description of a wife? I suppose she was a woman who'd been observed behaving like a wife around Captain Stephenson. Perhaps he was a bigamist, or a rogue of one sort or another. Anyway, whatever he was up to, he was lost in terrifying circumstances. He was attacked with some kind of weapon, suffered a violent, horrible death, and was thrown over the side, not necessarily in that order. It hardly bears thinking about – his officers and crew, his men and women, all lost. Or not. How can I prove whether it really happened?

And another thing. Who exactly were those people who got back to tell the tales as told in the two articles? Maybe one invented the piracy story to avoid being implicated in a mutiny. I suppose the article in the Gazette lends credibility to Trudy's piracy claim, but again mutiny is not out of the question. I'm going through so many permutations in my head, but one thing does seem pretty clear now. I have to get out to Indonesia and sniff around. I have to find the island of Carabatoo.

I'm dying to call my husband in Australia and tell him about the new developments in the saga of Salty Sam; but I don't think he'd appreciate being woken in the middle of the night. I bought him a Blackberry for Christmas. He hasn't quite got to grips with it yet, and continues to refer to it as 'My Raspberry Or Strawberry Or Whatever The Fuck It's Called.'

JANUARY 27

We must be ready to take off for Indonesian waters at the right time to avoid the monsoon, but at present the seas up there are bad. There are six men missing off Papua New Guinea right now. Even if we miss the worst of it, we're bound to have an uncomfortable journey from Australia to Indonesia. The captain has warned, "It's gonna be a bit lumpy going up there." He's working on our cruising permit for the region, but we have to be careful how we present our trip. The Indonesians are suspicious of people who want to dive on wrecks. Lately, treasure hunters have extracted considerable wealth from shipwrecks out there, and the Indonesians don't like that, because they want their cut. And there are so many wrecks in that archipelago: American, Portuguese, Dutch, English, all kinds of vessels came to grief. Either they ran aground, hit some rocks or faced terrible weather. It all makes me think fondly of Sam, that he was such a brave adventurer.

I have to admit that, as the reality of the contemporary threats out there begins to hit home, a part of me is afraid. In my heart I believe we're going to be okay, otherwise I wouldn't go. Nevertheless, it worries me that the captain, who's been told the piracy threat is overblown, would rather go unarmed. I'd prefer to take the weapons we already keep on board (a couple of AR15s, plus several Glocks and Sig 228 handguns), and I'd also like to follow Chris's recommendations that we have extra crew for security. In my opinion one just has to be prepared. It's like driving on the highway. You have to buy car insurance and a car that's in fairly good shape, and then you can relax and enjoy the ride.

But if I got killed by pirates on the high seas, it'd be a great story for my grandchildren! "Yeah, my granny was killed by pirates!" That would be quite a tale. One could look exotic with a story like that. Posthumously.

FEBRUARY 1, CIRENCESTER

I drove to Cirencester to visit Trudy Prior, who had an ancestor among the *Rosalie*'s crew and who first alerted me to the piracy story in Gozo.
I barely recognized her.

"I'm much better," she lied. "Having been poorly for over a year, starting off with lung cancer and recovering from that and then being told that I have it in the brain … but anyway, I'm fighting it and I'm not going to accept that I've got it, so I've told it to bugger off!"

I gazed at her with awe, touched that she could be bothered with my little quest when she herself was in the midst of such lethal combat. She had barely been able to climb the stairs to her little sitting room.

"Billy sends his love," I said, settling myself beside her.

"Bless him." She smiled.

I hesitated, feeling guilty about my need to ask for her help. "Well…" – it was now or never, I knew that, just by looking at her – "…I was so shocked when, out of the depths of Rosina's Bar, you suddenly announced it wasn't a mutiny. You remember? You told me it was piracy."

"That's right! You see, I passed Billy when I was walking the dog and I said, 'Please will you tell Pamela – it's something I read in her book that sent a shiver down my back.'"

So Billy knew about this before I did. He never told me.

"It was about the *Rosalie* and the connection, and your side of the story, that it was mutiny. It made a big impression on me, that we'd had a relative on the same ship."

Everything Coming Up *Rosalie*: Learning more from Trudy Prior, whose ancestor sailed with Salty Sam.

I asked her how she'd heard the story. She had grown up with what she referred to as a 'tapestry', but was really more a young woman's sampler. It had belonged to her father's mother and was always on the wall. Trudy's mother had related the tale when she was eight or nine.

"She passed on what she'd been told by her grandma, that it was a family tragedy. There had been pirates at the entry from the Sunda Straits and whatever cargo they had, it was taken and all the men on board had been lost. I can remember one day thinking of the girl who sewed the tapestry, one of my own ancestors, and I remember getting tears in my eyes, not knowing whether it was her father, brother, uncle that had lost his life at sea."

"What were their surnames?"

"Well, they would either be Adam, Adams – the 's' was dropped at some point – or Valentine. More likely Valentine … you see, all the tapestries I've got at home are by different members of the Valentine family."

I took out my photograph of the sampler. "At the top are the initials EA," I pointed out, "so even though she's written her name as Elizabeth Valentine at the bottom, the 'A' could stand for Adam? Or Adams?"

"Yes, my maiden name, with Valentine added on."

I mused that there might be other people sitting at home right now having a cup of tea and telling the same story to a grandchild.

"Yes," said Trudy, "those little moments in history that you can so easily dismiss … it touched me when I was young, but then that little snippet in your book started it all off again."

I filled Trudy in on my recent finds at the British Library. "Fascinating," she said. "You scratch the top of the story and you just go on and on And what a story. I mean, it was awful and terrible and obviously whatever it was that happened to our ancestors, they died under very violent circumstances. They were so brave. I mean, in those days to do what they did, to set sail knowing that they'd be gone for three or four years at a time, to brave not only pirates but the sea… They were tough."

"Tough stock," I echoed.

"Yes." Trudy stared through the window. "We're from salt-of-the-earth people."

"Absolutely!" I cried. "Look at you; you're someone who's saying cancer is not going to beat you."

"No, well it's not," she snorted.

"Where did that resilience come from? Probably from your ancestor who was on board the *Rosalie*."

Trudy promised to search for more evidence. "You're like a terrier," she said as she kissed me goodbye. "And I'm caught up in it now – so I'm the new Jack Russell."

FEBRUARY 2, LONDON

So far we've had no luck identifying the island of Carabatoo. I googled it, and found nothing, although there are a number of other islands in the Straits of Alas. I wonder why Sam ducked into these Straits, if the *Rosalie* was sailing east from Surabaya to the Moluccas, or Spice Islands as reported. That was definitely a southerly detour. Of course, without an engine, one couldn't sail anywhere directly.

I've emailed the captain to outline my plan. We'll sail north from Australia, look for clues in the Spice Islands, then go south-west to Java to search for

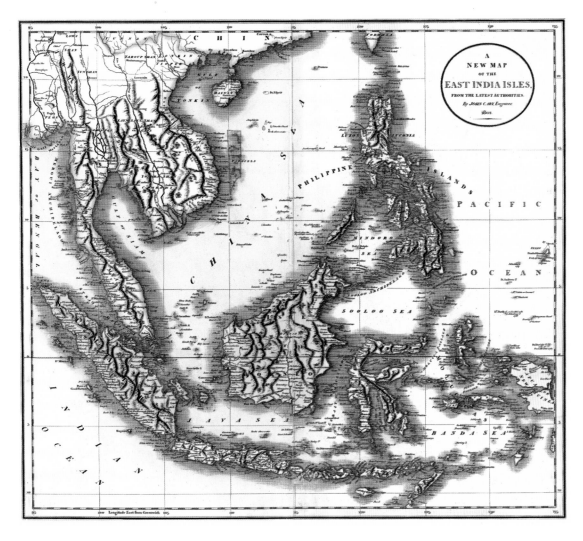

The Indonesian archipelago as seen by cartographers in 1801. Navigational charts often contained dangerous inaccuracies.

Sam's shipping agents and other clues in Batavia, as Jakarta was then known. From there we'll sail a little further east, to Surabaya where his other shipping agents were. Then we'll begin to retrace Sam's final voyage towards Moluku, maybe stopping at Bali for provisioning. Then a couple of islands to the east, between Lombok and Sumbawa, we'll enter the Straits of Alas, where we'll search for the island of Carabatoo.

I'm really excited about the prospect of finding out if there are any shipwrecks in the vicinity and diving on them to see if one might actually be the *Rosalie*. Of course pirates or mutineers – whoever they were – would probably have renamed and repainted her and taken her off elsewhere. But if she did run aground, some of the wreck might still be there. That would be amazing – to actually find the *Rosalie*, or even just her bell or anchor.

I feel we're on the right track now. The expedition will really begin from the north coast of Queensland, at Cairns, where all team members will join the boat, meet each other and, in one sense or another, get to know the ropes. The sailing crew will lead the man-overboard exercises, fire drills, watch-standing instruction and provisioning. Chris, our piracy advisor, and a new, on-board security officer will take us through a programme of piracy training – as far as we can without our weapons. The Australian police impounded my on-board firearms when the

Takapuna arrived in Brisbane, to be returned when we leave, so we will not be able to carry out any weapons checks in Australian waters. That will have to wait until we're at sea, right before we make landfall in Indonesia.

On the other hand, I've just learned about an interesting new anti-pirate weapon. It was recently used successfully by the crew of a cruise ship during an attempted piracy off the coast of Somalia. The MRAD (Medium-Range Acoustic Device) works by emitting an unbearable sound, pinpointed in the direction of would-be attackers over distances of up to 300 metres. It's impossible to load or fire a weapon while it's directed at you on full volume, and you can even add a 'phraselator', or recorded human voice in the language of your own choice, instructing intruders to back off. Sounds like a good alternative to bullets. Maybe I should get one. If nothing else, it would be useful at home during mealtimes.

FEBRUARY 3

As soon as I woke up this morning, I turned on my computer – and found out that the *Takapuna* has just been arrested. It seems ridiculous for a boat to be arrested, but it has been. What does that look like, I wonder? I mean, where do they put the handcuffs? Anyway, some person who tried to fix something a while ago and made a complete arse of it has managed to get a sheriff to go on board and make us post a bond for full payment before the boat can leave Brisbane. That will take time, yet in three days from now the *Takapuna* needs to be in Cairns.

"Let's keep me out of jail." The captain sounded tense over my cellphone.

The Cutty Sark, fastest of the Far East tea clippers.

"Yeah, well, I'd like you to remain this side of the slammer if possible!" I replied. "I've got an expedition to complete."

"Thanks," he drawled. "I'm glad you're on my team."

Next, an email informed me that our Ghurkhas, Dev and Tek, who were due to meet us in Cairns, have been refused their Australian visas.

"Do you have any ideas about where else they could meet us?" I asked the captain with some trepidation. He's made it clear he doesn't want the Gurkhas on board.

"We could pick 'em up in East Timor," he suggested, being in fact quite accommodating. "It's not much of a deviation. We could whack in there, snag them and be out in short order."

The final challenge for today was finding out that, in order to get one of the permits we need for Indonesia, applications must be made by each member of our crew in their country of origin, with their original passports. Now, on board will be an American captain, a Swedish engineer (Rolle), a British cook (Kayt), an Australian first mate (Dan), a Samoan doctor (Dr Ricky), a British stewardess (Sue), a Welsh security officer (Sean), two Nepalese security guards, Russ, who's English, and me (Australian passport), plus a whole recording team to be announced … you name it. With people on board from all over the world, there is no way that their original passports could go with them to the Embassies in their own countries to make these applications in time. I have no idea how to solve this one.

Instead of fretting in my room, I went down to Greenwich to visit the *Cutty Sark*, the celebrated tea clipper whose name was taken from the Robert Burns poem 'Tam O'Shanter'. I wanted to get a sense of what it must have been like on board a 19th-century trading vessel. The *Cutty Sark* was launched later than the *Rosalie*, in 1869. At 212 feet she was no doubt larger than the *Rosalie* and almost certainly faster, with a top speed of seventeen knots. Her sleek black hull and massive mast made my jaw drop, even in the grey light of a nasty, rainy day. As I wandered around, the ship did hint at conditions aboard in the days of her merchant runs. The deck cabins were tiny, and much of the equipment, especially the anchor winch, looked wicked. As for the complicated, lofty rigging – no wonder so many people fell off.

The *Cutty Sark* has a cavernous interior, but this used to be stuffed with tea, so there'd be little room to spare for all her crew. The hold now accommodates scores of visitors, who, like me, were marvelling at a wonderful collection of figureheads displayed along the bulkheads. The ornate and colourful mermaids, goddesses and other carved figures that once adorned the prows of sailing vessels still held the romance of bold voyages into unknown seas. I was quite taken with the guide's remark that they've not all been formally identified as belonging to a particular ship. So, it occurred to me, one of them might even have been from the *Rosalie*. Presumably she once had a rosy-cheeked French maiden leading her out into the oceans of the world?

On my way back from Greenwich I went to Paradise Street, Rotherhithe, to poke around the area where Salty Sam and his wife Ann once lived with their two children. There's little left from his era, although the restored Mayflower Pub is nearby. I guess that was Salty Sam's local watering hole. It's touristy, but I did feel close to him there. I'd never seen the Thames from that vantage point, and although the East India Dock and much of the land around the former hub of shipping are now posh digs for City bachelors, I was quite transported by the cobblestone streets, the narrow passages and the oily canal.

This restored Thames-side pub is at the Pilgrim Fathers' New World embarkation point, just round the corner from Sam's Rotherhithe home.

I managed to speak to Billy today. I'm glad his concerts in Australia are going well. But I know he mentions me in the shows, and sometimes I get paranoid. I mean, it's comedy, and I probably don't need to be worried, but I hate the idea of him describing our sex life or something to thousands of people. And he'd never confess it to me. I think I'm going to have to surprise him in Queensland. That's it: I'll sneak into one of his shows, then confront him afterwards.

Chapter 5 Ruling the Wives

FEBRUARY 4, LONDON

"Would you explain," I asked Admiral Sir Alan West, the First Sea Lord, "what exactly it is that you do?"

He was an exceedingly dashing man, with an impressive uniform. We had met through a mutual friend, so I guessed I had licence to be a little cheeky.

His eyes twinkled. "I am completely responsible, through the Chief of Defence staff and Secretary of State, to the Prime Minister for the fighting effectiveness and morale of the Royal Navy, Royal Marines and Royal Fleet Auxiliary."

"You're in charge of everyone, basically, aren't you?" I laughed. I told him a little about Salty Sam, beginning with the mutiny story.

He leaned forward. "Bodies thrown overboard presumably?"

That gave me pause. "Why, do you think they might have been given a chance?"

"It depends," he said. "I mean, pirates can be terribly bloodthirsty, but occasionally, if they thought there might be something in it for them, they might put them ashore somewhere." So it is possible Salty Sam survived.

On the subject of the second 'wife', the First Sea Lord smiled knowingly. "That did happen quite often actually, more often than they say. In Victorian times none of that was ever reported, but people were away for so long."

Often these relationships were not with English women, but they were still deep and long-standing, some of them. But in Victorian England, you couldn't possibly talk about something like that.

In 1800 the Navy had a very large fleet, including seventy four gun ships, for fighting Napoleon. It was a time of great innovation. For example, they introduced a block-making machine in Portsmouth that produced 40,000 blocks a year for the fleet. It was an enormous task to supply every ship with vittles, stores, nails and so on. Copper sheathing was invented for ships' bottoms, which meant they didn't have to be scraped so often. "At that time, in about 1810, we had, what, 110,000 men in the Navy," said the First Sea Lord. "When you think we only had a population of 12,000,000 people, that was quite incredible. And they all had to be fed. We were able to provide food, water, and lots of drink to chaps deployed all around the world. The French and Spanish couldn't really do all that.

The First Sea Lord commands the ideal counter-piracy vessels.

One of our toasts – we have a standard toast every night – is 'a bloody war or a sickly season'. War meant good promotion."

I asked about the interaction between the merchant sailors and the Navy.

"We relied on them, and they used to rather tease us, because in the merchant navy they'd run up aloft with say, six men, whereas we'd send thirty men aloft – because we *had* thirty men." When a war came, the Navy wanted merchant seamen so the merchant service had to pay their seamen even more than they normally did because they were desperate not to lose them.

"When Naval recruitment officers knew that an East Indies fleet was coming back from the Far East," said the First Sea Lord, "as soon as it came into this channel, we'd press the bulk of the men."

"You mean they press-ganged them?"

"Yes. So these poor sailors who had been out to China and all the way back … there was the UK in view and these rotten Navy people would come out and press them. It was particularly the top men we wanted, the guys who went right up the rigging. That required great skill and strength. It actually caused damage to their backs later in their life but they were very, very adept, with hugely powerful arms and legs and could run up the rigging very quickly. They were the *crème de la crème* of the seamen."

Salty Sam would probably have had just a couple of these top British men. Over time the rest of his crew might have become a mixture of Mauritians, Dutch, and some of the local indigenous population as well as Indian Lascars. And once he had his crew, where would Sam have headed, given that he was probably a man with an eye for the most lucrative cargo?

"Well, opium was one nasty thing that was happening," said the First Sea Lord. "It's unbelievable that Britain actually went to war with China because the Chinese were trying to stop opium being brought into their country. But judging people by today's standards is no good. And of course that was a nice little earner, because for that they could get amazing things in China. China was a treasure trove: silks, wonderful ceramics and so on."

The matter of finding the right price for one's cargo was always tricky. Today, a merchant captain's firm sends him an email by satellite instructing him to alter course because there's a better price for the cargo at such and such a port. But in Salty Sam's days he'd have had to get his information from coffee houses. Lloyd's of London was originally a coffee house where shipping people went, to pick up rumours of what was happening in the various sea ports around the world. But such information was unreliable. Salty Sam would have set sail for a particular port, but when he arrived he'd find out that if he went another 50 miles up the coast he could get an even better price.

The First Sea Lord took care to outline the extreme navigational challenges Sam would have faced along the way. With rudimentary charts, few lighthouses, and no GPS, Salty Sam would have used sun sights. But in overcast weather, he'd have had to work by dead reckoning. Some had magnetic compasses, but those can be 35–40 degrees off from a giro heading, and they didn't know how to adjust. "It was guesswork," he said. "In the time of your great-great-grandfather there were proper chronometers, but what he wouldn't have known, except from his own knowledge, was what the tides and other phenomena were doing. Yet a chap who'd been out there some years was way ahead of someone who'd just arrived. He knew that, say, going through a particular strait you had a huge current against you. Travelling north between Sulawesi and the southern Philippines for example, there's about 2 knots of stream running against you most of the time. And in some areas you get huge teak logs floating through. If one of them hit a ship like the *Rosalie* it would have caused serious damage."

As they say, a collision at sea can ruin your whole day. I realized we had no reason to believe Salty Sam had ever sailed to the Moluccas before. Perhaps he made a blunder, based on inexperience, that led him to run aground.

"What other challenges might he have faced?"

"Well, piracy was rampant and the Royal Navy was waging a huge war against it throughout the 19th century. There's a famous picture of forty of these bloodthirsty pirates having been captured by the British. They're all kneeling in a row with their heads chopped off lying beside them. By 1860 we'd pretty well stamped out piracy."

"So what's happened?" I complained. "Because they're back."

"You can't keep 'em down without a big nasty bully boy like the Brits were. We owned lots of places, and if pirates turned up we'd go into territorial waters and sort them out. There's no one like that now. These days some of them have fast boats, GPS and other new technology. Off Somalia it's risen dramatically. And they are quite cute. They know exactly how much money they want for a ship – an amount which ties in with the insurance rates. The firms say, 'Hmm, I'd rather pay that than a higher premium' ... so the pirates have got it to a tee. But the sad thing is, they will kill people."

I asked him what navigational issues I and my crew had in store.

"Well, I'm sure you'll sit down and read the Pilot, look at an overall planning chart, look at the weather patterns for it, and ask yourself, 'How close do I want to go to the coast here? Is there a tide running me on, running me off? Are there any shallow areas, any hazards? Do I want to go through there, at dusk, close in, where there've been lots of incidents? Where will I stop, since local people will know I'm here and moving on to there?' You need to think all those sort of things through. Archipelagoes are often more tricky than the open ocean. Then there's weather, and of course a fire at sea is absolutely awful. Is there always going to be someone on watch?"

"Of course," I replied.

"Some yachts don't always have someone on watch. I'm afraid even big merchant ships don't keep as good a watch as they used to. You want to make sure you can be seen on other people's radar and not ploughed through by something bigger. Then there's the whole issue of pirates."

"Well, I was wondering, are you going to have any warships in the general area during March?"

He laughed. "I'll put you in touch with a ship. I've got a carrier battle group going through into the Indian Ocean this year. I've also got a frigate, and I think I've got a nuclear submarine going out that way as well, so the answer is yes, there will be some ships around."

"The nuclear submarine sounds good," I smiled.

"I can't say I can provide one of those to look after you all the way through," demurred the first Sea Lord. "It's excessively expensive…"

"What, I'm not worth it?!" I pouted.

"…but if you see a periscope or something looking at you, you'll know what's going on!"

"I was just thinking it will be good to have those ships' phone numbers tucked into my bra at all times, just in case."

"When Ellen MacArthur went round the world, we had, on three or four occasions, an RN ship which I just tweaked slightly. Obviously we can't use

Modern pirates use fast boats, modern equipment, and automatic weapons. Grappling hooks aid boarding of target vessels.

public monies, or extra fuel, to do it…"

"I'll take all the tweaking I can get!"

"We do try to help people," he smiled. "I recently diverted a ship for a yachtsman who was rowing the Atlantic and got it all wrong. He was blown back and had completely run out of food so we stopped and gave him provisions (without assisting him in the race). We gave him a roast duck lunch."

"If I was your wife, would you let me go on this trip?"

"If you were my wife and I tried to stop you I think I'd probably end up in HASLAR – that's the Royal Naval hospital!"

That rang a bell. Billy is frequently approached by both men and women – on the street, in restaurants and backstage at his concerts – who congratulate him on 'allowing his wife to have those extraordinary adventures'. "Allow?" he always retorts. "You think I could stop her?"

"I would be nervous," continued the First Sea Lord, "if my wife said 'I'm doing a lone yachtswoman trip from Australia, through the Indonesian archipelago, across the Indian Ocean, round the Horn of Africa and up to the UK…' But you've got people with you, haven't you? And presumably you've got a couple of chaps who know how to use a weapon?"

"I've got a couple of chaps and a woman (me) who can use a weapon," I snorted. "We've got some AR15s on board, some flares, some hand guns, we'll have one of those MRAD 500s to make a nasty noise – and we'll have two Gurkhas, an ex-SAS guy and an ex-Royal Marines Commando."

"In that case I don't think you've got any trouble," he said, looking impressed. "The best thing though is not to get yourself in a situation where you have to use those weapons. If you have to do that, they're probably using weapons too, and that's not a good position to be in."

"So how would you avoid that, if someone's coming too close?"

"If they see you've got weapons and are prepared to use them, they are going to be careful about it. These people want an easy touch. They don't want to get their people killed. They'd much rather do a hit, take all your money and go away. But they can be pretty ruthless and violent."

I asked him what he thought had happened to Salty Sam.

"Well, first, what happened to the 80,000 florins?"

"As far as I know, the family never got it."

"The trouble is you can go into conspiracy theory in everything, can't you? But knowing that there were lots of rogues out there then, I'd have thought that someone, like an agent, who suddenly got 80,000 Dutch florins would want to keep it. If he knew where this ship was going, and if he had people working on board, it's not beyond the wit of man to set something up to get rid of the chap who owns the 80,000 – particularly if he's made another Will so none of that goes back to the wife in the UK. That was a lot of money, you know. What happened to the ship?"

"Nobody knows."

"They never found it? It would be unusual to burn the ship. That's worth a lot of money. One would assume it was still running somewhere, and again, with a shipping agent in Surabaya, one would smell a rat. Poirot, I'm sure, would get out there and find out what was going on!"

"To take the conspiracy theory even further," I said, "maybe the agent was in cahoots with the Raja on the island of Carabatoo."

"Or, you could run a completely different story, which would be that Salty Sam didn't want to go back to his wife in the UK and was happy with the one he had out there, and wanted just to disappear off the face of the earth, so to speak, and settle down with his 80,000 florins. You could disappear in those days. Raja Brooks, for example, was a Brit who really ruled Northern Borneo – it was his own kingdom effectively. Fascinating chap. Had head hunters working for him. He was one of those charismatic Men of Empire. There were lots of them, living all over the world. Outrageously behaved, but they must have been great fun."

"What might it have been like, the day-to-day sailing aboard a merchant ship like the *Rosalie*?"

"Oh, the constant movement, the constant noise, the creaking, the groaning, the fact that weather had such an impact, you know, the waves would come over the top quite regularly in bad weather, the fact that you are constantly changing sails, constantly changing course. They were all huggermugger in the bits they actually lived in, which were often wet and humid. Lots of irritations like cockroaches and rats. The drinking water would have been quite bad quality; it would soon have gone green and had things in it. There was heavy drinking of alcohol on board. The food would have been rough at times, although probably quite plentiful.

"The captain would have lived in rather more style. He would have tried to maintain a certain elegance, probably not so much as in a Royal Navy ship. Someone like your great-great-grandfather, who had been doing it for a while, was probably a man of some substance. But he would have always have to be careful where he put his money. Often the captain had a big money belt that he wouldn't take off, because you were always uncertain about some of your people.

"The smells on board would have been quite intense, especially if you were carrying a cargo of spices. You didn't wash much, and then there was the

'There were three ships...' A Royal Navy vessel at the start of the 19th century, would have been well manned.

smell of the spices, the smell of the sea, the smell of the cordage, lots of hemp, all the ropes. The smell of tar, the pitch and the decks…" I was mesmerized by the evocative sensory picture he painted.

"It must have just been amazing, mustn't it?" he said. "And the uncertainty must have been a real edge. Today we all like our certainty. I want to know roughly what the weather is going to be like later, but they didn't know what the currents were doing, they weren't absolutely sure if there was a rock ahead, or the weather might change suddenly and that would be it. You would be deeply religious because these were acts of God. Going down to the sea and seeing the works of the Almighty, as they would put it. If you came from a naval family, a merchant navy family or particularly if you were fishermen, a ship would just disappear and that was it. Often no one ever found out what had happened to it."

"Do you think there would have been women aboard Sam's ship?"

"In that sort of ship? Absolutely."

"So would every sailor have had a woman aboard?"

"No, but I think the bosun, the mate, the captain would often have had women. They would do jobs as well. They would help the chef, they'd do some tailoring. In the Royal Navy at the beginning of the 19th century, there weren't meant to be women but there still were. There were women at Trafalgar. They were married to crew members like the bosun and the gunner, the senior NCOs, the sail maker. So yes, there would have been women on board the *Rosalie*."

"So they would have all been killed too?"

"I wonder. A lot of them would have been mixed race"

"So they might have been taken by the pirates?"

"Yes, I don't think an attractive woman would have been killed by a pirate, even if he killed everyone else."

"We were pirates too, weren't we?"

"Yes, yes, it runs in the blood. One of our strengths, I think."

"It was funny," I remarked, "going to Panama and hearing Sir Francis Drake described as a 'terrible pirata'."

"Well, when you think what they did to the Spanish it was awful. Outrageous behaviour, but then it got a nice veneer, didn't it?"

"Romantic…"

"And it helped the nation, so it's amazing what you forgive. When Drake caught the big treasure ship, it was something like 12 billion of today's money – and the Queen had a big chunk of it, so she was happy."

Tonight I met the most paranoid man in the world. Nicknamed 'Q', he sells ballistic flotation vests, i.e. lifejackets that also protect you from bullets. Sean thinks we should get enough for everyone on board, plus helmets. After casing my hotel room for surveillance cameras, 'Q' hardly spoke, and would answer few of my questions. Honestly. You'd think we were doing a drug deal. After using his own arm as a measuring tape, he announced I would need a 'Large'. They don't even manufacture these things for the female shape. But where else can a girl get accessories like a Fire Retardant Outer Cover, Level IV Armour Plates, Anti-Stab Panels, Detachable Ballistic Collar and, my favourite, Detachable Ballistic Groin Protector? All this plus a handy carry bag!

"What colours do they come in?" I asked.

"Navy, olive, black and orange," replied 'Q'. What a conundrum. Did we want to take navy so we'd be less visible to pirates, or orange so we could be seen by a rescue boat?

FEBRUARY 5

I'm looking forward to being on my sailboat *Takapuna* again. All right, I'm a spoiled bitch, having such a thing of beauty. She is named after my birthplace in New Zealand: 'Takapuna' is a Maori name that means 'high place by the water', and is associated with a legend about romantic longing. Recently she has had a great deal of TLC in a shipyard in Brisbane, including a new paint job, teak decks and improved rigging. She is an Italian-built Valdetarro, a steel-hulled, 112-foot cutter-rigged sloop with a 26-foot beam, and was British-designed by Laurent Giles. Her mast is 130 feet high, and she has three sails: mainsail, staysail and Genoa. She draws only 9 feet, a helpful quality when navigating shallow lagoons.

The *Takapuna* has a large, enclosed pilot house with two navigation stations, and a fore and aft deck. The aft deck leads to a swim platform, and a lazarette (garage) where dive equipment is stored. Below is a large saloon, plus a galley with a crew mess leading to the engine room. With five cabins forward and six aft, she has an unusually large interior volume for a sailboat – one of the qualities that make her an ideal expedition vessel.

A comprehensive satellite capability means that communication by telephone, email and fax is possible anywhere in the world, while her navigational equipment is state of the art. The *Takapuna* has the ability to just sail, just motor, or motorsail – a combination of both. In the engine room purrs a 348 horsepower MTU engine, two John Deere Kilopack generators, plus one large and one auxiliary Village Marine water-maker.

Rolle keeps everything in his domain absolutely spotless. He's a mad, shaggy-haired Viking, whose eccentric sense of humour, lateral thinking and wicked cackle keep his fellow-sailors amused. Beyond that, he is an excellent engineer, a realist with a power of straight-shooting communication, and a kind-hearted softie. He also makes a lethal Mojito, when Kayt lets him into the galley.

Kayt, our cook, is a young Englishwoman from Liverpool. She is beautiful, sweet-natured and brave – and accomplished in the galley, on deck, or at a hundred feet deep. Her food is great – except for one fault: she says that she's terrible with meringues. Not that we'll be eating anything that fancy on this voyage. Kayt's not the only British woman on board. Sue is a slim blonde sailor from the Isle of Wight who takes care of the boat's interior and manages the accounts.

There always has to be an Aussie crew member on board a sailboat. We found first mate Dan, our latest addition, driving jetboats on Sydney Harbour. Out of respect for his new, anonymous bosses, he cut off his beloved dreadlocks. Two days later he found out it was me and Billy – who would have preferred him the way he was. Bummer, dude.

FEBRUARY 7

A few friends turned up to wish me luck and fair weather. It was short notice, but I'd told them, hey, they'd better turn up because after this I could be eaten by pirates. One of my pals, Theo, had wanted to know if there were any bits they'd spit out. It felt like a children's birthday party, all of us in pirate hats and eye patches. I cut the cake with a scimitar, then swashbuckled my way onto the Heathrow Express.

FEBRUARY 9, GOLD COAST, QUEENSLAND

The last time I saw the Miami of the southern hemisphere, the *Takapuna*'s engine was acting up and, in the absence of a breeze, we were forced to limp into Surfer's Paradise. It's Queensland's 'party central'. From way offshore we could hear the screams of people riding rollercoasters at Dreamworld, Sea World and Wet 'n' Wild. This time I took a taxi from the humid airport, along the hotel-lined esplanades where meter-maids were once kitted out in gold lame bikinis to launch a tourist industry that has never looked back. Ah, it's good to be in the sun again.

After a nap, I sneaked into Billy's Surfer's Paradise concert to surprise him – and more particularly to find out what he's saying about me on stage.

It didn't work.

"I had a feeling you might be in the audience tonight," he said after a stunning concert that he edited just in case. Bugger. He's obviously clairvoyant.

Above: King of Comedy reduced to drive-in performance – Billy's Surfer's Paradise billboard.

Below: Reunited with the *Takapuna*.

FEBRUARY 10, CAIRNS

Billy and I took a morning plane hop to Cairns, where the *Takapuna* was waiting, having been released from her "arrest" to travel north in time to meet us. My husband ensconced himself on the aft deck with his banjo and a cup of tea, while I began my task of sorting out and stocking our cabins. Do I have enough sunscreen aboard? Shampoo? Long-sleeved shirts for covering up in Muslim countries? Bug spray? Hormones? (I wouldn't want to perpetrate low-oestrogen mood swings upon fellow-mariners!)

Back in London, Russ is pulling together the expedition partners and finances, Lisa is creating a promotional DVD, and Lucy, our Project Manager, has miraculously managed to solve our visa situation. Here in Cairns, every crew member is busy with last-minute provisioning, stocking and prepping the boat. Rolle is tinkering with the engine and water-maker, Kayt is putting aboard food and galley supplies. Sue is trying to prepare the berths for the largest number of people we've ever had aboard: seventeen! The captain, as always, is wrestling with the electronics and communications, Ricky is counting out anti-malarial tablets, while Dan always seems to be up the mast in the bosun's chair playing with the rigging. This is our last-chance town.

This evening the whole *Takapuna* crew went along to see Billy's show. It was brilliant, but I was so jet-lagged I kept nodding off. I don't think that impressed people sitting nearby. I'm sure they were saying, "You'd think his own wife would try a little harder." Afterwards, the crew said I'd had a few mentions, not all of them so flattering. At least Billy left our sex life out of it for a change. Apparently he does this hilarious thing about how I can speak volumes with a silent look. It's true.

On Yer (collapsible) Bike – Scottish comedian sells car to buy yacht.

FEBRUARY 11

Billy brought his collapsible bicycle on board, but when he tried to assemble it to go for a quick ride, he'd forgotten how. He spent several hours trying to work it out. The crew was amused by all the swearing – although no one dared offer to help. But they were impressed, I'm sure, at his perseverance.

I must say, my husband's being very good about the fact that I'm about to take off for ages to parts unknown. He's worried about my safety – although he does seem to have confidence in my ability to take care of myself: "Them pirates don't know what they're up against."

Chapter *6* Kiwi Gold

FEBRUARY 12, BAY OF ISLANDS, NEW ZEALAND

I said goodbye to Billy, who's off to open his concerts in Sydney and Melbourne, and left for New Zealand. We're used to separations, although it's always easier when each of us is leaving to do something we're passionate about. In my opinion, a good marriage leaves room for each partner to fulfil a mad dream occasionally, even if it doesn't happen to be shared. Billy does not quite see why I want to follow the Salty Sam trail. But I love him all the more because he is so understanding about my need to do so. He knows I won't be able to rest until I've followed this adventure through.

After arriving in Auckland, Robin, Ricky and I took a helicopter up the north-east coast to the gorgeous Bay of Islands, site of New Zealand's first European settlement. On the way I was able to enjoy a brilliant view of my birthplace. I spent many happy childhood days on the beach at Takapuna. It lies opposite the volcanic island of Rangitoto, where I learned to fish. The *Takapuna* sailed triumphantly past its namesake last summer, with my ninety-year-old Uncle Bill waving from the balcony of his seaside apartment.

After landing near the town of Russell, we trekked along the waterfront where Salty Sam's son established a trading store. He and Hira lived close by at Tapeka. I find it interesting that Samuel Jr found a local wife, thus unknowingly emulating his father's likely relationship with an Indonesian woman. Or did he discover that secret when he sailed to Indonesia to try and unfreeze the family assets? Did he keep quiet to protect his mother from the painful untruth?

Christ Church, in Kororareka, the Maori name for Russell, is New Zealand's oldest surviving church, finished around 1836. Samuel Jr and his wife (whose European name Ada Charlotte appears on her headstone) are buried here. So is Salty Sam's wife Ann, who came out here to join her son but died shortly afterwards in 1842. My cousin Joan plays the organ at Christ Church. It is a wonderful little place of worship, with needlepoint cushions depicting local flora, fauna and vistas. On one outside wall is a large hole made by a cannon ball, fired from HMS *Hazard* while its officers attempted to stop the sacking of the town by the chief Heke. The town of Russell saw many clashes between Maoris and Europeans, and in the middle of it all were Samuel and Hira. As a bi-racial couple they must have had some particularly difficult marital challenges at that time.

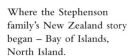

Where the Stephenson family's New Zealand story began – Bay of Islands, North Island.

Pompalliar House, a substantial, two-storeyed colonial building with lovely verandahs, sits on the bay. Named after a bishop who lived there, it was originally the headquarters of the French Catholic mission, and is the oldest surviving building associated with the history of the Roman Catholic Church in New Zealand. In the early 1900s it was owned by my great-uncle Henry, one of Salty Sam's grandsons. He made the house a bit of a showplace, complete with ornamental cannon and flagstaff.

I walked on the beach at Tapeka, where on Aprli 1, 1836, Samuel Jr purchased 30 acres of land from Chief Rewa in exchange for one cask of tobacco, one double flint gun and one piece of cotton. With a frontage of 650 feet along this sandy beach and bounded by a freshwater creek, it was a killer deal – and an ideal site for his home. It sat beneath the enormous Norfolk pines he planted, and chatted to my cousin Brett, who collaborated with my father on the booklet about Salty Sam's son. He shocked me by being the first to point out Hira's legacy to me. "She too was a woman capable of taking off from her family for long periods," he smiled. "Remind you of anyone?"

FEBRUARY 13, AUCKLAND

I visited Auckland's Maritime Museum today. It is wonderful, but there was nothing relevant to my great-great-grandfather. They have a marketing 'character' called Salty Sam, designed by one of my relatives for their educational programme. From the look of this individual, with white beard and navy blazer, he may be based on another sea captain in my family: one of Salty's grandsons, who was my great-uncle. Captain Edward Stephenson (known to his friends as Ted) took passengers on an elegant summer cruise aboard a 300-ton Northern Company steamer called the *Ngapuhi* (pronounced na-poo-he) round the northern beaches of New Zealand. From 1904 to 1908 up to ninety passengers at a time, dressed in bonnets, long skirts and stiff suits, would embark from Queen Street wharf in Auckland. Captain Ted steered them across the Hauraki Gulf, up the coast to the Bay of Islands and back again. It was *the* cruise. On the way passengers picnicked beneath spikey red pohutukawa blossoms, raced horses uphill, bathed in mineral springs, and dined rather well.

After comparing this picture with one of Samuel Jr, I can now visualize my great-great-grandfather. As far as I know, there is no existing portrait of Salty Sam, but nevertheless, there seem to be sufficient family likenesses between these two ancestors and my own father to get a sense of his defining features.

Captain Ted's photo shows him as a handsome, imposing man with whitening beard and moustache, his arms folded over a tight-fitting, slightly rumpled uniform. With his collar and tie, a peaked cap bearing the company insignia, and a jacket with polished buttons, he seems the epitome of a charismatic and reliable sea captain. Facially, he looks like my father, with somewhat hooded eyelids. As for his expression, there is a no-nonsense air about him, perhaps a little bit on the grumpy side. He looks as though he's about to say, "Just hurry up and take the damn photo!"

FEBRUARY 14, WELLINGTON

Absolutely amazing luck. It turned out that the Alexander Turnbull Library here has many original documents relating to Samuel Stephenson, including letters from Sam Jr and his brother-in-law in England, plus all the legal correspondence that went back and forth between Batavia and London over Salty Sam's Will. Best of all, I found my great-great-grandfather's financial accounts for several years leading up to his disappearance.

This is the best haul of information so far. In these accounts there are clues about a previous ship Sam had owned, details of cargoes he'd bought before leaving Surabaya, and what his income and outgoings were. It's going to take me a while to decipher it all, but it's absolute gold! There is no mention of opium but, of course, if he was being a bad boy, it wouldn't be in the books.

Captain Ted Stephenson (front centre) poses with Ngapuhi cruisers.

I did notice there was a lot of booze aboard. As a matter of fact, there was so much mention of gin (50 cases), brandy (23 cases), and Madeira (12.5 doz.) that when I came to the last line of the seventh account I misread it as: 9 doz. of claret and several old drunks (trunks). The rest of his cargo was more sober: rice, sugar, straw bags, nuts, cheroots and Bengal chintz. Perhaps the most interesting aspect of the accounts for the years prior to 1821 is that, before the *Rosalie*, Salty Sam owned a ship called *Wolfe's Cove*, that seems to have been lost, because recovery expenses are listed. Not only that, but he lost a legal battle with one of the mates from the *Wolfe's Cove*, which makes me think a little more about the mutiny story.

At the end of this fantastic day of findings we flew back to Cairns, after spending a delightful Valentine's Day evening in the Qantas lounge at Sydney. Oh well.

But at least it gave me a chance to peek at the letters written by Salty Sam's son to his brother-in-law Richard in London. On December 20, 1827 Sam Jr expressed great satisfaction in his colonial life at Tapeka, and relief in being away from England.

> *The accounts we hear from Europe are dreadful particularly America and England. Nothing but bankruptcy… I expect you will all be obliged to emigrate to this land of freedom to live upon fish and potatoes… I am happy to say I enjoy excellent health … about forty inches around the belly – think of that. Dear Richard don't you envy me? When will you be so great a man?*

By 1843 it was a different story:

> *Men are going about the country glad to get work for their food and many living with the natives. When I arrived here they were getting four pounds per month… There is no employment for vessels just now. The depression appears to be the same everywhere.*

That same year, Samuel wrote of fighting between Europeans and Maoris:

> *My Dear Richard,*
> *Herewith you will receive a letter for May and also newspapers giving the particulars of … a dreadful massacre near Nelson, one of the settlements on the South Island … there has been a great sacrifice of life amongst the Europeans … twenty-three … dead and several missing…*

On 6th September, 1842, when Salty Sam's widow Ann had been in the Bay of Islands for very little time, he wrote:

> *My Dear Richard,*
> *With grief I wish to inform you that my dear mother is no more. She breathed her last on Saturday 3rd of September… Sensible to the last. And with the greatest resignation, with a smile on her countenance, which she retained for the day of her buriel, which took place this morning… Her complaint was a disease in the urinary passage and bladder… She has been a great sufferer for some months but I hope I feel assured she is in heaven. This has been a dreadful affliction to me in my solitary home and what will it be to poor Mary? I have not written to her, I cannot muster resolution, I must therefore leave it to you to communicate the melancholy news… I shall forward to poor Mary by the first opportunity direct our father's miniature and other relics…*
> *Believe me to remain yours in affliction, Samuel Stephenson*

Resting place of Salty Sam's
wife at Christ Church,
Kororareka, New Zealand.

Where, oh where, did that miniature end up? It was possibly the one
and only picture of Salty Sam. Did it make it back to England? Or is it lying
in an attic in Russell?

FEBRUARY 15

Time to bring in the Big Guns, historically-speaking. Russ has persuaded Anne
Bulley to do some research for us in London. She is an expert on the 'Country
Traders', independent Captains who traded on Indian-built vessels between India
and the Far East and has written a marvellous book about one of them.

Salty Sam was not a Country Trader. But, with yesterday's new information
from the Alexander Turnbull Library, Anne has been able to trace more details
of Salty Sam's previous ship, the *Wolfe's Cove*. Lloyd's Register indicates that she
was a 350- or 356-ton, single deck copper-sheathed ship, built in Quebec in 1812.
She was surveyed in London as A1 and sailed for the Isle de France [Mauritius]
on April 25, 1818 as a 'licensed India ship' (owner C.Waltham). Sam may have had
yet another ship, called the *Helen*. Was he the Onassis of Rotherhithe?

Chapter 7 A Flaming
Nuisance

FEBRUARY 16, CAIRNS

The mood on the boat is not good. We are about to take off for the dodgy waters of Indonesia with more people aboard than we've ever had. Chris, my ex-SAS security advisor, arrived today to supervise our piracy drills. Sean, an ex-Royal Marines commando, who will remain on board as our chief security officer, came with him. A dry-humoured Welshman resembling a bald bear with freckles, Sean will be our best defence against pirates, terrorists or anyone else who threatens the *Takapuna*. He's just done a year's duty in Baghdad, so make a loud noise and he'll hit the deck.

The captain is extremely worried about the trip. And when the captain is edgy, there is a ripple effect on everyone else. He thinks he's going to end up in an Indonesian jail, because that did happen recently to an Australian skipper who was visiting Bali. But the reason was that the Australian didn't declare his weapons when he arrived. Rumour has it he fired a crew member who became disgruntled and dobbed him in to the Indonesian authorities.

Another thing weighing on my captain's mind is the thought that even though we're going to play it by the book, there could still be trumped-up charges. From what we understand of Indonesian government bureaucracy, the head honchos in different ports can be as creative as they like in interpreting the rules, sometimes in the cause of receiving large bribes. Now, that's their culture and that's just the way it works. We have all kinds of nefarious business practices in our own society and I'm not criticizing the Indonesians for that. But it does mean that we are up against the unknown. For example, we have the correct paperwork for our weapons, but we don't know whether somebody might say, "I don't accept your paperwork" and either ask for huge sums of money or accuse us of weapons smuggling.

Tonight we had a crew outing to the pub, where the local entertainment was a night of cane toad racing. We had heard on the radio that a bucket of cane toads could be exchanged for a sixpack of beer, but this was the first time I'd seen one of the critters up close. The cane toad was introduced to Queensland in 1935. The idea was to do Australia's sugar cane industry a favour by wiping out the beetles that were threatening crops. But someone got his wires crossed during the research phase. The plan had worked in Hawaii, where the offending beetles were ground dwellers and therefore easily snapped up by hopping amphibians. Unfortunately, the schemers had failed to notice that the Australian sugar-eating beetle lived higher up the cane – in fact, well beyond the reach of the cane toad. Meanwhile, blow me down with a boomerang if those giant toxic froggies didn't multiply to numbers beyond anyone's imagination – to the extent that they are now rampant, and marching south to Sydney as we speak.

But the fact that the creatures lack predators and have multiplied to plague proportions is hardly their fault. It certainly doesn't excuse the mishandling they were subjected to this evening in the name of 'fun'. I slunk away, after a miserable few minutes in which I saw someone actually blow air into the amphibian until he almost exploded. That competition was rivalled only by a 'beauty contest' in which participants were publicly rated by a sozzled audience. Frankly, I'd rather be naked on 'Big Brother'.

Mr Toad's Wild Ride: Cane critters race in a Queensland pub, not my idea of fun.

FEBRUARY 18

Anne has found out that, before Salty Sam owned her, the *Wolfe's Cove* was pirated in 1813 by a privateer vessel called the *Grand Turk*, then later snatched back! Then, in 1818, she was a licensed India ship that made a voyage from Java to Mauritius and back again. But get this: in January 1819 she was driven on shore in Mauritius, but was refloated and sold after her masts and spars were saved first. Was my great-great-grandfather a bad driver, or what?

Today my cousin Alistair, another descendant of Salty Sam, drove up to visit me. He's a New Zealand farmer who now lives on the Queensland coast. As a child he teased me mercilessly, and I was fascinated by him because I rarely heard his name spoken without the words "That naughty ..." in front of it. At seven years old, for example, he tried to sell his older sister to a gang of Maori boys for the equivalent of two weeks' pocket money. He was incorrigible, yes, but also open-minded, honest and kind hearted. Nowadays he is an outrageous party animal with a repertoire of shockingly uncouth and politically incorrect stories that immediately engaged the whole crew in a game of 'What's he going to say next?' This evening, on the aft deck, he treated us to a *Haka*, a traditional Maori war dance that he adapted for the occasion:

We are from Takapuna, best boat on the sea
Skull your beer, skull your beer – More! More!
We have the balls – Bigger! Bigger!

What followed is unprintable, but it was performed with a great deal of stamping and chest-slapping; at the end he dropped to one knee and, with the veins popping out above his ferociously staring eyes, waggled his tongue in and out for a good half-minute. I saw a new-found respect beneath the disbelieving faces of my fellow voyagers: "He's your first cousin? No kidding?"

FEBRUARY 19

In 2003 there were 133 attacks on vessels in Indonesia. Today, Chris briefed us all on piracy issues. I've noticed, though, that some of the crew refuse to believe there's a threat. I only hope they're right.

There are other threats too. We are all being vaccinated against diseases including rabies, Japanese encephalitis, hepatitis A and B, cholera, typhoid and yellow fever. We will also be taking anti-malarial tablets, and arming ourselves with insect spray to avoid being bitten by mosquitoes, which can carry dengue fever. Currently there are concerns about avian flu in Indonesia and China, so Ricky's trying to find supplies of Tamiflu. He has been assembling a comprehensive ship's medicine chest and medical kit that will cover most eventualities. In addition, we will be carrying a defibrillator and a Tempus 2000. The latter is an electronic box, complete with video camera, that can relay patient information such as blood pressure and electro-cardiogram to the Medlink remote medical network for fast additional assistance.

Kayt has been stocking the galley fridges and pantries with enough food to keep the crew happy for several months at a time. We normally catch fish while travelling, and thus we have fresh daily protein. As time progresses, we will have to rely more and more on vegetables and other staples bought in the regions we'll be visiting.

Something old, something new: good old-fashioned paper charts will come in useful as well as the state-of-the-art electronics installed in the *Takapuna*'s starboard navigation station.

The captain has been obtaining charts of all the areas where we plan to travel, as well as arranging for cruising permits, visas and guides. He has been talking with local people to find safe anchorages and marinas. Rolle and Dan have been tinkering with the winches, obtaining special bladders in which to store extra fuel for the longer journeys, and making sure every aspect of the boat is 'shipshape'. Our new camera person, Pete, arrived today to replace our first cameraman Robin, whose girlfriend has offered him an ultimatum. Pete's a tall and rugged young man from Surrey, who has never sailed off-shore. Will he get seasick? I fear there's money down on that.

FEBRUARY 20

This week the TAFE Queensland Institute here in Cairns is offering a sea safety course I'd always wanted to do. With a little time on our hands while we wait for weather, Ricky, Pete, Sean and I began the Standards of Training, Certification and Watchkeeping (STCW) course, an international requirement for professional mariners that covers sea survival, on-board safety and firefighting.

Today was entirely a classroom experience, but later in the week there will be two days of firefighting. On Friday we'll go off-shore in a training boat, leap over the side, and try to make it into a life raft before being eaten by crocodiles, which are prevalent up here. These waters are also known for the lethal irukandji, and its big cousin the box jellyfish. The latter has forty-six brains and sixty arseholes, and I'd like to avoid meeting up with even one of its orifices.

After school, I went with Sean to meet the crazy Q, who has arrived to clear our body armour through customs. He was as weird as ever. Since his literature claims the vest will right an unconscious person on their back, I made him put on one of his expensive 'ballistic flotation vests' and threw him into the hotel pool to see if it worked. He hated that, not because he found my actions unnecessary, but because he didn't think the chlorine would react well with the anti-ballistic fabric of the plates. Is it just me?

FEBRUARY 21

The second day of our STCW course. We studied Effective Human Relationships on Board, Approach to Duties, and Accident Awareness, all of which seemed extremely *a propos*. In the afternoon we began our fire-fighting course, focusing on the various types of fire and the Containment, Control and Extinguish protocol. We were shown a video of a room catching fire, and another of firemen fighting an out-of-control blaze aboard a docked cargo ship. Scary stuff.

Russ arrived halfway through the afternoon. It's great to have him here. He's been getting to know the boat and crew, and I think his energy and positive outlook are a blessing. I'd like to spend time with him this evening, but I have to study all night for my exam tomorrow. Since the local newspapers have got wind of my attendance at this course, it would be awfully embarrassing if I failed.

'Q' tipped! Our mystery supplier of body armour was not impressed when I had him thrown in the pool for a buoyancy test.

FEBRUARY 22

The *Cairns Post* this morning has a ridiculously large portrait of me on the front page with the headline "Mrs. Connolly's World Tour". Oh, God.

We took off for TAFE and sat our written exam, which thankfully turned out OK. The next heart-starter occurred at the local fire station to begin the practical side of our firefighting course. 'Boundary Cooling' – what a concept! A frightening array of fires for us to extinguish. I rather fancied myself straddling the hose in a yellow helmet, doing a sort of equestrian side-step with my fellow hoser. The worst bit, though, was getting to grips with the Self-Contained Breathing Apparatus. I seem to be technically challenged when it comes to valves, screws and tubes. It's essential to get it absolutely correct, because not only are we going to be tested on it, but tomorrow we're going to be pushed into a burning tunnel. One mistake and we'll fry.

Hah! I learned something today that has provided me with ammunition to be evil. Rolle is our designated fire-fighter, but I discovered that no one with facial hair should use the breathing apparatus because it is impossible to get a proper seal. I may yet see our Viking clean shaven!

FEBRUARY 23

That wasn't funny, today. The firemen set a raging furnace inside a narrow, metal cylinder which was a mock-up of a crashed, burning plane. Then they made us crawl inside to fight 'the burn', as they call it. We approached the hissing doorway like men conscripted onto a reckless rocket to Mars. "A few of you might get minor burns," warned Don. "But we're up to that, right?" No one answered.

The heat was beyond cruel. I could actually feel my knees being singed as I crept along the searing-hot steel grid, trying to keep low enough to prevent my helmet visor from melting. I was aware that Don was shouting instructions about where to point the hose, such as "Paint the wall!" or "Paint the gases!" but it was hard to differentiate the commands. I could barely see and the roar of the flames was terrifying. At one point I disgraced myself by accidentally painting the fire instead of the wall, sending hissing, scalding steam backfiring on top of us. Terrible firemanship.

As evening fell, I was put in charge of a hose and asked to advance upon a racing, billowing wall of fire. Approaching within three or four metres of it, I have to confess I became mesmerized by its living allure. It was beautiful and terrifying, all at the same time: a roaring gold-and-scarlet Medusa with green flecks and a violet heart. At one point, in the midst of imminent danger, I lost my

Below left: A creation for Ladies' Day at Ascot, with visor and anti-singe hood.

Below right: Great Walls of Fire! Advancing on a raging inferno during the Queensland fire-fighting course.

mind, being suddenly incapable of working out which way to turn the hose valve. Nasty moment. Fortunately there was a professional by my side. I just pray I never have to deal with a fire at sea. Way worse than pirates.

Back on board, Russ, the captain and I discussed our route to Indonesia. It seems best to head for the city of Kupang, in West Timor, clear into Indonesia there, then sail north-west to the Banda Islands, the former centre of the nutmeg trade. After Banda we would continue further north to Maluku, the former Moluccas, stopping at Ambon and Ternate, where the clove trade once flourished, then wind our way south to Jakarta and Surabaya, where Salty Sam's shipping agents were. Finally we will retrace what we think was Sam's last voyage, eastwards to the Straits of Alas, to try to find the island of Carabatoo and what remains of the *Rosalie*. All the while we would be searching for clues, and it is my hope that the captain and crew will be flexible enough to alter course if something comes up.

I'm afraid Ambon is going to present a big, big problem. I've been advised by an Australian friend who knows these waters that if Ambon appears on our application for an Indonesian Cruising Permit we'll become the subject of an intelligence investigation and will probably be refused entry to Indonesia altogether. He recommends we bribe someone in nearby Northern Sulawesi to sanction a side trip. Sounds very dodgy. The captain and several others don't want to go to Ambon under any circumstances. Well, it is considered risky, due to civil unrest, and my marine insurance won't cover it.

FEBRUARY 24

We all got through the sea survival course, but I hope I never have occasion to get in a life raft again. It's horrid. Apart from being bounced around like a sneaker in a washing machine, the training video made it clear that you would lose all personal dignity. It even showed a man simulating taking a dump in front of his fellow survivors. "Everyone should have a bowel movement within the first twenty-four hours," said the voice-over. Nice.

This evening my classmates and I met at a local pub for an 'end of course' party. All the cute young girls there, who'd been chatting up Pete, Ricky and Sean throughout the week, were decked out in their mini skirts and bare-tummy tops.

Hope the crocodiles are colour blind... Sea survival training in Cairns.

"How did you get your job?" I was asked by a pushy, petite blonde.

"I just slept with the owner," I replied sweetly. She didn't get it.

At one point I crept up on Sean, surrounded by wide-eyed chicks, telling tales of his recent security gig in Baghdad. "Guess you lost a lot of good men out there…" I said, repeating a line used by the leading characters in the movie 'Wedding Crashers' to pull women. Okay, my comment was in terribly bad taste, but I couldn't help myself. I'm a bad-ass bitch.

FEBRUARY 26

We went for a sail today. It was wonderful just to get out of the dock and feel the breeze – a real morale-booster. I think our newcomers were surprised at just how much we were heeling over as we sailed along. Pete asked me, "It'll be pretty much like this at sea, right?" I didn't want to frighten him, but it was about a twentieth of how intense the sailing experience can be, especially in bad weather. If I tell him the truth he might turn tail.

We've accomplished a lot this week. It's been hard, and I've still got a blistering burn on my knee. But I feel a great sense of achievement that I've completed the STCW course, and I'm pleased the others did too. It also sends a message to the professional sailors on board that the FNGs (Fucking New Guys, as Sean calls them) are willing to learn, and take on-board safety seriously.

An added bonus is that, through meeting others doing the course, I've found an underwater videographer for our team. Tessa is an outgoing and athletic young Australian from Port Douglas, who'll do triple duty, being also stewardess and production secretary. But we still need one more crew member, an able hand who can work both on deck and below. Oh, and they've got to fit in. This is supposed to be a Prima-Donna-Free Zone.

A first sailing trial for new expedition members, Cairns.

The weather's deceptively pleasant, considering there's a cyclone moving toward the north-west corner of Australia, close to where we are. Before we leave we'll have to make sure we aren't running into anything like that. I trust the captain to keep checking on the situation but the region where we'll be heading is exactly where those nasty tropical storms start brewing.

I'm worried about Billy. He sounds really sick. At first I thought it was just bad reception on the phone. He caught a virus and now he's practically lost his voice. It's a good thing he had a day off or he might have had to cancel the show. I was telling him I can't wait to get going. I just want to be at sea, getting close to the Spice Islands, and find another clue. Instead I'm moping about the boat trying to keep busy, trying to learn Indonesian, trying to exercise. I did a few press-ups today, girlie-style, not too low, and I boxed a couple of rounds on the stern with Ricky, which nearly killed me.

It's been a pressured week for everybody. I felt bad that everyone had to work today, Sunday, but we had to go out sailing so that Russ could experience it

Problems with the sail have Dan working 110 feet skywards.

before he leaves tomorrow for London. He'll rejoin in Kupang, after stopping off in Mauritius, where the *Rosalie* was built and registered, to see what clues he can pick up there. We'll probably depart either on the weekend or on Monday. My crew won't leave port on a Friday or a Sunday, due to a sailors' superstition – probably created to avoid missing a weekend piss-up.

MARCH 2

Frustrating news. It looks like we are definitely not leaving here this week and probably not before the end of next week. At least we are no longer under arrest; the lawyers have sorted that out. There's been a big cyclone brewing up north, but the worst thing was that we've had problems with the mainsail. We've had to drop it three times in the last four days. It's been away to the sail maker for repairs, and has returned in better shape, but now we have to tune the rigging. We are also still waiting for a few shipments and deliveries. At least the underwater scooters came today. We've received four very cool Sea-Doo Seascooter Explorers, in bright orange, that will enable us to zoom around during our wreck dives much faster than we could swim.

One reason why the captain is worried about all the extra people on board is that it's hard to keep track of everyone's whereabouts. Someone could disappear off the stern and nobody would know. As an added safety precaution I've ordered some personal man-overboard devices, small McMurdo transmitters that you wear round your neck with your life vest. If you fall overboard they emit a signal, so that somebody on board knows your location, and your GPS position is transmitted to a satellite. It's not a good idea to fall overboard at sea. Frankly, your prospects aren't great.

Although I'm sure everybody just wants to leave, there is actually a lot to do. Rolle's repairing the bow thrusters. The captain is juggling a great number of things, and his anxiety level continues to be high. In fact, at the moment he's rageful. Somebody left some chocolate biscuits on the galley floor two nights ago and he just read the riot act. I'm sure it seems petty to people who have just come on board, but there is a point to it – which is that when fourteen or fifteen people are living in a small space and sharing one tiny galley, they have to be respectful of each other and tidy up after themselves.

Sean is still trying to deal with the fact that not too many Takapunians are interested in security. I think that's hard for him. He wants to be respected as a valued member of the crew, but that cannot be achieved while people are ambivalent about whether or not they want – or need – to be protected. I think Pete and Robin too are struggling with feeling like outsiders, but that just takes time to correct. I have to believe that when we go to sea we'll be more of a team. I noticed that, when it was time to drop the mainsail this week, everyone lent a hand. That was positive.

Dan and Ricky have been working hard on deck. I help them when I can, but today I've been organizing my cabin. You'd think that after nearly two years I'd be used to living in such a small space. In fact I'm very happy in there, since it feels so womb-like. But because I'm writing, recording the journey, and running things on shore as well, I've had to cram in a lot of papers, books (thirty-two so far) and technology (computers, cardboard file and a hard drive). And there's all my crap from last year, when I was travelling round the South Pacific, in little hidey holes. It was so badly stowed that when we went for a sail and started heeling everything began to fly around and I got a real wake-up call.

I received a very 'to-the-point' email from Billy today. It just said "Dear Pamsy, where are you? Love Billy." I've lost my cell phone, so he hasn't been able to call me. Ricky came to see me this evening with a sad face, having just received the following email from Trudy's daughter:

> Hi Ricky
> I am e-mailing you as I can't reach Pamela but would be grateful if you would pass on the very sad news that Trudy has passed away. Her condition deteriorated slowly to the point where she needed to be admitted to hospital where she was very happy and comfortable for 10 days. Her condition became critical on Thursday 2nd; she went to sleep at 17.45.
> We would be grateful if Pamela would pass this news on to Billy; Mum was very fond of them both.
> Fiona

MARCH 5, GREAT BARRIER REEF

The Ides of March. I wonder who's stabbing whom in the back, on board the *Takapuna*? It's extraordinary that I have this beautiful boat, yet I had to get away for the weekend.

So many elements are conspiring to make this expedition stressful for the entire team. We're not just engaged in sailing the boat, nor are we limited to protecting ourselves from the ravages of the sea; we're also preparing to ward off piratical human threats. On top of that, we're trying to record the expedition. And first and foremost I'm trying to find out what happened to Salty Sam, which in itself carries problems and dangers. Certainly we are

Taking time out for some
much needed thinking.

attempting something extraordinary. We're sailing to areas of the world where hardly anybody goes, even today. The Straits of Alas, Java, and Maluku are not on the tourist beat. In fact, these are serious no-go areas for Westerners – especially in a yacht.

One of my biggest problems is self-doubt. Am I the kind of leader that I need to be? Really, I'm a one-woman band, but in this situation I'm not in sole charge. I pay the captain's wages and I rely on him to run the boat – but privately I'm not enthralled by his approach. I know that males and females do have different leadership styles. Women tend to manage groups of people by networking, by empathizing, by getting on the same level with their employees and bonding with them. They'll self-disclose, and will use all kinds of particularly female techniques to motivate people. My captain's brand of leadership is the opposite: the male gorilla approach.

The man's a brilliant captain in so many ways, and I understand his anxiety; in fact I think it covers up fear. He's afraid of the unknown, he's never been up to Indonesia and he's heard conflicting stories. He's understandably worried about the large number of people on board, especially since several have never had sailing experience. And he's legally responsible for them. That's a huge load.

I want to do everything I can to help him. But anxious people need to control their universe and, as his boss, I'm his worst nightmare: a woman he can't control. I've talked to him endlessly, but we have serious differences of opinion about several aspects of this journey. Big issues, like security. Honestly, I am so close to putting anti-anxiety medication in his tea. I wish the man would smoke dope or something. I feel he wants to leave. Should I ask him to? I honestly don't think I could find somebody else and get them up to speed in time for us to get this journey done. Hmm. What would Hemingway do in this situation? Or Conrad?

What usually happens in a crisis is I look to myself. What can I do to improve the situation? The only thing I know is to sit down with people, both one-to-one and in a group, and get to know what their concerns are. That doesn't seem to work here. How am I going to pull these people together as a team? How am I going to make this a palatable journey for everybody, including myself? Because right now I don't even feel like going.

I'm glad I've got Ricky to talk to. He's my best pal on the boat and I moan to him a lot, poor man. I'm sure he's fed up with me. I can't talk to Billy about the problems on board because he'd probably just say, "Well, you're no day at the beach yourself" (which is true, of course) or else, "Why don't you just come home?"

> Dear Pam,
> My Blueberry has committed suicide without warning so I am stuck with the bloody E mail. Drop me a line and tell me how the journey is shaping up.
> Billy

MARCH 7, CAIRNS

We still haven't worked out which island in modern Indonesia was formerly Carabatoo. Without this information we can't confirm our route, because we don't know our final destination. Naturally the captain is anxious to know.

Even Andrew Cook, the expert from the British Library, has been unable to find the island. Having gone back to records from the 17th and 18th centuries, such as the East India Directories and the Admiralty Pilot, he came to the conclusion that Carabatoo was not necessarily a name for an island, but rather a descriptive name for an area. Since *karrang* means coral and *batoo* means rocky shoal (rocks that don't break the waves but are perilous to ships) he thinks 'Carabatoo' refers to an area that local sailors might have named.

Anne Bulley thinks that if the survivors were mutineers they would not have wanted anyone to identify the island. They may have had a hide-out there where they stored their booty and were, therefore, being purposely vague. Or they may have been talking about another island for which their code-word was Carabatoo. Lucy feels we'll have more luck in finding out about this by visiting The Hague. She plans to take Anne over within a couple of weeks. It's funny – I always thought 'Carabatoo' sounded too romantic to be a real place.

MARCH 8

We have a very full boat, and there's more to come. Right now, besides the captain and me there are five sailing crew: Kayt, Rolle, Sue, Dan and Dan's friend Scotty who has just joined us as our long-awaited extra hand. A cool, lanky, long-haired Aussie, Scotty is a veteran of tall ships. He can cook, identify every planet in the solar system, and find the hippest nightclub anywhere in the world. Since he's six foot seven, his feet stick ten inches out of his bunk.

Among other crew members, Ricky will not only be our medic, but also attend to watches, winches, deck duty, and tender-driving. In Kupang, Sean's security team will gain our two ex-Gurkhas, Dev and Tek – if they can get their visas. To help record the expedition, Pete and Tessa will be joined by Russ and Jim, who'll likewise come on board in Kupang. Jim will be an added boon to our security team since, before he was a cameraman, he was in the SAS.

There is not a lot of improvement in on-board relationships between sailing crew and Fucking New Guys. Lately, people have split into factions. Each team watches the other for cock-ups, such as leaving a camera in the pub (video crew), and falling into the harbour after drinking a lot of vodka (sailing crew). I took everyone to task after I saw a tally score chalked up in the galley:

Boat crew = 1, Visitors = 2. There was, of course, a common denominator for many of the 'incidents', which is alcohol. It's a good thing we'll be dry at sea.

I have tried to educate everyone about the different tasks each team must carry out. I know there is a difficulty for the creative team, who by definition may find it harder to switch into practical gear at a moment's notice. Not everyone can jump instantly from right-brain to left-brain activity, and I can foresee conflict, not to mention safety issues, looming once we're underway.

There are many rules on board. Everyone must take a watch, clean up after himself, and help in the galley. Then there are all the safety precautions, abandon-ship protocol, and all emergency procedures specific to the *Takapuna*. Dan has taken the newcomers through the watch-keeping orders. He has stressed that they are expected to be awake and alert fifteen minutes before the watch, wearing a life-vest. Before the watch is handed over, the previous watch keeper must pass on full information about our position, heading, sails, and wind, tide or current, weather warnings, and the position and movements of other vessels in the vicinity.

There are hundreds more rules about beacons, buoys, overtaking and rubbish disposal but the most important rule for a watch keeper is maintaining a proper lookout at all times, and by all available means. Not only must they constantly scan the horizon, but they must also learn to read navigation instruments and plot our course every hour – tasks that take some considerable effort of study.

Even though FNGs will always be partnered with a more experienced watch master, all this is still a sizable learning curve for our neophytes, so I'm pleased that Dan is so patient with everyone. Rolle showed equal understanding when he took all FNGs through the engine-room checks. Other rules that will take some getting used to are those that involve living with others in confined quarters. People who are used to having someone pick up after them will soon get a rude shock.

Kayt has issued a flyer headed, 'CONGRATULATIONS! YOU ARE TODAY'S GALLEY BITCH!', outlining all the tasks required by her 'helper' of the day, a job that will be shared by most. It involves helping to prepare meals, and serving, doing dishes, and cleaning the galley floor. The need for life on board to be efficient does take some getting used to. We have to remember to keep our portholes closed at sea, practise extreme water conservation and stow personal items and equipment carefully. Given the high cost of satellite communication we must keep phone and internet use to an absolute minimum. Plates or utensils must be washed up and put away immediately after use. The other night, a teacup lying in the galley sink rolled around and woke everyone in the crew quarters – leading to a blow-up the next day.

I know some of these expectations seem petty to people who've never been at sea. But one reason why the captain and sailing crew can be uptight about seemingly small matters is that they are gauging each person's ability to respond safely, accurately and fast in an emergency. At sea we all have to count on each other to survive, and if the captain sees someone repeatedly leaving stuff lying around he will make the assumption that he or she is disorganized, sloppy, and not to be relied upon. It's a precarious life in the middle of the ocean.

So it's become my task to explain the reason for each rule, to encourage people to get their act together, and to smooth any conflicts when they arise. But I hear grumbling all day, and I'm sick of it. I'd like to suggest that complaints are made directly to whoever is causing the problem, but I'm afraid that might be done in an offensive manner and cause even more problems.

Kangaroo court – Aussie Dan and crew discuss teamwork issues.

I think some things can improve if I go on encouraging people to communicate. The captain complains that I don't communicate with him, and from time to time that is true, partly because I'm not close at hand, sometimes because I forget, but mostly because, if the truth be known, he makes me nervous.

MARCH 9

Today I reached the end of my tether. I'm close to abandoning the whole trip. We can't go to sea in this state. I'm excited about the Salty Sam journey but I am not looking forward to all the crap that may come my way, nor trying to protect everyone on board, least of all from the real, serious dangers.

I called an early meeting, and said I was extremely unhappy, and that people needed to get all their wingeing over and done with, and make up their minds whether they wanted to come or not.

"If not," I said bluntly, "get off the boat and give us a chance to find someone else. You decide." I then left the room, having asked the captain to initiate the airing of problems and to let me know who still wanted to be on board.

Big mistake. It just turned into another bitching session. In the end, though, all members did say they wanted to stay. But I'm not convinced. I have a bad, bad feeling, and I don't know how to fix it without jeopardizing the entire expedition.

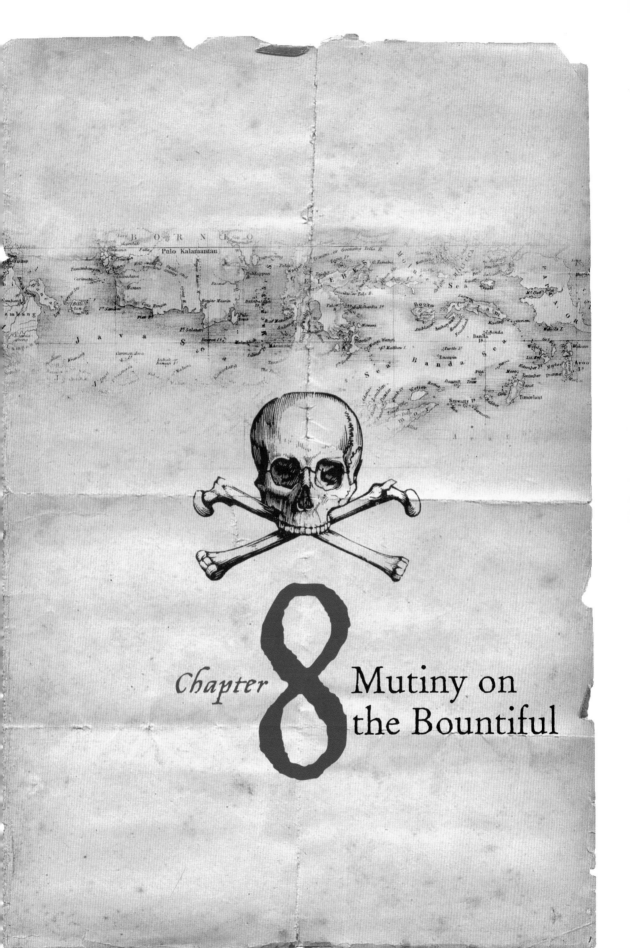

Chapter **8** Mutiny on
the Bountiful

MARCH 11, CAIRNS

The old Aborigine guys fishing on the other side of the marina know a thing or two. For a start, they know enough to do their fishing up high where the crocs can't get them. Secondly, they managed to land the mother of all barramundi just last night. The smartest thing they're doing, though, is staying on dry land. They're not going off to sea while the cyclone season is still hanging on up north and another bad storm is brewing round the galley table.

But we are.

Our camera person Robin left, with few regrets, I think. He wrote a farewell missive on the galley blackboard: *Bon Voyage, Takapuna! Try not to kill each other!*

The captain, Rolle, Dan, Kayt, Pete, Tessa, Ricky, Sue, Scotty, Sean and I sailed out of Cairns around noon. The Customs officials had come on board at 7.30am to deliver my guns and ammo, while Kayt and Sean had hit the market even earlier for last-minute provisions.

I was excited, but also shockingly nervous. The boat is ready, but honestly, I do not feel we are psychologically prepared. I confess I had to go shopping to calm my own anxiety. I bought three cowboy hats from the Ken Done shop, and a couple of cheap watches at the mall. Interpretation? I need more time – and protection for my mind. Deep.

We left in sunny weather, streaking out along the Cairns River towards Port Douglas. Within an hour or two it was overcast, with rain. Just off Four Mile Beach there was an illuminating break in the clouds, and breathtaking light on the hills before we slid into a maroon sunset and darkness beyond.

Lying on the aft deck I was just starting to feel good and relaxed when Sean came to me and complained that the captain had demanded the keys to the weapons closets. It's started already.

MARCH 12, GREAT BARRIER REEF

It was nice to wake up to calm seas. Not so calm on board, though. I was on watch with the captain at 5am, so I decided to address the crisis of the weapons keys. It did not go well. He's hopping mad because Sean refused to give him both sets of keys when he asked for them last night. The captain actually used the word 'mutiny'. Trouble is, no one seems to know the correct protocol for storing weapons when there's a security officer on board. It's Sean's job to clean the guns and keep them safe. But, at the same time, the captain has a right to make decisions about on-board safety – which includes the storing of weapons. The worst aspect of all this is that I have two aggressive men spraying the territory, and I'm stuck in the middle. Honestly, I'm scared.

I finally managed to contact Chris to ask what the usual protocol is. Woke him up somewhere in the Maldives. He said that no one on board should have the ability to load and fire a weapon on their sole initiative, and I totally agree. Also he said it was usual for the security chief to hold the key to the weapons, and the captain to have the key to the ammunition. Then, when a threat level escalates to a certain point, the security chief will discuss this with the captain and they'll mutually decide to make the weapons ready.

Mutually decide?!! These two sacks of testosterone couldn't decide anything together, even if all our lives depended on it. And it may come to that.

I'm scared. Beside myself, actually. Honestly, I am beginning to understand what it must have been like aboard Salty Sam's boat, with forty or so men all drinking and staking out their territory.

So next, the captain threatens to leave the boat if he doesn't get his own way which means holding both sets of keys. Then I hear Sean on the phone to Chris saying he'd like to throw the captain overboard. Jesus. And I'm upset because no one's listening to me about what the accepted procedure is, even though the weapons actually belong to me, and I hold the licence to carry them. Fucking hell. Right now, mutiny seems more likely than piracy. And I'm not just talking about the *Rosalie*.

MARCH 13

Calm weather, I suppose partly because we're still inside the Great Barrier Reef. But I'm not feeling good.

We had some drills and training sessions today, especially for the FNGs. There is still an uncomfortable division between the old and new team, and I'm not happy about the way people are behaving – on both sides. I'm feeling so inadequate. I'm a psychologist, for heaven's sake. I should be able to sort this out. The fact is, I could – if I were not under the pressure of getting this expedition finished before June.

It's funny, but with all this strife I feel closer to Sam. I feel I know something about his struggles that I could never have read in books or any archive. Of course, his role must have been even more challenging, because he captained his own ship. He was responsible for the lot. I got to thinking, though, that maybe it was better not to have to deal with a captain. If only I was Ellen MacArthur, I could sail this thing myself and be a true one-woman band. But then, the *Takapuna* cannot be sailed single-handed. It's just too damn big.

Right before we left Cairns I'd received a Fedex package from Anne Bulley. Today I finally opened it, and found copies of early Dutch charts of the Straits of Alas and surrounding islands, plus some sailing directions for that period. Interesting stuff. I was surprised at how detailed the directions were for the Straits themselves, with warnings about the quirky tides and currents. Nevertheless, they may have been more frequently visited by Europeans in those days. I also found a reference to them among the writings of Major William Thorn: "It is the safest and most convenient strait east of Java, having soundings, whereby ships are enabled to anchor when necessary, with moderate tides; and the plantations and villages on the coast of Lombok, which is low to the sea, afford supplies and refreshments."

Off the far north coast of Queensland we passed the site of the wreck of HMS *Pandora*, the frigate sent by the British Admiralty to find the mutineers from HMS *Bounty*. On her way home in August 1791, with fourteen mutineers captured on Tahiti locked in a holding cell known as 'Pandora's Box', the ship struck a reef. Against the captain's orders, a crew member threw the prisoners a key to their cell just before she sank. God, what a predicament: being humane, against committing mutiny plus the possible threat to your own life if everyone survived. I wish we could dive on the wreck, which lies at 33 metres, but Australian rules dictate that we'd have to clear out of a major town afterwards which would cause us further delay. I am particularly interested in seeing the *Pandora*, because she is so well preserved, with cannon, two anchors, an oven and copper sheathing visible when conditions are good.

The coast of Australia is littered with over 5,000 shipwrecks. Some, such as the *Batavia*, flagship of a fleet belonging to the Dutch East India Company, have yielded fantastic treasure. Carrying gold, silver, coins and jewels, in 1629 she

19th-century sailors toiled
to keep Booby island a
haven for shipwrecked
mariners.

struck a reef – and that was just the beginning of their problems for the 315
passengers, soldiers and crew. They were under the command of skipper Jacobsz,
a brutal rapist, and Cornelisz, his murderous and mutinous cargo officer.
Accounts of the plotting, treachery and unbridled barbarism that unfolded on
land after the Batavia sank make a sobering read for anyone at sea with a bunch
of men who are at each other's throats.

MARCH 14

Today we turned the corner of Australia and are now sailing west, past its north-
eastern tip. We have a couple of fuel bladders on board, and one of them, which
we've named 'Fred', was drained into the main tank today. As usual, I was helping
along with the draining process by jumping up and down on Fred when Rolle
stopped me. "That's enough," he said. "No need to rape him." So now I'm taking
out my frustrations on inanimate objects.

We passed Booby Island, named after the brown birds who are the only
residents. The name reminded Dan of something he was going to be missing
for a long, long time. Gazing longingly at a passing passenger ship, all lit
up as dinner was being prepared, he imagined the tanned single girls aboard.
Single, married … who cares? He considered his options. "If I jumped
overboard now, that passenger ship would have to stop and pick me up."
That didn't say much for our own Man Overboard capabilities, but I got
his meaning.

In the 19th century, before the lighthouse was built on Booby Island, passing
ships used to land stores of food and water. They were placed in a dry cave for
the benefit of shipwrecked sailors, which gives a hint as to how frequently ships
foundered on the rocks over there. Letters were also landed and collected, so
it was a sort of mail-drop cavern. I wonder if Salty Sam knew about it?

That's the last we'll see of Australia for a while. I lay on the aft deck and
watched an apricot sun, flecked with silhouetted birds, heading fast for a clear
horizon. Lovely night.

MARCH 15

When I came on watch at 5am the stars and moon were still out. There was enough wind to put out all three sails, and we had an enchanting, pink-tinged ride as the sun rose. It's a bit rough, though. Poor Tessa spent the night sleeping on deck. She's been allocated the most forward crew cabin, the one where the bow rises and falls mercilessly, even in good weather. Later in the morning I sat on top of the pilot-house roof. From my vantage point I noticed there was a lot of crap in the ocean – plastic baskets, polystyrene, and a large pinky-brown sea snake. Or did I dream that last one? God, I'm horny.

Around 11am we spotted Indonesian fishing boats off to port. They sit on the border between Australian waters and their own territory. There have been a few tussles lately, with each nation complaining that the other has overstepped the boundary. I suppose that would partly explain the very visible presence of Australian customs vessels and aircraft.

With six days to go before we reach Kupang, we're making slow progress, but people are at least settling into a routine. Mid-afternoon, when the wind had come up, Scotty reported that some bolts had slid out of the staysail furler casing. The captain, Rolle, Dan, Scotty and I donned harnesses and went forward to inspect it. The halyard seemed to be misaligned and required some creative winching to restore it to the point where we could get the bolts back in. The boys are still scratching their heads about that one. I knew we were in trouble when they asked me for some white nail polish. Offering them a choice of Chanel or Sally Hansen, I was impressed when Rolle chose the former and instructed me to paint lines to mark the position of the bolts so we could check if they loosened later on … just like they do for aircraft. I had to explain that the application required two coats plus a top coat. Honestly, don't they know *anything*?

Dan has injured his toe and has a mega-bruise on his side from being thrown against a cleat. Ricky says it's not serious, but our first mate is obviously in pain. Breakfast was Vegemite toast. For dinner, Kayt made chicken curry. She's a miracle. It was delicious, but the captain hates curry so we had to call it 'hotpot'.

As predicted by our captain, the seas are a bit lumpy now, but the air is balmy. An email from a landlubber pal put it all into perspective:

> Sounds fun to be at sea. Though horizontal snow in Toronto is of course really nice at this time of year.

MARCH 16, ARAFURA SEA

I can dance the hornpipe. Useless talent, you might sneer, and I would have to agree that I rate it along with my other pitiful party tricks, such as my ability to twist my elbow clockwise until it faces my hip, screech low and crazy like a kookaburra, and fit an entire chocolate Wagon Wheel biscuit in my mouth without gagging. The point is that when I learned to dance the hornpipe at, oh, around eight years old, I had no idea that its history and mine were entwined. Sailors used to caper on their tippy-toes with arms folded to relieve the tedium on long voyages round the Horn – although how they managed to remain on their toes amid the squalls and furies of that particularly nasty piece of water I can't imagine. It was hard enough to balance myself in my own bunk last night, sailing west on the slightly less notorious Arafura Sea, just south of the equator between the north coast of Australia and Papua New Guinea.

The Arafura Sea is a confused sea, as Dan puts it. Take a plastic bowl, fill it with greenish-grey water (like you get in your glass after quite a few dippings when you're painting with water-colours), plonk half a pea-pod in the centre for a boat and sit it in your kitchen sink. Now take three or four hairdryers and aim each of them at the water, facing in different directions. When you turn them on (don't try this at home), the uneven turbulence surrounding your little pea-green boat will resemble what we are currently experiencing on a grand scale. Here at their intersection, the Indian Ocean, Timor Sea, South China Sea and several other opposing swells seem to be fighting over our passage. Frankly, I wish they'd kiss and make up; 20–30 foot waves breaking over our bow hardly make for a pleasant ride.

The Arafura Sea is a mean sea. It bitch-slapped my porthole at around 9.30 last night, and I was convinced we'd had a knock-down, with the mast hitting the water. I'd just been dozing off when my cabin took a dive and the whole world flew. I staggered on deck and found our watchkeepers scrabbling to reef in the mainsail. Forty-five-knot winds followed – nearly ten knots above tropical storm speed. It was a tense night.

A flying fish lay dead on the foredeck this morning, and a tiny, hitchhiking booby had landed for a rest on the caprail last night before disappearing off into the blackness. Tessa has been sick and dehydrated again. So has Pete, as well as several others, although they won't admit it. Worst of all, as we feared yesterday, we've definitely got a problem with the staysail furler casing. When Rolle went forward to check on it, the nail polish marks were misaligned, showing that something is horribly wrong – so much so that we cannot continue the voyage in this state. The captain and I have been considering where we should put in for repairs. There is the choice of returning to Cairns (least favourite), Thursday Island (may not have a big enough crane to get the halyard down), Gove (big bauxite mining town) and Darwin. The captain chose Darwin as the most likely to provide us with support for the repair we need to do, although I must say the idea of a town full of lusty miners held a definite appeal. But that's just me.

At the intersection of several opposing bodies of water, the Arafura Sea gives mariners a bumpy ride.

MARCH 17 (ST PATRICK'S DAY)

Today I honoured the Irish with sage camouflage cargo pants; in fact my outfit *du jour* is dedicated to Hotlips from 'Mash'. Several people got pinched for not wearing green, and it serves them right. They have no respect for Leprechaun Day, and claim they're only in it for the booze. Which reminds me – Dan says Darwin has just two pubs, but one is closed. Just one big crane would make this girl happy.

As I came on watch at 5am Pete was watching the dial incredulously as the wind climbed to forty-five knots. Nasty, nasty. Thirty-foot waves. When I stood in the pilot house looking forward, they blocked the horizon. We have to pull back the throttle as we approach the trough of these giants so we can climb them slowly and don't slam down on the other side. Now we're only making five knots at best. That speed and our current heading truly make this the slow boat to China.

There's a vicious cyclone brewing at our tail. If it decided to head our way we'd never be able to outrun it. But we're poised to fly north just in case. Trouble is, we need to go south to get our repairs done in Darwin. Some people couldn't care less. "Yeeha!" cries Scotty at the helm as we fly over a real bigun. "Air time!"

Thank heavens the *Takapuna*'s a sturdy old girl. For centuries, mariners have known about what they call 'white squalls', yet modern observers are only just realizing these are random microbursts of wind that can be destructive even to large ships. All day I observed them coming in, first brewing black billows that undulated close to the horizon, followed by darkening throughout the sky and a chilling, ethereal moan as winds picked up at a frightening speed from, say, twenty-five knots to forty and rising. The mainsail would start complaining furiously, banging and flapping into a full-blown tantrum. Then the rain would start, a massive volume of water being vomited from the sky with the resonance of sonic drumming. Every now and then a skyscraper of a wave would whack over our bow. The captain reckons the wave pattern can never be predicted, that it defies mathematics. "It's chaos theory," he says solemnly. "They just come from nowhere."

"How long will we need to be in Darwin?" I asked him as he was calling the people who serviced the furler for information and drawings.

"Hopefully just a day or two," he said. "It'll be like stopping in at Auntie's for tea and cakes."

"Well," I scowled, "I trust Auntie's got a darn big crane…"

Submerged! The *Takapuna*'s decks are underwater as giant waves crash over bow and stern.

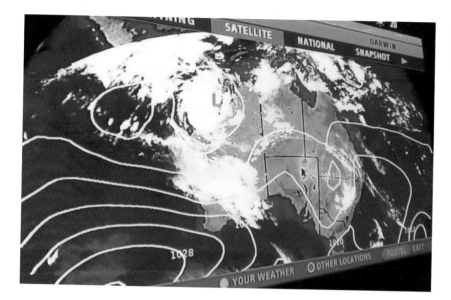

Major Depressions –
brewing trouble spots
predict more problems
ahead for the *Takapuna*.

MARCH 18

At 9.45 this morning we had reasonable conditions for a change, so we turned
off our engine for a bout of pure sailing. We even managed to pick up the
television footprints for Australia, and tuned into the Weather Channel. That
little 'tropical depression' behind us has now become a full-sized grown-up
called Larry. Tropical Storm Larry came of age off the east coast of Australia
and is now turning cartwheels towards the north Queensland coast. In other
words, if we were still near Cairns, we'd be making a run for it. The captain
timed that brilliantly.

The standard of radio communications round these parts is known to be less
than professional. We soon found out what that meant. On the emergency
channel, a fisherman began describing a recent engine-room fire to his taciturn
mate on another vessel. The story could have been gripping if it weren't for
the fact that the teller's vocabulary was rather dependent on words that begin
with 'f'- which made it simply hilarious. Australian Customs guys flew over
and buzzed us again. They must think we're idiots, still out here and heading
into more bad weather. One hinted heavily over the radio: "It's not gonna get
any better." I tried to imagine what we must look like from the air. I suppose
if I were flying over a sailing boat in such obviously dodgy seas I'd be quite
impressed by the bravery of people in such a lonely part of the globe, being
thrashed around for days on end.

Sean emerged from his bed at lunchtime, having drawn the short straw in the
graveyard watch stakes. Since his cabin has become the unofficial armoury, he was
rained on by flying helmets and body armour when we changed tack last night
– and that kit is heavy. During the afternoon conditions became even worse.
Kayt, Ricky and I attempted to make and serve banana smoothies without
incident. Not a chance. With the galley see-sawing like a funfair ride we ended
up screaming with laughter, and with pale yellow slime all over the floor.

Pete has been falling asleep all day, so I've taken pity on him and dropped him
from the 5am watch, though Ricky thinks I'm being too soft on him. This afternoon
Pete made the mistake of trying to crawl onto the foredeck to shoot some footage
of waves crashing over the bow. One full-on body blow and he was back in the pilot
house with his life vest inflated round his ears like a huge yellow rubber duckie.

'Category Five Monster's Trail of Destruction' – Cairns is hit just after we leave.

Ricky pointed out today that I have hairy toes. I retorted that body hair removal is a low priority out here … but I suppose I should try a little harder.

My Dear Pamsy,
I hope the fun legs are holding up as sea legs as you cross the raging main. I just read in the paper today that the Americans just had a battle off Somalia with some more of those pirates. Apparently they are ripping off the aid that is being sent to their own country since it is in a state of emergency, fancy that eh, ripping off your own people who are starving to death. The government of Somalia has run off to some neighbouring country in fear of the warlords who now completely control the country. They also control the piracy!
I was sorry to hear about your latest hold up, it must be a real pain in the arse at this stage in the game, but everyone I speak to who is in any way familiar with the life aquatic seem to think that this type of thing is pretty much par for the course, so I just nod sagely as if I knew what I was talking about. Look after your wee self and don't put yourself in harms way if you can possibly avoid it. Stay as sweet as you are,
Love Love Lovexxxxx
Bill Bill

MARCH 19

The seas are still enormous. It was a bad night for everyone, with the boat being pitched around like a cup in a jacuzzi. All day the wind kept us guessing, with sudden fifty-degree shifts, which made it hard for us to maintain our speed and heading. Actually, it's miserable out here, but at least we're well fed, reasonably dry, and not in a life raft clutching a 406 EPIRB (Emergency Positioning International Rescue Beacon), hoping someone will fly out to pick us up.

My watch this morning, from 5am to 8am, was uncomfortable, but relatively uneventful. The captain informed me that there's another problem with the boat: a crack in our exhaust that will have to be fixed in Darwin. Also, bolts are falling out of the Genoa furler casing as well as that of the mainstay. Honestly. I thought the boat was ready, after all the money we've spent on her recently.

Anyway, I'm looking forward to Darwin, a city I've never visited. We should be in the harbour by tomorrow night. I'm betting that we won't get in and out in less than a week, not once those boys get near a pub.

I consulted our *Rough Guide to Australia* and realized that Kakadu National Park, a place I've always wanted to visit, is right near Darwin. I became excited by the notion of a safari into the bush, and a (hopefully distant) sighting of some big, bad crocs. Then there's the possibility of a trip to the gym, and a meal in a nice restaurant. Suddenly I saw the good side of stopping in at 'Auntie's'.

Scotty's an optimist too. This morning, despite the heavy seas, he attached a bright pink lure with wicked plastic eye to our fishing rod and let out the line. I asked him, "Would you catch me a Lobster Thermidor?"

MARCH 20, DARWIN

We weren't allowed into the smart marina in Darwin. Not sure why. But I like it here in the 'fish pond' as they call it, a noisy working dock full of fishing boats. It turns out there are way more than two pubs in the city and, more importantly as far as I'm concerned, the best cappuccino joint in Australia.

I just had to do the 'crocodile cruise'. Dorky, I know, but it was quite something to see those monsters leap in the air for a piece of meat. This was dangled on a stick by a man in a safari suit. The commentary was priceless. They'd given all the crocs in the vicinity terrible names like 'Snappy' and 'Leapin' Lizzie'. Some of them had heads a metre long, and could pack 6,000-7,000 lbs of pressure per square inch.

Great White invades 'fish pond' – Takapuna is forced to berth in fishing industry docks in Darwin (left), but I manage to fit in a trip to nearby Kakadu National Park to see some jaw-dropping sights (below).

MARCH 21

I have been refused marine insurance to enter the Port of Jakarta, and also Ambon. Essentially, both ports are regarded as war zones. We received an email that has not soothed the captain's anxiety one jot. In fact, I'm expecting, for safety's sake, he will refuse to take the boat to either port.

Travel Advice for Saturday, 21st March. Summary.
- We advise you to reconsider your need to travel to Indonesia, including Bali, at this time due to the very high threat of terrorist attack. We continue to receive a stream of reporting indicating that terrorists are in the advanced stages of planning attacks against Western interests in Indonesia against a range of targets, including places frequented by foreigners.
- In December 2005, Indonesian authorities warned publicly that terrorists in Indonesia may be planning to kidnap foreigners.
- Terrorist attacks against Westerners in Bali and Jakarta indicate that these areas are a priority target for terrorists in Indonesia. Suicide attacks against locations frequented by foreigners in Bali and Jakarta have killed and injured many people. Further terrorist attacks cannot be ruled out and could occur at any time, anywhere in Indonesia.
- An extremist website posting discussed possible terrorist tactics including terrorist attacks against foreigners in the Kuningan area and other locations across Jakarta
- We strongly advise you not to travel to Aceh, Maluku (particularly Ambon) and central Sulawesi due to the very unstable security situation and risk of terrorist attack.
- In the past year there have been human cases of avian influenza in Indonesia.

I didn't want to add that, a few weeks ago in Sulawesi, three schoolgirls were beheaded by Muslim extremists. It was all over the Australian papers, along with the death sentence received in the case of Australian kids accused of drug smuggling.

Yes, I know it's a dodgy place to go, but I still want to find out what happened to Salty Sam. So I've come up with a compromise. Instead of hanging around Darwin for about a week while the repairs are under way, I have decided to fly to Java for a day or two to search for clues. It will save time, and we may then avoid taking the boat into Jakarta.

Dear Pamsy,
I don't know if you are at sea or still hanging around in the deep north, but wherever you are I hope you are well. I must say that the weather forecasts that I have seen do not exactly fill me with joy. I just hope that all of you are as correct as you are confident. Drop me a line if you can,
LOVE LOVE LOVEXXXXXXXXX
Bill Bill

9

Chapter

A Sip of Java

MARCH 22, JAKARTA

Around midnight, Pete, Ricky, Sean and I landed in Jakarta. As the capital of the Indonesian Republic, it is a smog-blurred centre of commerce inhabited by nearly ten million people. Pretty soon we found ourselves negotiating our way through a gargantuan metropolis, whose massive freeways and high-rise glass buildings contrasted with the shanty towns squeezed into every tiny orifice. It's been yonks since I was here, and I had no idea the city had developed to this extent. It is so far removed from the Batavia of Salty Sam's day, I hardly feel like I'm on his trail at all – except I know for a fact that he did sail here and trade in this city.

The traffic was terrible, even this late at night. When the taxi meter reached 100,720 I reached for my currency converter in alarm. "It's only about ten dollars US," soothed Ricky, who's managing our finances.

Sean had insisted we stay at the Marriot, and, when we pulled up, I realized why. We underwent a thorough security search before we even got close to its opulent foyer. The Marriot, he says, is the most protected hotel in Jakarta. But it was bombed in 2002, with twenty people killed when a suicide bomber made it to the ground-floor coffee shop. The terrorist's head was found on the 7th floor.

MARCH 23

I'm beginning to feel connections here with Sam and his world, especially after visiting Batavia, the original trading city during the spice-trading years, and the old port of Sunda Kelapa. We left at 6.30am in a nondescript minivan with curtains over the windows – by order of our Welsh Man in Jakarta. Sean's nervous about the security situation. His buddy at the recently bombed Australian Embassy told him there's currently a serious threat of kidnapping, theft, terrorist attacks and drive-by shootings. If he could, Sean would prefer to have a four-man team with advance reconnaissance. He made me cover my blonde hair with a scarf tied Muslim-style, telling me, "You stick out like a whore's drawers."

The city of Batavia was the heart of the Dutch empire out here; in fact the whole island of Java was the main source of its opulence and strength. Batavia was built by the Dutch as their show-off capital; the "Queen of the East" was known for its filthy-rich inhabitants and posh buildings, as well as its high-powered wheeling and dealing. It's funny, when you think how the good burghers of the Netherlands lived at home – far less extravagantly, it seems, than abroad. "These people," wrote Major William Thorn, "who have been proverbially plain and frugal in Europe, were as much distinguished by the splendour of their foreign establishments." Perhaps that's why the Dutch were so gung ho about making sure no one else had a piece of the action out here; this was their Las Vegas, an expression of their shadowy side.

Outside Batavia, the Dutch established forts throughout Java, strategically placed to keep an eye on nearby native kingdoms. And, from their point of view, just as well. I was intrigued to learn that one Sultan's residence, at what is now Jogjakarta, was guarded by an army of 300 Amazons – agile horsewomen armed with spears. My kind of gals.

Meanwhile, with extraordinary zeal, and any amount of warfare, manipulation, bribery, cruelty, torture, and genocide that they deemed necessary, the Dutch protected their interests throughout all of what is now Indonesia – especially the islands of Sumatra, Banda, and the former Moluccas, now Maluku.

Not surprisingly, the Dutch were feared and hated by the locals. But the heyday of the Dutch East India Company, or the *Verenigde Oostindische Caompagnie*, best known by the acronym VOC, was over by the 1790s, well before Salty Sam arrived. The British, French and other powers had always been nipping at the heels of the Dutch, and the British had managed to get a foothold in several strategic locations. After the annexation of Holland into France, the British upped their bid for Java, and moved in with a vengeance to avoid a French takeover – although they gave it back to Holland in 1816.

But the fall of the VOC has been attributed mostly to corruption and the decadence of life in the city of Batavia, with its palatial residences manned by slaves, its 'moral decline' and the challenges of living in the tropics. European-born Batavians had no idea how to adjust to the climate. They thought fresh air was bad for them and pooh-poohed the idea of taking cool baths. In 1775 the government supported the disinclination of soldiers of the garrison to bathe, even once a week. Not realizing that alcohol caused dehydration, gentlemen started their day by drinking a large glass of gin on an empty stomach. As a supposed prevention against

The Raffles-style Café Batavia, in a restored 1730 Dutch building.

disease, along with pipe-smoking, they took the same medicine several times a day. The Dutch even insisted on continuing to wear their winter woollies. Personally, I think the VOC fell because of heat rash.

It was a good idea to leave before rush hour. Jakarta traffic becomes gridlocked after 7.30am. We had breakfast in the Café Batavia, a restored old Dutch building of 1730. It is now a two-storey bistro with quirky, Raffles-style décor and a cocktail called a 'Blow Job' that costs over a million rupiah.

"Would you pay a million for a blow job?" I asked the Dutch tourist peering over my shoulder at the drinks menu.

"Absolutely not," he said. "In Amsterdam we get them for free."

While we were drinking coffee in the Café Batavia I received a call from Deborah, our 'fixer' in Indonesia, who had some wonderful news: she may have located the island of Carabatoo. Her husband is a sea captain based in Bali and, in the course of pouring through local charts, they have found two islands in the Straits of Alas that are likely contenders. One is Batukarang, whose name is very like 'Carabatoo' pronounced backwards and means 'coral rock'; the other is 'Kere Batu', which sounds even more similar. Batukarang is at the northern end of the straits, and the other is more southerly, just off the east coast of Lombok. It now seems sensible to search for the *Rosalie* in the vicinity of both islands. This is exciting information, and I'm relieved to be able to give the captain a more complete route.

We left the Batavia Cafe and walked across the cobbled Fatihillah Square to the Jakarta History Museum, in a bell-towered, two-storeyed building, completed in 1627, that was once the *Stadhuis*, or

Dutch city hall. Inside, a class of Muslim school children was languidly eyeballing dark, ornate, wooden furniture from the Dutch period. They perked up considerably when they were taken to the dungeons and water-prison and given detailed accounts of Dutch atrocities. Prisoners were forced to stand in dirty water for weeks on end, their blood being sucked by leeches. Then they might be subjected to a whole creative range of terrible tortures, ending with death by impalement, guillotine or sword. Stooping low, I entered the airless dungeons where people had once been packed in, with more than 300 prisoners in this building at a time. Many were slaves, like Suropati, whose crime was that he fell in love with Susan, the daughter of his owner. She was sent home to Holland by her angry father, and died on the way.

Since the *Stadhuis* was once the centre of legal affairs in Batavia, I wondered if this was the place where hearings were held concerning Salty Sam's Will. Certainly Sam would have known the building. I gazed out of a window overlooking the square. Dutch judges once sat up here on the balcony, sweating in their European regalia, to watch the executions they'd ordered. In 1740, 500 innocent Chinese citizens were butchered just below the balcony. The Dutch had encouraged the Chinese to settle in Batavia, but unrest arose between them and the rest of the population over unemployment and other issues. The VOC tried to limit incoming Chinese, whereupon thousands of illegal Chinese residents ran away into the woods and formed bandit brigades. In the fighting that followed, ten thousand perished, many of them right here. The place felt nasty.

Overlooking the canal and the old harbour is the Bastion Columbourg, a 17th-century lookout on a site used by Portuguese even before the Dutch. It was a coral stone keep from which soldiers could watch the seaward city entrance. I climbed to the airy observation room of its restored tower, with the ubiquitous and strident Moslem call to prayer whining from massive, distorting speakers, and gazed down. Until the early 18th century, ships could sail right up there. I could still see the whole waterway, and below me was the roof of an old VOC warehouse. Salty Sam must have done business around here; bought charts, met with Mr Jessen, his shipping agent. The stench of the canal, a thick soup of the city's waste, wafted up. Did my great-great-grandfather stand here and survey the port, his handkerchief to his nose, just like me?

Below: Lights on, nobody home. The National Archives building in Jakarta was once a Dutch residence.

Below right: View of Batavia canal from an early lookout post.

Above: A crew member sands the hull of his *pinisi*.

Left: Inspecting the *pinisi* – Bugis ships berthed ready for loading in the Coconut Harbour. The narrow wood planks form precarious gangways.

The maritime Museum Bahari is housed in some fine Dutch buildings that used to be the *Westzijdsche Pakhuizen*, or west-bank warehouses. Built in 1645, this is where the VOC kept its stocks of pepper, coffee, tea and cloth. On display in the museum were lovely models of traditional vessels – some of them make-believe, such as the fantastically carved Kalimantan Dream Ship. Shaped like a bird, with its bowsprit resembling a beak and a colourful tail carved at its stern, it supposedly carried the spirits of the dead from this world to next. I was also taken with a display about the local vessels called *pinisi*, to me the most romantic ships in the world. Made of sturdy ironwood from the forests of Kalimantan, they are the preferred vessels of the nomadic Bugis people from Suluwesi, who were pirates. Even now these sea gypsies live aboard their *pinisi*, on which they can travel vast distances.

Seeing my delight in these ships, Sumardi, our guide, sped us further seawards, to the old harbour, Sunda Kelapa, or 'Coconut Harbour'. Lined up along the dock we found scores of modern-day *pinisi*. These brightly striped war-horses of the sea are now essentially cargo ships, each of similar design, with a large-volume open deck, a raised wheelhouse, and crew quarters towards the stern. The hull sweeps upwards at the bow, where a long bowsprit points its finger into the oncoming sea. No one needs to put these superbly resilient vessels into dry dock for a refit every year; they're simply pulled up onto the beach so skilled members of the crew can scrape and repair the hull right there.

On one *pinisi* I could see men carrying large bags.

"What cargo are they loading?" I asked Sumardi.

"Semen," he replied solemnly.

"Semen?" I repeated in surprise. "Where, or what, did that come from?" He didn't understand.

"That's semen?" I questioned him again.

"Yes," he insisted, "Semen." I would have been left wondering about that for the rest of my days if, later on, I had not spied English lettering on one of the bags. It read: 'Cement'.

Our final stop of the day was the National Archives building. We had heard we would find good records of the Dutch East India Company there, dating back to 1790. It's a really fine Dutch building. In typical style it is closed and austere from the outside, but its interior is grand and spacious, with impressive ornamental arches and a stately staircase. But to my great disappointment we were told the archives have all been moved out to another location, over three hours drive away. Instead, the building now contains furniture and other items relating to the Dutch colonial period.

After taking a disinterested peek at the incredibly ornate carved cabinets where the archives were once housed – the fanciest filing cabinets in the world – I was about to walk out when I noticed a sign. Being tired, I almost gave it a miss, but something led me upstairs to where I found a temporary exhibition of early charts and prints. It was thrilling. There were several old etchings of Batavia in Salty Sam's day. One showed Chinese houses on fire during the troubles in 1740, while another depicted the spinhouse, an institution set up by the Dutch 'for the encouraging of virtue and the suppression of debauchery of lewd women.' From the looks of it there were a lot of them about in those days. Perhaps that's where Salty Sam got his 'wife'! The spinhouse had no windows (presumably so they couldn't make advances to passing sparrows) and the women were allegedly reclaimed from their lewdness by keeping them continually at work under the tuition of a governess.

There were pictures of Onroost Island where the Dutch had a substantial fort, and some of the port of Bantam, where we're going tomorrow. One 18th-

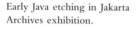

Early Java etching in Jakarta Archives exhibition.

century print showing the port of Ternate in the Moluccas depicted the eruption of the volcano Gamalama, raining lava on European ships lying beneath it in the harbour. This whole archipelago has a tendency to vomit fire; Krakatoa is not so far away and growing again, having drawn the whole world's attention to itself in August 1883; and right now there's a volcano on this very island, Mt Merapi, that looks like it's getting ready to perform.

I spent an hour or two wandering around these treasures, with Sean, Pete and Ricky shuffling their feet in boredom. But here was the entire, bloody history of the spice trade told in rich visual panoramas. The charts really gave me a sense of the old sailing days round here. What a struggle it once was for mariners to know what the archipelago held in store for them. Most cartographers worked for only one power, and jealously guarded their work as top secret. Alternatively some charts were made deliberately misleading, so great was the competition for land and goods. I can't imagine what it must have been like to run into an isthmus when you were expecting the straits next to an island. It would be so easy to run aground, especially at night. Not that we ourselves are headed for a nice summer cruise. Even our own charts contain out-of-date information and the Indonesian Government is not terribly interested in supplying hydrographic aids to outsiders like us. But at least we have radar and Max Sea.

> Dearest One,
> Got your e-MAIL. Nice to see that you are still alive and roaming the planet. I hope you are all right in Jakarta. Keep up the good work.
> LOVE LOVE LOVE XXXXX
> BILL BILL

MARCH 24, BANTAM

Once again we're hitting the road early – a road originally constructed under Napoleonic rule, with an estimated loss of life of 12,000 local workers. In the inland areas back in Sam's day the jungle was thick, the Blue Mountains region virtually impassible, and the monsoons irregular. Along the coast the climate was sultry, while some of the inland areas could be cool enough to warrant an indoor fire. Rice fields extended throughout the lowlands, and the mountains yielded timber lofty enough for the masts of ships, while teak, also perfect for ship building, abounded in the forests. Exotic plants such as sago, bamboo, mangosteen, jack fruit and betel were plentiful. Deer and antelope were hunted in the mountains, wild hogs and monkeys lived in the jungles, while in the forests roamed the Royal Tiger (as large and powerful as its Bengal cousin), as well as a species of black tiger, and the rhinoceros. Scorpions lurked in the marshes, and voluminous snakes were said to swallow sheep whole.

Bantam, to the west of Batavia, was once an impressive and diverse market selling all kinds of spices, along with wares including Indian cloth, Chinese silk, porcelain, and Japanese lacquer. There's not much left to show for it, but the 16th and 17th centuries saw the height of Bantam's splendour and wealth, which collapsed at the end of the 1700s when Batavia took over as the main centre of trade. So I'd be surprised if Salty Sam came here at all.

There was no sign of a town, although an ancient mosque towered over a few street stalls and a tatty museum. The surrounding land was very flat. I wandered round the remains of a Sultan's mother's palace; it had been destroyed in 1830,

"The sea should be here!"
A confused moment amidst
Bantam's faded glory.

but there was still a certain beauty in its ruins. Angry clouds roamed above the palm trees. A flock of geese scuttled across our path, but apart from them the place was deserted. According to Sumardi, the empty stone swimming baths once featured gold-plated taps.

"Where did the water come from?" I asked Sumardi. But he just smiled mysteriously and walked on. I was confused; I had thought Bantam was a port.

"Come this way," he beckoned, leading me through an overgrown field by an old stone bastion. Suddenly, we came to a hole in the wall, and he disappeared inside. I did not want to follow. I was hot, tired and grumpy – in no mood for dark places and lurking mosquitoes. But, coaxed by Ricky, I found myself following an old Dutch tunnel. Surprised to hear it once led to the sea, I climbed up onto the bastion, where guards and cannon once guarded the port. To my left was the red-tiled roof of a 16th-century Chinese temple, one of the oldest in Indonesia, with two enormous dragons facing each other off on some plaster clouds. I turned right – and suddenly, there was the sea, a long way in the distance. Ah! So all the early sketches of Bantam I'd seen were taken from right there; remarkably, though, the water has receded. I fail to understand the science of this; I thought sea levels were rising round here. Certainly I've heard that many of the 'thousand islands' in Jakarta Harbour (there are actually closer to 260) are disappearing.

On our long drive back, Ricky found a *Jakarta Post* article about a conference on piracy, currently being held in Singapore. Representatives of several nations are convening to discuss their inability to control crime at sea. The main reasons were given as lack of reporting, refusal to share information, and insufficient funding for patrols. Well, at least they acknowledge there's a problem.

MARCH 25

We took an early flight to Surabaya. I always wanted to visit the place that inspired 'Surabaya Johnny', the haunting Kurt Weill song from Bertolt Brecht's Threepenny Opera:

> *Surabaya Johnny, is it really the end?*
> *Surabaya Johnny, will this pain never end?*
> *Surabaya Johnny, oh, I yearn for your touch…*

Teguh, our guide, is a delightful, tiny man with pop-eyes and a broad gummy smile. A veritable poster-child for the Indonesian tourist industry, and upbeat to the point of mania, he kept us heartily entertained all day.

"So sorry if I'm so energetic," he began, "because today is a lovely day. I hope you can have some fun." He whisked us off to the 'Museum', which turned out to be a Phillip-Morris-owned factory making local clove cigarettes. So that's what they do with their spices these days.

"You will be amazed how you can make 4,000 of the most expensive local cigarette in Indonesia," warned Teguh, and sure enough, we were. Rows and rows of women were busy hand-rolling the reefers, employing a riveting, full-body shaking that made them resemble a couple of hundred robots with Parkinson's disease.

'Surabaya' is a Sanscrit word meaning 'shark-crocodile', and the symbol of Surabaya is the two creatures in battle. "This is the characteristic of Surabayans," said Teguh. "More energy, frankness, and temper."

The city seemed far less built up than Jakarta, with considerably less Western influence. I was enjoying the noisy, tarpaulin-covered street stalls and the buggies drawn by pompom-covered horses until a truck pulled up with at least two dozen motorbikes on board. Ear-splittingly loud pop music blared from its speakers aimed at passers by. "It's a marketing strategy," explained Teguh, who constantly surprised us with his command of businessman's English.

By contrast, the spice market was a jewel of down-home trading. Sited in an enormous warehouse, it was stuffed with an enormous variety of colourful produce. Giant bundles of cinnamon, sacks of nutmeg, pepper and almonds, bowls of saffron and chillies, and racks of dried fish were all illuminated by a soft glow falling from skylights and mixed with a fine haze of spice particles, to produce an extraordinarily beautiful effect. I sat with some women and helped them peel their garlic heads. Friendly, talkative, and seemingly happy, and they frequently tugged at my hair; you don't see too many blondes round here.

In Sam's day, Surabaya was a prosperous town, with a mint producing silver and copper coins, large forests providing timber, and a flourishing ship-building industry. We walked along the litter-laden canal, a former centre of maritime trade. It's reminiscent of Amsterdam, with many early Dutch houses and offices still standing. People were bathing, but Teguh wanted us to know he disapproved. "A lot of people take a shower, and shit in the river," he complained. "So stupid."

On one waterfront corner a wonderful, skinny Dutch building bore a plaster shark-crocodile insignia of Surabaya. We ducked behind it and found a warren of alleyways lined with badly damaged Dutch colonial houses. Despite the heat, the naked wires, the stench, and the buzzing trucks that squeezed into even the

Tobacco rows – Surabayan women rolling clove cigarettes for local markets.

Right: *Becak* (trishaw) gridlock at market time in Surabaya.

Opposite: The spice market in Surabaya.

narrowest of closes, I felt compelled to explore. Somewhere along here were the offices of Salty Sam's shipping agents. Salty Sam walked these streets. Maybe somewhere close by, stuffed in an attic, are 80,000 Dutch Florins that belong to my family. I just found out that in today's money that's worth just under half a million pounds.

I contemplated the aftermath of Salty Sam's disappearance. The Dutch side, so the story goes, didn't believe he was really dead, so a massive battle started between Dutch and British lawyers. And there was poor Ann at home, trying to cope. Those letters from the Turnbull Library give a sense of how frustrating it must have been for her, trying to deal with it all.

We had attracted an entourage of giggling children. "Hello, Mister!" was applied to us all at every turn. I asked one her name – "*Siapa nama anda?*" – which led to a lengthy and jovial all-inclusive name-sharing session.

That prompted me to head to a bookshop to see if I could find the name Stephenson in a phone book. No luck, although I suppose if Sam had stayed and had descendants here he would have changed his name. Then I looked for the names of his lawyers and shipping agents. Most weren't there, but I had a shock when I found a Jessen, one of the names in my father's pamphlet. There is still a company, now called Jebson & Jesson, operating in both Jakarta and Surabaya; it appears to deal in cables and maritime technology. Surely the Jessen partner is a descendent of the original agent? Jessen is hardly a common name. It's Sunday, but I might just knock on their door tomorrow. Ask what they've done with the money.

Tanjun Perak, or Silver Harbour, is a wonderfully grungy port, and home to ships of all types and nations. It was from here that the *Rosalie* set sail in 1821. Since Surabaya is to the east of Batavia, it was almost certainly Salty Sam's last Javanese stop before he headed off for the Spice Islands. I sat on the dock and stared out to sea, past the rusting hull of a well-travelled island-hopper. The *Rosalie* actually lay in this harbour. My great-great-grandfather was here, awaiting cargo, provisioning, repairing, planning his next voyage. If the article in the *Prince of Wales Island Gazette* is true, he sailed out of here in 1821. The wind lifted the sails, bore him on an easterly tack – and he never came back.

Above: Walking the plank – Ricky coaxes crazed woman down from ledge.

Right: 'Hope-for-the-best' cargo-loading in Surabaya.

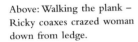

Besides Tanjun Perak, Surabaya has its own *pinisi* harbour, not far from a smart marina with heavy security. As in Jakarta, Buginese crews were hard at work loading the ships. One man invited us aboard. He showed me a model of the ship in full sail, so I finally got a sense of how she was rigged. There were five triangular sails, and two rudders, one each on port and starboard stern.

I'd wanted to board this ship, but as usual the gangway was just a rickety plank of wood, one of the highest, steepest and narrowest I'd seen, over utterly toxic-looking water.

"What the hell?" I said to Ricky. "I'll white-knuckle it."

"You sure?"

'Yeah. It's not so much the drop; you fall in that water, you die anyway." I put my hand on his shoulder and managed to board at a painful pace, while men on another plank beside me were virtually running up and down with four or five enormous bales of cloth loaded onto their shoulders. At the top of the gangway a man with pencil and paper was recording each piece of cargo. No such thing as computer-calculated load distribution here.

With Teguh translating, I asked the overseer of the cargo about the number of crew. He said there were 50, and that the vessel was bound for South Suluwesi. As I glanced up at the wheelhouse I saw a young woman emerge and lean over the railing.

"How many women aboard?" I asked.

"No women," was the reply.

"Then who's that?" I pointed.

"Ah," smiled Teguh. "Just one. For the captain."

"What do you mean?" I asked. There was a brief conference. "Escort," smirked Teguh at last. "Private escort." This situation had more in common with Salty Sam than I ever imagined.

"How do you know she's not his wife?" I asked.

"Hundred percent," replied Teguh knowingly. "I'm a local and I know very well. Everywhere – truck, ferry – women always accompany the men, sometimes for the captain, or even for others. This is a three-day journey." I resisted the urge to compliment the crew on solving the 'frustration-at-sea' problem, because I thought it might get horribly lost in translation.

Instead, I turned my attention to the challenge of walking the plank. It was far worse on the way down. In fact, my embarrassingly shaky disembarkation, only accomplished by hanging onto Ricky for dear life, brightened the day of a number of giggling *pinisi* crew members. They took time off from their busy schedule to enjoy the sight of a terrified white woman in the grip of a full-blown panic attack. It was better than 'Baywatch'.

MARCH 26, JAKARTA

Back in Jakarta, Ricky informed me that the *Jakarta Post* has reported the death of a one-year-old girl in Western Indonesia from bird flu. That makes 23 deaths in Indonesia from H5N1. The total number of people who've died from bird flu world-wide is 105. Is this truly a time bomb, a pandemic about to explode? Or just another way to sell pharmaceuticals? I'm sceptical, but I still don't want to kiss any hens.

On our way back to the hotel we came upon a huge demonstration by religious groups opposed to an upcoming pornography bill. As we passed the crowd, we Westerners slunk lower in our seats, being perhaps considered purveyors of all such 'evil'. Sean would not let Pete film it. Instead, he took me to a department store where I bought a black wig and a kebaya, a lacy traditional top with long sleeves. It's not always been like this here. When the Dutch first arrived in Java the women were bare-breasted. They were told to cover up in order to protect the morality of the Dutch soldiers. Since I now know the latter never bathed, I imagine it was a good thing all round. Unfortunately, though, it probably took more than a bit of lace to fend off a horny Dutchman with B.O.

Finally, I visited the antiques market, where several stalls specialized in maritime wares. I began to scour these for ships' bells, compasses, sextants and telescopes. There were US Navy diving helmets, and a wheel from Greenock – all kinds of intriguing nautical items. "How old is this?" I would ask. The answer, curiously, was always "Seventy years". I know it's ridiculous, but there was a tiny part of me that hoped I just might find something from the *Rosalie*. The storekeepers were extremely solicitous. Every time I said the word 'bell' hundreds of clanging objects appeared: Chinese temple bells, bicycle bells, gongs, and even a few ships' bells, mainly from the Japanese Navy. Turning my back on Sean doing a ghastly Quasimodo impression with a large bell from a ship called the *Pelayo*, I picked up an unnamed bell and asked, "Which ship did this come from?"

The vendor thought for a moment, until his eyes suddenly lit up. "The *Titanic!*"

For whom it tolls – hunting for the *Rosalie*'s bell at a maritime antiquities stall, Jakarta.

MARCH 27, DARWIN

Flying back from Jakarta we stopped over for an hour in Denpassar, Bali, where we were able to meet Deborah. She has been working hard preparing for the *Takapuna*'s arrival, and turned up at the airport with a full chart of the Straits of Alas. Batukarang and Kere Batu certainly seem to be likely contenders for the island of Carabatoo, but the fact that they are at opposite ends of the Straits of Alas once more begs the question: "Why did Salty Sam enter those Straits?" If only we were there now, not stuck in an airport lounge with the *Takapuna* still thousands of miles away.

MARCH 28

I like Darwin. We were invited to Government House to meet Ted Egan, the Administrator of the Northern Territory, and his partner Ms Nerys Evans, as well as Annette Burke, the Mayor of Palmerson, a nearby city that happens to be twinned with Kupang. The captain, Sue, Ricky, Tessa and I drank tea in the drawing room while I told the story of Salty Sam. Annette told us a little about Kupang, which is our next stop, and promised an introduction to its Mayor, her counterpart there. It was a relief to know that we have a high-level connection at our first Indonesian destination.

Nerys impressed me as a dedicated local patron of the arts, with a lively sense of humour. Upon hearing that Ricky was from Samoa she said, "Did you know that after Western Samoa beat Wales for the first time one Welshman was heard to say to another, 'Thank God we weren't playing the whole of Samoa!'" She gave us a tour of the Residence and showed us some stunning aboriginal art, plus an impossibly well-constructed model of a ship in full sail made out of matchsticks by a prisoner, and the bedroom where the Queen stayed.

Takapuna's crew hard at work as we leave Australia for the second time.

MARCH 29

Last night a notice was posted above the companion way for all to see:

0530 tomorrow: ALL HANDS ON DECK. U/W (Under Weigh) For Fuel Dock.

0900 ALL HANDS ABOARD For Customs

We left Darwin around 11am. I barely lifted my head from my computer. I refuse to believe we're off until I get to Indonesia. So many false goodbyes. So many stops and starts. I'm jaded, pissed-off, and I need a shag.

Chapter **10** Shooting the
Breeze

Rear Gunner – target
practice off the stern.

MARCH 30, TIMOR SEA

Since it was a calm day, and we're out of Australian
waters, Sean and I decided it would be a good time
to test our weapons. This, of course, required verbally
wrestling the captain for the keys. We loaded our
magazines under the cover of Sean's cabin. I was
surprised to see him collecting his first aid kit and
putting on his bullet-proof vest, not usually needed
for target practice.

"Since I'm shooting with a woman…" he said,
making a stupid face. After inviting him to have
intercourse with himself I sneaked on deck and
tried to make it to the stern platform without
being noticed by the rest of the crew. A couple
of AR15s and several handguns are pretty hard to
conceal, so we weren't surprised to find we had
an audience as we locked and loaded. I practised
fast drawing from my holster and firing my Glock
in double-tapping mode at a floating cardboard
container until I was satisfied that my target-
shooting was up to scratch.

"It's a pirate box!" laughed Rolle.

All the while, Sean irritated me by hovering too
close as if I were a novice. But I wasn't the one who
ended up with bleeding thumbs from mishandling
the Glock. "Watch you don't shoot me in the foot
when you draw," he said. "Well, move your foot,"
I snarled. To make him back off I fired my weapon
at just the right angle to send a shower of burning bullet-casing in his direction.
It worked. Then I let loose with the semi-automatic weapons until the waves
made my day. It was almost orgasmic.

MARCH 31

Woke up feeling purged. We're enjoying a lovely sail to Kupang. Cyclone Glenda
seems to have taken all the whirling energy away from this place, inflicting it instead
on the good people of the West Australian seaboard.

Today I saw the weirdest ship. It looked like something out of the movie
'Waterworld'. Patched together and rusting, like two ships stapled together, at first
I thought it was a pirate ship, but it was probably just a live-aboard fishing boat. To
our starboard is the 'natural gas station' from which a pipeline goes all the way to
Darwin, feeding propane to the barbecues of the Top End. At night it shines like
Bollywood bling.

APRIL 1, KUPANG

We arrived in Kupang Harbour just after lunch. Rows of smokestacks grew
above a sprawling metropolis. I was astounded at the size of it, and the modern
buildings lining the shore. "Well, it ain't no sleepy hollow," said the captain.
Kupang is the capital of the Indonesian province of East Nusa Tenggara, which
comprises West Timor and several eastern Indonesian islands including Sumba,

Flores and Komodo. There are two or three hundred thousand people here. Captain Bligh landed briefly in 1789 after being set adrift by the mutinous crew of the HMS *Bounty*. He had survived 4,000 miles in an open boat. Less than three years later, the officer who met Bligh experienced a sick kind of déja vu when survivors of the wreck of the HMS *Pandora*, some of them mutineers, also turned up in Kupang in an open boat.

Right away, we had problems with customs. Two unsmiling uniformed Indonesian officials came on board and scrutinized our passports, paperwork and permits over several hours. At one point my cabin was searched when I wasn't present, which was particularly upsetting, because they went through my underwear drawer. They have a perfect right to do so, but I would have preferred to have been present, rather than suffer the humiliation of hearing how everyone enjoyed a view of my variously coloured G-strings.

There were some tense moments when the customs men inspected our weapons. At one point I became aware that Sean was counting out all the ammunition in front of them, and I hastened to help. Later, the captain told me that the paperwork was correct when we entered Australia, but that Sean had bought more since then, without adding it in. That was a big no-no that could have had serious consequences. It was all sorted out eventually, but, naturally, the tension between Sean and the captain has escalated.

Left and below: Customary greeting – scenes from our arrival and clearing-in at first Indonesian port, Kupang, West Timor.

APRIL 2

I went ashore to look around, which involved clambering over a moored *pinisi* and, once again, negotiating a narrow plank on the shore side. I wore a scarf to avoid offending the Moslem population, but it was quite unnecessary; the town was full of uncovered women and Christian schoolchildren. Kupang is pretty in parts, with an obvious, and somewhat disturbing, polarization of wealth and poverty. But I love eastern cities, no matter what, and am always fascinated by them. On our way into the centre of town we drove behind a man on a bicycle with a line of dead chickens strung along a stick. So that's how you spread avian flu.

We visited the market place, a busy and colourful chequerboard of vegetable, fish, spice and clothing stalls. They were tended by people of all ages, from silent, sleeping grannies to cheeky teenagers posing on their motorbikes while they drummed up passing trade. By a butcher's stall I spied a blonde Indonesian woman, obviously with European blood, and wondered again if Salty Sam had borne children here. I bought a wonderful bamboo-stringed musical instrument for Billy, called a *sasando*, a bit like his autoharp.

We all went out for a delicious meal of coconut crabs. I believe the nightlife here also features karaoke brothels … for men who like to sing on the job.

APRIL 3

Teguh arrived today from Surabaya to act as our guide and interpreter for a while. Hengke, an Indonesian crew member from Flores, has joined us too. He's shyer than Teguh, but very charming. He has a local captain's licence, and will be enormously helpful with translating, piloting, and our official port communications.

The captain is furious, and not just about the extra people we've now got on board. Last night someone didn't attend properly to his watch and we dragged anchor 200 metres. We could have 'hit the bricks', and I don't blame him for getting tough.

"The next time that happens, whoever was on watch will get off at the next port," he announced. "That's how we'll solve the accommodation problem."

The stickiest space issue is that it seems Kayt has been counting on using the forward port crew cabin as an extra pantry, so there's one less berth than I thought there was. With this number of people on board, we can't do more than a four-day sail without that extra food-store. Yikes. Something's got to give.

APRIL 4

My two favourite Indonesian expressions are now '*Pelan Pelan*' (Slow down!) and '*Hati Hati*' (Watch out!). A jaunt out to the village of Soe, about 110 km outside Kupang, turned out to be a great way to kick-start your adrenal glands. Our driver saw to it that we were rarely travelling on the two-lane road without at least a couple of other vehicles abreast of us: critical, near-miss overtaking seems a matter of honour in these parts.

After a full two hours of this it was disappointing to discover that, instead of the traditional village promised in the 'no-date' guidebook, Soe is in fact a large town adorned with screaming Japanese motorbikes, concrete buildings and a one-way system. In the surrounding villages, however, we did find people still living in traditional 'beehive' houses: tall, palm-thatched

Above: Roadside couple, West Timor countryside.

Right: Hive of domestic activity at *lopo* houses near Soe, West Timor.

cones with tiny doorways, like stretched, brown igloos. Small children holding even smaller children stared shyly at us, then turned to race back inside their smoke-filled *lopo*.

With the Mayor of Kupang coming to dinner on board this evening, it was all bustle on deck, and, by the time we shook off the dust of Soe, Kayt had cooked a five-star meal. Unfortunately, the ruling official chose not to attend. When Scotty and Ricky arrived at the dock to pick him up in our freshly washed tender, there were three snappily dressed officials staring down in horror at the size of the bouncing dinghy and the long rubber ladder leading down to it.

"Can't you bring the big boat over here?" asked the Minister of Tourism.

"No," snarled Scotty, eyeing the rusty steel stakes jutting out of the berth. "This dock's not suitable for the yacht."

"Well," stammered the Mayor's right-hand man (his boss was no doubt sitting behind the tinted glass windows of the waiting vehicle), "anyway, we just came to tell you that the Mayor cannot make it tonight. Maybe tomorrow." They swiftly retreated.

Meanwhile, the Mayor's welcoming party waited on the stern. That included myself all decked out in a purple silk sarong and kabaya, but with dirty hair due to new water restrictions on board (the harbour is polluted, so we can't use our water-maker).

"What do we call the Mayor?" I asked Hengke.

He made a phone call. "*Bapak Walikota,*" he decreed, translating it 'Mister Mayor'. "You can greet him with '*Salamat dating, Bapak Walikota.*'"

I practised this parrot-fashion, until I spied the tender returning with no one more illustrious on board than our good doctor and our second mate.

"Who's going to tell Kayt?"

Ricky, Scotty and I played 'paper-stone-scissors' to decide. I lost. "What, 'maybe tomorrow night'?" she fumed. "He can kiss my arse."

So there we were, all dressed up and no *Walikota*. In the end, everyone on board shared the five-star meal, and very nice it was too. A party ensued. Dirk, the boat's plastic blow-up penguin, played the role of the Mayor for the evening, and (confidentially) there were a few sore heads the next day.

In the middle of this social calamity, our Gurkhas arrived. Dev and Tek turned out to be two compact Nepalese look-alikes wearing the shiniest shoes in the world. I found it difficult to tell them apart and asked if they were related; but there is some mystery about that, even though they have the same last name. Anyway, they seem very pleasant. I tried to imagine them in battle, turning nasty with their famous *Kukri* knives, but they seemed far too polite. What's more, their table manners are immaculate, and put the rest of us to shame. I, for one, have been so long at sea I eat hunched-shouldered, from habit guarding my plate against a possible slide-away with the crook of my elbow.

APRIL 5

This morning, right off the bat, I had a major row with the captain about our accommodation problems, which escalated into a full-blown humdinger. By lunchtime I had calmed down, and decided to adopt the addict's practice of accepting the things I cannot change. One thing I can improve is my vertigo, so this afternoon I went up the mast in the bosun's chair to try to assuage it by 'flooding'. It's a psychological trick, like getting back on the horse when you've just fallen off. A hundred and twenty feet up, I white-knuckled it for forty minutes while the wind whistled all around. It seemed to work, but it was nasty. Fortunately the *Takapuna* didn't roll too much. Hate that.

As if to compensate me for such a rotten day, Ricky returned from town with a Roti Islander's hat. This is a straw cowboy-style confection with a conical antenna for attracting messages from the heavenly spirits. The people of Roti Island decorate these hats with plastic flowers – which must look pretty strange on a farmer up to his knees in the rice paddies.

At 4.30pm, Pete and I raced to the airport to pick up Russ and Jim, who were arriving from Bali. When we emerged from the tender beside two stunning *pinisi*, the car we were promised was nowhere in sight.

'Whose motorbike is this?' I demanded, pointing at an electric-blue Suzuki standing by the dock ladder. The owner quickly offered to lend it … for a price.

"OK, Pete, let's do it!" I grabbed one of the helmets and the handlebar.

He was looking at me strangely. "What? Are we going to fight about who's driving?" I smiled.

"Yeah," he replied tersely, "I'm driving."

I was about to retort "Wanna bet?" when fortunately my frontal cortex flipped in. "Neither of us knows the way, right?"

"Nope," replied Pete. We both retreated. Luckily, at that point we were descended upon by two motorbike taxis – savvy riders who took each of us, in badly-fitting helmets, on a pillion ride along mud-rutted thoroughfares.

Russ and Jim were lounging on the sidewalk as we drove up. "Sorry."

Jim turned out to be a lanky Englishman with the whitest skin in Kupang and a proper grown-up. He has been chosen to join our camera team not only for his stunning creative abilites, but also because he was in the SAS for 24 years and knows a thing or ten about security.

Russ was ebullient as ever, with fabulous news from Mauritius. "I'll tell you about it later," he said. But in the car back to the port, like a child with an exciting secret, he couldn't wait to off-load.

"I found out the tonnage and other details of the *Rosalie*," he announced as we sped past schoolchildren, spray-painted buses, market stalls and army barracks, under a reddening sky. It turns out that the *Rosalie* was built in Port Louis, Mauritius, in 1815–16, during which time only one other ship was constructed

Above: Public transport, Kupang-style – the motorbike taxi.

Right: Food fight – trying to land a mahi mahi for lunch.

on the island. The reason why Salty Sam lost the *Wolfe's Cove* is that on January 25, 1819, Mauritius was hit by a hurricane! The ship was driven on shore, after which he managed to get the spars off, and eventually retrieved and sold the rest of her. He then bought the *Rosalie*, a 298-ton, three-masted ship, around 100 feet in length, and left Mauritius on June 2, 1819, aboard her, bound for Sumatra. Whew! So the loss of the *Wolfe's Cove* couldn't have been Sam's fault.

APRIL 6, SUNDA SEA

We left Kupang before it was light. The day started badly when the captain growled at me as soon as I'd walked on deck and I responded to him in kind. "How long have you two been married?" winced Pete.

Poor Russ, who must be unbearably jetlagged, was an hour late for his first day's watch, and Rolle decreed that his punishment should be cleaning the shit tank. "Better get your snorkel," he said with an evil cackle.

This morning I caught a mahi mahi. These fish are nature's way of telling you you're under-buffed. It fought like buggery, but with the captain's neat gaff job

we finally landed it. It took forever to die because, due to its high bump-head, those intent on dealing out the *coup de grace* couldn't quite figure out where its brain was. At one point the captain even wanted to summon Ricky from his bed (he had been on night watch) to provide a physician's opinion of the location of the brain. But in the absence of timely professional advice, there ensued a bloody scene involving a Swedish engineer, a steel spike, and a lot of flinching by horrified onlookers. God, life is savage out here.

We can see the faint outline of East Timor, just off to starboard.

As the unfortunate person without a bunk, Teguh is managing well, but I feel bad for him. Despite this discomfort, he is so accommodating and so grateful to be on board, it breaks my heart. Like all good Moslems he gets up at 4.30am to pray, then says his reverences again at noon, 5pm, 6pm and 7pm. He brought his prayer mat on board, but took care to explain to me that if he happens to be working during prayer time he doesn't need to stop. "I just pray in my heart," he said.

I asked him about his food requirements. He doesn't eat pork or indeed anything with a cloven hoof. Nor does he eat pets such as cat or dog, so I shall issue strict instructions to Kayt not to cook up any domestic animals whilst he's on board. Teguh and Hengke say that on Monday night they will cook Indonesian food. Excellent. This trip is going to be a great food experience if last night was anything to go by, when Dev and Tek produced a Nepalese curry. They're Hindus, so I'm not sure why it had chicken in it, but it was one of the best I've ever eaten. Trouble is, if Billy hears about it he'll be so jealous he'll want to visit. He absolutely loves curry. And although I miss him, I really don't want him here with all these people on board. He'd head-butt anyone who got too close.

It was dead calm today. Almost eerie. We're like a penny in a pond. Tonight I lay ruminating under a gorgeous moon and brilliant stars, utterly mesmerized.

APRIL 7, BANDA SEA

Same again: it's weirdly calm, humid and still. Not enough wind to sail, and we're burning fuel at a ridiculous rate. I've been teasing Russ this must be his fault, that he brought these doldrums with him. If we were in the 17th century I'm sure someone would have strung an albatross around his neck by now.

Nevertheless, his information, hot from Mauritius, amazes me. For example, I always wondered where the name 'Rosalie' came from. Now I know it actually comes, like the ship herself, from Mauritius, where there's a village called Grande Rosalie. This settlement draws its name from an old sugar estate, no longer operational, thought to be the first working plant established there during the period of French rule; its chimney bears the date 1744.

That's just one of the gems Russ unearthed last week. He also found a document, a 'Bibliography of Mauritius', that covers the printed record, and the manuscripts, archivalia and cartographic material, for the period 1502–1954. It was from this that he found out the tonnage of the *Rosalie*, along with when and where she was built. Mauritius, in 1810, had become a British colony so it was an ideal time for Salty Sam to do business there – and a good time for Frenchmen to sell up. According to this document, Sam bought the *Rosalie* from a Monsieur Boudret in 1819, and indeed my great-great-grandfather's name is down there, in faded brown and white, as both master and owner.

This afternoon we stopped for a snorkel at a tiny volcanic island called Gunung Api, all by itself in the middle of nowhere. It's one of the Romang group

Above: Fishermen in the cove at Gunung Api, the volcanic island known for its colony of sea snakes, watch us curiously as we snorkel.

Right: Charts solved the mystery of two volcanoes with the same name – one in the Romang Group, the other in the Banda Islands.

of islands. What a privilege to be able to visit it. Thousands of brown boobies zoomed around their rocky home, but no humans live there – unless there is someone hiding out in one of the many caves that line the shore. We swam in water that changes from indigo to turquoise and is home to hundreds of sea snakes. I always thought those creatures were shy, but one headed for me quite alarmingly, and swam right between my legs. Or did I just dream that? Later, I observed Pete, who has a snake phobia, free-diving beneath me. He almost had a head-on collision with a particularly large silver and blue specimen, and his double take and frantic backstroke were worthy of Jim Carrey.

I spent an hour poring over the chart in confusion. Gunung Api is mentioned in historical literature, but it did not appear to be in the described geographical location. I finally realized that there is another Gunung Api – a more famous one – at our next destination, Banda Neira. The latter has always been volcanically threatening to nearby inhabitants, and was very active at the beginning of the 17th century, when the Dutch and British were just arriving. Then it was said to yield "… nothing but cinders, fire and smoake. The hill cast forth such hideous flames," wrote one observer, "such a store of cinders and huge streames that it destroyed all the thicke woods."

We shall be in Banda Neira in a couple of days. The island was once the very centre of the nutmeg trade. Procuring the spice wasn't in fact a life-or-death mission, but it seemed so at the time. Nutmeg was once considered a life-saving drug: a cure for the plague. This was no pumpkin-soup garnish: think 'AIDS cure' and you'll get the picture. That's why men braved the seven seas to fill their cargo-holds with little brown nuts. If they made it home, they could buy a football team.

Chapter **II** Trial By Fire
Mountain

APRIL 8, BANDA SEA

The Banda Sea is a bland sea. B for boring. It's almost as if we do not deserve to be so comfortable in the middle of the ocean. No wind. No sails. Just chugging through mirror-water while the sun beams benevolently on our barely visible wake.

Back in Europe, Anne and Lucy have been searching for clues in The Hague. They found no mention of shipwrecks in any of the literature they read, but yesterday they discovered an interesting entry under a 'Surabaya Departures' listing in the *Bataviasche Courant*. Adverts for Salty Sam's agents were in the back of this fortnightly newspaper: Peter Jessen, George Haswell. They were also listed as part of the Sea Assurance Society. The following listing appears in every issue going back to February 24, 1821: 'NED – SCHIP ROSALEE, S. STEVENSON SCHEPEN LIGGENDE TER REEDE' – 'Netherlands Ship … situated in the harbour (docked)'. Also, on the 25th of August 1821 under 'Surabaya Departures' was the following: 'NED – SCHIP ROSALEE, S. STEVENSON NAAR AMBOINA' ('Netherlands ship … heading for Ambon').

In other words, in 1821 the *Rosalie* was anchored in Surabaya for a whole six months! What was Sam doing there all that time? Repairs? In late August he set sail for Ambon. Yes, Ambon! Another piece of the jigsaw. We've got to go to Ambon. To hell if it's dangerous.

Meanwhile, researchers at the British Library have turned up a book called the *Mauritius Calendar* for 1816. This too lists the *Rosalie*'s port of origin and her owner before Salty Sam. An associate in Mauritius has also tracked down information about a Claude Francois Boudret – whose wife's name was Rosalie. This man was an armateur; in other words he financed privateering ships that wreaked havoc on the British. Understandably, he left Mauritius soon after the British conquest, in 1811, so perhaps it was a different Boudret who built Sam's *Rosalie*.

We'll be in Banda tomorrow. I just found an account of my friend Lawrence Blair's brush with pirates in these very waters. Five years ago, while cruising this eastern part of the archipelago in a 100-foot *prahu*, he was boarded at night by twenty-five local men armed with *parangs* (machetes) and drawn bows and arrows.

> *A single wrong move and both the captain and first mate would have been full of arrows… People fully dressed for the part – muscular, wearing red-bandanas and wielding splendid* parangs *and longbows – poured up over our sides and forced their way aboard. The firebrands amongst them rushed to our tanks and diving equipment and accused us of pirating their reefs.*
>
> *Though they were soon persuaded that we were not, as they claimed to have thought, Thai or Javanese hit-and-run cyanide-and-reef-bombing pirates, it still took an hour and a half to talk them off the ship. When they left, in high spirits, most of our canned drinks, sunglasses, penknives, and anything else that wasn't nailed down went with them.*

Lawrence also made the point that, lacking official protection, these men should be congratulated for so bravely defending their reefs.

APRIL 9, BANDA NEIRA

My worst hour ever aboard *Takapuna*. I completely lost it, and I'm thoroughly ashamed. I awoke feeling something was not right and immediately looked out of my porthole. There were the islands of Banda within a few hundred yards. I ran on deck and was met with an impossibly beautiful sight: two or three of the

most gorgeous volcanic islands I've ever seen, and approaching us two stunning, carved *Kora Kora*, or war canoes, each manned by forty men, waiting to escort us into the harbour. I immediately broke down, and started sobbing, and shouting, "Why didn't anyone wake me up?"

It seemed completely irrational to everyone around me, but I was heartbroken. My first glimpse of the Spice Islands should have been a far-off, first sighting – a purple dot in the distance that I could enjoy seeing closer and closer over a period of hours. 'A virginity of sense,' in the words of Robert Louis Stevenson. As it was, I felt cheated. I had stayed up as late as I could last night, but succumbed to sleep in the early hours. Of course, it was nobody's fault except mine, and they would never understand why I was so devastated. I demanded the captain turn round and sail out to sea again, then retreated to my cabin. Russ knocked nervously on my door – God knows what he made of me. I feel such an idiot now, and Russ will never believe such an open display of emotion is rare for me. It is as if all the tension, fear and anger of the past three months have finally caught up with me.

Eventually I emerged and witnessed half the journey I had longed to see. It was in fact wonderful to be flanked by men paddling beside us, singing and chanting as we sailed in to Banda Neira. I jumped into one canoe and joined the paddling into the shore. Waiting for us was the King of the Bandas, whose name is Des. His nose was thoroughly out of joint too, because he didn't get to organize the *Kora Kora*. He complained that the men should have been minus shirts to make it authentic. I'd go along with that.

Besides his day job as King, Des Alwi is an historian, linguist, and curator of the local museum. He is highly motivated to preserve Banda's heritage … well, the Dutch bit anyway. There are two cars on the island, and he took us for a ride round the tiny town. It's very picturesque, and delightfully devoid of modern Western influence. Colonnaded Dutch colonial buildings line the seafront, and many old houses in the village have also been nicely preserved or restored. The town is dominated by Gunung Api, the lofty Fire Mountain, that meets the stunning harbour at a ribbon of palm trees. Light breezes ruffled the bougainvillea blossoms.

Des and I had watched the *Takapuna* slide gracefully round the harbour, searching for a place to anchor. "You put up your sails in the afternoon and you can smell everything," he said, "… spice, nutmeg, mace."

Above and opposite:
A Banda welcome –
local *Kora Kora* war canoes
escort the *Takapuna* into
the harbour.

Below left: Urchins fishing
for urchins.

Below: Banda Neira village.

We climbed up to the five-point star shaped Fort Belgica that Des had restored and wandered around its battlements. The Portuguese arrived here in 1512, and soon afterwards the Banda Islands became the centre of the nutmeg trade to Europe. The Dutch came next, in 1599, and soon afterwards the British turned up and grabbed the nearby island of Rhun. This annoyed the Dutch, who wanted a nutmeg monopoly throughout the Banda Islands. Fighting ensued, with the poor Bandanese people stuck in the middle. Thousands of them were killed by the Dutch, so that by 1621 few were left. "I'm amazed you guys are even speaking to us," I said to Des. "So much carnage over little brown nuts."

We moored in a lovely, sheltered part of the harbour. "A Japanese warship was hit at sea and, instead of staying where they were they put in right where you're anchored," said Des. "The thing blew up at midnight, killing 27 of our people. See the cloudy water? That's all the metal and debris from their munitions." It was awful to hear how foreigners had disturbed the beauty and peace of this place, but Des wanted us all to enjoy it.

"If you climb the Fire Mountain over there," he pointed to the enormous rock-encrusted cone dominating the small harbour, "and swim across the channel, I will grant you citizenship of Banda." That promise encouraged the planning of an early morning climb up Gunung Api, daunting as that seemed with the mountain's broad slash of fresh, brown lava from an eruption in 2000. We ate dinner ashore in the hotel restaurant, and after the meal Des sang with the band. "I am the Perry Como of the Bandas," he said modestly.

APRIL 10

We left the *Takapuna* in the tender at 5am, slid across the bay to pick up our two guides, then unloaded our band of climbers at the base of Gunung Api. I was feeling nervous about the ascent. I'm pretty fit, but Des had told us that, in recent years, two Dutch guys had died while attempting the summit. "There are no high places at home," he said. 'So every time they see a mountain, they want to climb it." He announced that the best round-trip time so far was forty-three minutes, achieved by a couple of north-country British hill climbers. I wondered if there was an easy, rambling track; but no, the only route was 660 metres straight up the face.

We set off at a pace I knew I could not sustain. Tek, who'd climbed the Himalayas back home in Nepal, showed some of the laggers how to keep their legs apart to reduce the strain – but unfortunately I missed that important piece of information. After half an hour, when the sun was up, many of us were flagging, and we were less than a quarter of the way there. Behind us a scorching mist rose above the cooler harbour.

Des had warned us that the last 60 metres were the worst, but by then I was thinking that if I was going to have a heart attack, I probably would have had it already. It was terribly humid. We hauled our aching bodies up the final ascent, and sat on hot rocks to enjoy the view.

We circumnavigated the immense crater. No peacefully sleeping giant this, but a restless, fire-breathing demon. The ground beneath us was steamy, and hissed alarmingly in places. As I lay on the summit, the hot stones felt good on my back. Proud of making it to the top, we had been fooled by tales of how easy it was going down. The pressure on our knees was intense, especially when light rain began to fall and created a steep glacier of slippery mud. In the end I sat on my backside and slid most of the way. They need 3,000 mm of rain every year to grow their nutmegs here, and I'd say they wouldn't have been far short this morning. By comparison, the two-kilometre swim across the harbour was a doddle – and a welcome cooling off.

In the afternoon Des introduced me to his delightful pet cockatoo, who took a painful fancy to my hair. When the day cooled off, he whisked us across the harbour in his regal barge for a stroll round his nutmeg plantation. His love of his trees, especially the very old ones, was touching. He seemed to have intimate knowledge of their gender and sexual orientation – and pointed out which were the male, the female, and even the 'gay' trees.

This evening Des came aboard for dinner, and presented us with our certificates of honorary citizenship. In full King mode he congratulated us for conquering the Fire Mountain, and confirmed that we were now entitled to marry on Banda, and to invest there. He presented me with a small Chinese porcelain plate that had been washed up on a nearby shore. I was hoping he might know someone at Ambon, our proposed next stop. There has been a great deal of discussion on board about the dangers of the place, and even Sean feels

Below: A mature nutmeg tree and its fruit – the red membrane is mace.

Below right: With Des Alwi, King of the Bandas.

we should not risk it. Luckily, Des does know someone who will meet us there, and escort us round. He also mentioned that there is a library and some archives at the Church of St Saviour, and that his friend the ex-Bishop would receive us and help with our search. That did it. We've got to go to Ambon.

Hi Pamsy,

I hope the erstwhile cruel sea is being kind to you. I also hope that you are getting along with your motley crew, they seem like a rather jolly bunch of salty sea dogs, but then, as they say, you know what sailors are. In your last communication you seemed to be having a good time, and it was nice to hear, as you headed in the rough direction of scary spice, I hope it turned out well.

Life here is lovely in its nothingness. I have just had a lovely time with Cara and the kids up here at the house, they had a great time. Sometimes, when I see little Babsy sitting on her haunches, or should I say, hurdies, I am taken right back to the times when we watched our own kids in the busy busy position. Doesn't life just love repeating itself?

Celtic have done me the great honour of asking me to present the team with the league winners trophy at Celtic Park next Sunday. I'm very nervous, but at the same time absolutely delighted to be so highly thought of by them.

The snow continues to fall here. I think perhaps the seasons have decided to change order, just when we thought we had it down about Global Warming. In fact, a wee touch of global warming would be just the thing round here!

Good luck to your sea legs, and all your other vital bits and pieces,
Love Love Love, Bill Bill

APRIL 11, RHUN, NAILAKA

Although some of us were sore today from yesterday's climb, we decided to sail to the island of Rhun and take a look around. The British had a toehold here from 1601, and in 1616 the Englishman Nathanial Courthope established command of it, right under the noses of the Dutch. But Courthope and his men were virtually under siege for the next few years, constantly under attack, and with little food or water. Some of his crew mutinied, taking one of his ships, and eventually he was down to thirty loyal men pushed onto the adjacent islet of Nailaka. Fifty years later, the British returned the island of Rhun to Holland in exchange for the island of Manhattan in North America. The most famous swap in history meant that nowadays New Yorkers wouldn't be seen dead in clogs.

Des had arranged an introduction to the Chief of Rhun. We wandered through the village until we found his house, and waited until he returned from a wedding. He arrived wearing traditional Muslim garb – a sarong and a high-crowned, black oval hat. After greeting us warmly, he disappeared to a back room, then returned in a moth-eaten woollen jumper and a leather hat. Since the temperature outside was now over 100 degrees, we were baffled by this change of costume – but assumed he was trying to present his Western side. He led us up many stone steps to the site of the early fort that overlooks the main anchorage. On the way we passed an empty street stall sporting a painted sign that said simply 'Free Sex, Free Love', but neither the chief nor anyone else on the island had any idea what that meant.

The chief of Rhun shows us round his island.

Above: Our lean-to shelter on Nailaka.

Right: Nightfall on Nailaka.

Russ, Ricky, Pete, Tessa, Jim, Sean, Teguh and I stayed the night over on Nailaka. It was Russ's idea to experience what the besieged British contingent had had to put up with on their islet. A makeshift lean-to was constructed by those members of the party who knew least about such things, while our two ex-military men watched in horror from the shady comfort of their expertly constructed jungle beds. A fire was built, Ricky and Teguh went off in a canoe to get some fish, and Tessa cooked an excellent dinner. Unfortunately, though, the island turned out to be inhabited by a large gang of fearless rats. A small expedition was mounted to inspect the interior of the island, led by Russ with a bottle of whiskey in one hand and a machete in the other – a truly scary sight. But he made up for it later that evening, after the whiskey had been demolished, by performing a marvellous entertainment called the Dance of the Flaming Arse.

The wee hours saw the establishment of a clothing-optional rule on the island and, if I mention the phrase 'Lord of the Flies', you'll get about a quarter of the picture of drunkenness, debauchery and running amok that ensued. Naturally, I was perfectly behaved throughout – and I can say that, because it is I who am writing this book. Don't even *think* about asking Russ his side of the story.

Chapter 12 Cheese and Whine

APRIL 12, BANDA SEA

We left noonish for Ambon. Around 5pm Ricky and I were going though photos in my cabin when there was an urgent knocking at the door. It was the captain. His eyes were bulging, and shifting furiously.

"Hey, can you talk to Russ … about food?" he asked.

"What now?" I replied, probably revealing my impatience with this latest in the long line of petty complaints about the FNGs.

"He went into the galley and cut himself a piece of cheese this big," he said, holding his hands about ten inches apart. "There's almost none left for the rest of us." He retreated, leaving Ricky and me dumbfounded.

"What?" I turned to Ricky. "Am I going to go to my fellow adventurer and say, 'Don't eat so much cheese?' How ridiculous."

The main thing on my mind was that, if Russ really had eaten that amount of cheese at one sitting, I was going to be giving him a wide berth. The man was about to cut the cheese in quite a different manner.

From then on, the incident began to be re-told in winks and whispers. By dinner time Russ's slice of cheese had grown to be an entire wheel of Brie. No doubt this will forthwith be known as the Great Ambon Cheese Incident.

APRIL 14, AMBON

As we were sailing into Ambon we realized we'd made a huge mistake. It was Good Friday, and it occurred to us that a Christian holiday was perhaps not the best time to visit an island where Muslims and Christians have been relentlessly bombing each other for years. On January 19, 1999, riots began in Ambon, just at the end of Ramadan – a time when traditionally Christians and Muslims would shake hands.

Still standing – the church of St Saviour in Ambon, Maluku.

Instead, one house was burned, then another in retaliation, and it just escalated from there. At Christmas 2002, Muslim extremists blew up the Rehoboth Church.

We anchored in a filthy harbour, and met our guide, Hans, and his daughter Helena. "What's the situation like now?" I asked as we set off for St Saviour's Church.

"It's better," they said, "but you never know." I noticed they wore crosses round their necks.

"Are we going to drive through the Muslim section?" I asked nervously.

"Yes," they smiled. There was an uncomfortable silence, during which Russ and I glanced nervously at each other. "Our house was burned down in the riots," said Helena. "Look, can you see all the holes in the buildings? People had rifles and home-made mortars. Children were killed here."

The centre of Ambon was a torn-up, bullet-marked, crumbling mess. You could see how it happened: Christians living across the same street from their Muslim neighbours.

"After the riots we moved out of town," said Hans, "but then we had to cross the mountains on foot – four hours every day. After a while people made a small path for motorcycles."

We were handed a photocopied document entitled *Ambon Guide To Tourists.* "Today," it said, "Ambon is becoming an attractive tourist destination." The keyword was obviously 'becoming'.

At least there were some thoughtful tips for travellers:

Manners
The local citizens of Ambon Island and City is a very polite and eversmiling people. Handshaking is widely used when meeting each other, on introducings and greetings.

A HINT FOR VISITORS: When visiting offices, especially government offices, be yourself and dress casually.

When it came to producing some PR for the spice islands of yesteryear, the poor writer really had to scrape the barrel:

Maluku has a variety of tourist attractions widespread in the islands, attractions which are still untouched, still natural. Natural in the way of living and in the environment.

I remembered that, before the riots, there was a famous yacht race – the Darwin-Ambon Race. "Do you think it will be back?" I asked.

"People are talking about it," Hans said. "And there are some good signs." Helena, through the Maluku Interfaith Humanitarian Institution, was involved with an initiative aimed at encouraging the youth of both sides to talk and pray together. We stopped off at the newly re-opened *Baku Bae* 'Market of Reconciliation' where I was glad to see Muslims and Christians have begun to shop side by side again.

At the Church of St Saviour the choir was preparing for the Easter services. We stepped out of the heat into a small library building, where a thin Dutchman greeted us. This was the man Des had recommended to us, who had been Bishop there in past years. I told him my mission, and he showed me some wonderful old books containing illustrations of the port of Ambon during the Dutch period. But Salty Sam's story called up nothing new.

A bullet-pitted Ambon residence (top) and city centre building, damaged in the race riots.

A photo of the Nailaka bonfire revealed mysterious faces among the flames.

There were no records here, he said, of shipping movements to and from Ambon – they would probably be in The Hague.

Another blow. We had risked so much to come here, including the good will of the sailing crew, but had gained nothing. When we got back to the boat, Rolle was in a terrible state about the threat the polluted harbour presented to our generators and water-making capability. Since nothing more could be achieved in Ambon we left shortly afterwards for Ternate, a little further north.

I was standing on the stern munching on one of Kayt's hot cross buns when Russ brought me a photo he'd taken on the island of Nailaka. It was a picture of our bonfire.

"What do you see?" he asked.

"Faces," I said, without a moment's hesitation. I had thought they were distorted pictures of us all sitting round the fire, but they weren't. In fact, they were unmistakable, and unexplainable, images of a skull and a couple of other strange heads right in the flames.

"Perhaps it's the ghost of Salty Sam and his crew!" I was only half joking.

APRIL 14

Dear Pamsy,

Life goes on pretty much as usual here in the windswept north of the United Kingdom. We are awakened most mornings by the shrill cries of the multi-coloured Macaws as they prance around in their seemingly never ending fertility dance on the roof of our unpretentious albeit enormous dwelling place. The grunting in the night of the more voracious crocodiles can be tiresome, but the negative side is assuaged by the knowledge that they do a great job in keeping down the size of the families of our more irritating neighbours. As for my own wellbeing, a subject close to your heart. I am doing as well as can be expected of a man of my advanced years, although it must be stated that I am in my usual physical state which on any given day borders on the legendary, as you well know. I hope the waves are staying below their normal terrifying height for you, at least during mealtimes.
Until our next epistle, heave to me hearties,
Love Love Love, The Yin

Bill Bill,

Ahoy from the scariest Spice Island: Ambon. With all the travel warnings we've had about Christians and Muslims roasting each other over burning buildings it was a serious anti-climax, with nothing more invasive than a floating plastic bag that seeped into our sea-strainer and shut down one generator for an hour or two.
I hope the Easter bunny keeps off the lawn and deposits nothing more than chocolate.
I miss you.
Love Love Love, Pamsy

APRIL 15, MOLUCCA SEA

Dear Pamsy,
Glad to hear that you are rising above the ever present threat of violent death inflicted by peace loving religious types, a threat that assails us even at Scottish football matches.
Don't stand up in your hammock,
Bill Billxxx

Early this morning we crossed the equator. Since there were a few people on board for whom this was the first 'crossing of the line' we had to find a way to mark the occasion. It is usual to humiliate such novices via any number of sadistic rituals (in the Navy one used to get a broom handle publicly shoved up one's arse), but here on *Takapuna* we chose to be kind. The first-timers – Tessa, Scotty, Teguh, Tek, Dev and Russ – were forced to wear revealing costumes of Polynesian grass skirts and coconut bras that I keep on board for just such an occasion. Russ added a military helmet – a touch he decided upon because somebody warned him that a symbolic equator line might be shaved around his head.

The captain played the part of the mighty King Neptune, in Sue's sarong draped like a cape, a cardboard crown, and the gaff as a makeshift trident, and I was his shell-crowned consort. Rolle, in a wicked Viking helmet, was Neptune's henchman. He began by painting a large equatorial ring on each participant's stomach with tomato sauce. Then a bottled message from the Deity of the Deep arrived via fishing line:

Neptune's Message
Avast there, you ruthless land-lubbers, you miserable mortals who have never before crossed my median strip that ignorant folks call 'the Equator'! I have watched your pitiful crossing of my Arafura Sea, my Banda Sea, and my Ceram Sea, in your doom-laden search for my servant Salty Sam. I and my royal court have observed with great amusement your many human foibles: all your nonsensical tantrums, fights and grumbling; your pathetic midnight nudie-dips, your wimpish bouts of boxing, your loutish wakeboarding, and the cutting of the cheese. I am displeased. You have tried to assault my kingdom by the unauthorized catching of my creatures, you have daily disposed rubbish into my depths, and you have even dared to shoot my waves with lethal bullets. You pathetic earth-crawlers can never defeat me. I will always win. One strike of my trident, and a mighty storm will arise to swallow you deep into the bowels of my fair ocean. Beware. To appease me, and guarantee the safety of your journey, all first-time equator-crossers must fall to their knees in reverence of my Majesty. After being anointed with syrup, a sacrificial lock of hair will be cut from each of your heads and flung overboard, and each one of you will pray to me in turn. Kneel and repeat:

Then each novice was expected to kneel and repeat the following oath, while a sacrificial lock of hair was chopped off by Rolle and flung into the waves:

Right: Equator crossing
ceremony – Neptune
initiates (L to R) Teguh,
Tessa, Pete, Scotty, Tek
and Russ.

Opposite: Russ with an
ancient clove tree on
Mount Gamalama, Ternate.

Oh Mighty Neptune, I acknowledge your power and might.
Worthless mortal that I am, I tremble before you. As your humble
servant, I swear to help guard your oceans in our quest for Salty Sam.

As the last sufferer was plastered with a nasty mixture of sauce and cheese
(Russ was made to eat his), we began to enter the harbour at Ternate. "Quick!"
I said. "Finish and clean up. This would take a lot of explaining to the locals."

Ternate was one of the early centres of the clove trade … that is, until the
Dutch decided to make Ambon the one and only clove centre, to try to keep
their monopoly, and consequently burned all the clove trees here. But they
missed a few: they say there's a 400-year-old clove tree on the side of Gamalama,
the live volcano I've seen depicted in early etchings.

Our guide, Mr Sam, took us immediately to the reigning Sultan's palace, which is
also a museum. Sir Francis Drake came by here on the *Golden Hind*, and blew the
Sultan's mind by showing no interest in cloves. The reason was, his ship had already
been stuffed with Spanish gold he'd pirated elsewhere, and he had no room on board.

We had been told we might be lucky enough to have an audience with His
Highness, the current Sultan.

"His new wife," Mr Sam told me, "is young like you," thereby earning a lot of
brownie points and, for sure, a large tip. But the Sultan was a no-show, and we
were told to return at ten tomorrow morning.

Royal rug – the Sultan's
bejewelled crown, featuring
'live' human hair that
requires an annual trim.

APRIL 16 (EASTER DAY), TERNATE

That Sultan is one elusive ruler. He did not show up as promised, and I honestly
don't think he was anywhere near Ternate, unless he was busy entertaining his
new young wife.

"Well, could we please see his crown?" I asked the Royal Guard. The crown
is legendary, a kind of jewel-encrusted turban with human hair attached to it.
It is said that this hair actually grows, and has to be trimmed annually by the
palace handmaidens.

"I'm sorry," replied the Guard, "but the Keeper of the Crown is not here."

"Where is he?" I asked.

"Oh, he is travelling with the Sultan."

"Really?" I said. "Can't we just peek at it?" Not surprisingly, the rules say the Keeper has to be present when anyone views the crown.

Instead, we were granted an audience with the Sultan's oldest sister Rini, which turned out to be a blessing. She appeared at the doorway of an inner room, a petite elderly woman dressed like a bohemian New Yorker.

"My real name is Scheherazade," she confessed. "You know, from The Arabian Nights." As a child she had spent a few years in a convent in Brisbane, hiding from political enemies who wanted to assassinate her family.

She listened carefully to our story. "You must go to Manado," she instructed us. "Talk with Professor Lapian. He knows about such things." Before we could leave, Mr. Sam insisted on taking us on a whistle-stop tour of Ternate, which included visiting a fort built by one Sultan in the shape of male genitalia as a present for his wife. Was he trying to tell her something?

APRIL 17, MOLUCCA SEA

Sultan's sister knows best, I hope. The city of Manado is just a day's sail from Ternate, so we left Maluku almost immediately and headed for North Sulawesi. There's grumbling among the crew because of the sudden change, but I know they'll be happier having a night off in Manado. For a start, there'll be a big supermarket for Kayt, with frozen food; there was nothing in Ternate or Kupang.

Still, I can only empathize about the strains and stresses of life on board. Someone posted a 'Quote of the Day' above the companionway: "The next time I have sex it's going to be the best damn sex ever."

Arrival in modern Manado – the new waterfront development.

APRIL 18, MANADO

Just as the mosques were calling 4pm prayers, we dropped our anchor in Manado opposite the massive Ritzy Hotel and a new waterfront retail development. This is a cosmopolitan city. The streets were stuffed with trucks, taxis and smart cars, although some motorcycle riders had substituted coolie hats for helmets. Nearly half a million people live here in the north-west corner of Suluwesi.

Indonesian intelligentsia – with Rini, sister of the Sultan of Ternate, and Professor Adrian Lapian.

Russ and Jim flew off for a few days in the UK. Meanwhile, I managed to make contact with Rini's Professor. Adrian Lapian was waiting for us at the dockside: a charming, cherubic seventy-six-year-old. I was thrilled to hear he is a piracy expert. In his view, it is worthwhile, even necessary, to study Indonesian history from a maritime perspective.

"Dutch history about Indonesia was written from the decks of VOC ships," he said, quoting a colleague, "but I think we must all go sailing to have a fresh, comprehensive look at our past." Having taught south-east Asian history at the University of Indonesia from 1961, he was invited in 1966 to study in the Netherlands. In 1963, meanwhile, having joined the historical section of ALRI, the Indonesian Navy, he became its head.

"Do you know what VOC stands for?" He winked. "Not the *Verenigde Oostindische Caompagnie* (Dutch East India Company) but *Vergaan Onder Corruptie*, which means 'bent down because of corruption'."

We chatted for a while over coffee at the Hotel Ritzy (it was!), then travelled inland to his house in the village of Tomohon beneath the stunning Gunung Lokon volcano. After lunch by the crater lake, he showed me his superb library of history books and even entrusted me with some tomes on piracy, the spice trade, the building of *prahus*, and underwater archaeology.

The Professor's Tomohon residence.

"That Resident, or Regent, who received the survivors at Bima," he said, after hearing the whole story of our quest, "– I may be able to help you get his report from the archives. That may shed more light on the story. In those days, Bima was administered by Makassar – why don't you go there next? I shall be attending a workshop there on Tuesday, and I could meet you."

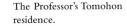

A farmer's hut stands amid windswept rice fields – the road to Tomohon, Northern Sulawesi.

We made a plan to sail down the Sulawesi coast to the port of Makassar, stopping on the way at the Professor's beach house at Amarang. His library of maritime books is there, and he may even be able to give me a copy of the Buginese people's *Law of the Sea*, a fascinating set of maritime rules written down by the chief Amanna Gappa in the 1600s.

As we talked on his veranda at Tomohon, downing tea and banana fritters, the Professor led me to a long-overdue epiphany. He said the Buginese were always superstitious about negative moods at sea. It was considered terribly unlucky to go to sea with a bad vibe, in fact they could not even build their ships if there was an argument. This information affected me most deeply.

Late this evening I decided I will not allow the voyage to continue under such a negative cloud.

APRIL 19

At 5am I woke from a fitful sleep with an overwhelming sense that it was time the captain and I parted company. We chatted at length then mutually agreed that he should step off the boat and enjoy a well-earned rest. Dan will become interim captain, and Scotty will become first mate. The Law of the Sea has prevailed.

Chapter **13** Bogey Men

APRIL 20, CELEBES SEA

There's a different atmosphere on board now. In fact, today we had some of the most delightful sailing I've ever known. I'm proud of Dan, and the rest of the crew, who are getting on with the job in a most professional manner. With Professor Lapian on board, we sailed 36 miles down the west coast of Sulawesi to his beach house. I'm quite in love with that old man; he's such a glowing, positive force. When we arrived, around fifty local men, women and children were waiting to greet us. The local officials were a welcome change from those in Kupang; two shy, smiling men waved from their canoe, each wearing a navy T-shirt with '*Polisi*' on the back.

The Professor invited us to inspect his maritime library, and lent me more of his precious books. In one I found a paragraph that solved the mystery of the Dutch flag. I had always wondered why it was depicted in Trudy's tapestry. It turns out that, in Salty Sam's time, all ships operating out of Batavia were required to fly a Dutch flag, whether they were from the Netherlands or not. The Professor says there's a museum in Makassar that we might find interesting. On Tuesday he'll introduce me to the head of the Jakarta archives, who is also attending the workshop.

Meanwhile, Alain Huron, our researcher in Mauritius, has found some references to the Boudret family. Evidently there was a Claude François Boudret (1767–1824), a trader, printer and shipowner who settled in Mauritius in 1790. In 1794 he married a cousin, Rosalie Boudret. Around that time, Boudret purchased the *Jean Bart*, which was renamed *Rosalie*, possibly in honour of his young wife, and in 1796 he and an associate are

Take my picture, Meester!
North Sulawesi children.

Our welcoming committee near Professor Lapian's beach house and maritime library at Amarang.

further recorded as owners of a privateer ship named *Rosalie*. But what happened to that *Rosalie* after 1796? Alain found no record. Anyway, it's not OUR *Rosalie*, as she was built in 1816 – unless Salty Sam was cheated. Could he have been sold a tarted-up, twenty-year-old ship, passed off for new? Surely he was too smart for that.

APRIL 21, MAKASSAR STRAIT

Bonjour Matelot
Dearest one,
The weather has taken a turn for the worse, just when it looked like things were on the way up, a stiff breeze up the string vest certainly gets your attention in the morning. Cara has been hinting about a shopping trip to Edinburgh to get some nice things for the kids, it sounds like it could be a great wee diversion, I think I'll go ahead with it, it's time I left the house anyway, I'm becoming a hermit these days. Well my dear, since I know nothing of any value to you about the sea and its many interesting facets, I'll sign off with a manly wave and a rousing *High Ho Silver*! And gallop off into the distance.
Splice the mainbrace,
Bill Bill xxxxxx

APRIL 22

Everyone's getting along better, which is a great relief. I've been able to instigate group meetings without fear that they'll go horribly wrong. This morning's went very well indeed, and was a good opportunity to air any problems and share information. Pete, for example, received a good-natured ribbing for starting the washing machine at six this morning and waking everyone up.

APRIL 23

Tek has expressed concern about the riots back home in Nepal. As the older of our two Gurkhas, he has informed me that although he and Dev miss their families, neither wants to go home for a break in case he is not allowed to leave again. I am resolved to keep them on board as long as possible.

I've been reading about the politics of piracy. Fascinating. The year before Salty Sam was lost, a Dutch official named Elout was advocating the urgent establishment of European posts at all 'Native Ports' to provide policing. This was vital, he claimed, "in order to repress the piratical practices of the Malays, who are all pirates…" By 1824 a treaty had been signed between the British and the Dutch, who agreed "to concur effectually in repressing Piracy in those Seas: They will not grant either asylum or protection to Vessels engaged in Piracy." This was, of course, way too late to help Salty Sam.

There were certainly plenty of pirates around – although, as the Professor has pointed out to me, one must be careful not to apply European value judgments to Asian social and economic phenomena, i.e. a pirate's only a baddie if you apply your own moral concepts, or if you're on the receiving end of an attack. "In the 19th century," writes historian Nicholas Tarling, "there were often differences or doubts as to the proper application of the term. The fact is that … it tended to involve an unfavorable moral judgment passed by Europeans on non-Europeans."

There is a striking similarity of dress between residents in the 17th century, as featured in Van Linschoten's *Itinerario* (below), and today (opposite).

Whatever you want to call them, people who carried out attacks at sea presented a big problem for traders like Salty Sam – and, just like today, there were large numbers of them clustered around the Indonesian archipelago.

There were the Sulu Pirates, 'the hardy and ferocious race' that inhabited the islands between Borneo and the Philippines. The Jahore Pirates launched annual fleets of *prahus* to lie in wait for traders travelling northwards to Penang, 'plundering them of all they possess and murdering indiscriminately all on board'. Another group of pirates was the Ilanuns, a distinct race inhabiting the coast of the Mindaneo Bay and using the lake behind it as their stronghold. They lived on board their *prahus* with their wives and families, and their booty came principally from selling captives around Borneo and the Makassar Straits.

The Molucca Straits, still feared today, presented security dilemmas for Europeans and local traders alike. It was believed that "at certain times of the year piratical *prahus*, each carrying 90 to 100 men, proceed in fleets of 10–20 from islands at the southern end of the straits, each accompanied by 3–4 fast rowing boats."

Although the Dutch ruled the larger centres of trade in Salty Sam's time, there was a Raja, or chief, in charge of each small province or island group – many of whom, it seems, supported the pirates. Possessing little money, they often preferred to invest it in piratical adventure than to risk it on 'the uncertain and tedious profits of commerce'. Upon each *prahu*'s return, the Rajas would claim fifty per cent interest on all cash loaned to the pirates, plus a portion of the booty – including all weaponry of certain types – and the pick of the female captives.

In the 18th century, the disruption brought about by Europeans jostling for control of the spice trade had led many local Rajas, deprived of legitimate

income, to plunder and raid throughout the archipelago. One incident in 1821 is particularly reminiscent of the story about Salty Sam in the *Prince of Wales Island Gazette*. The *Seaflower* was a trading vessel that embarked on a voyage in the Archipelago just three or four months before Salty Sam left Surabaya on the *Rosalie*. At Sulu Town it was well received, and its Captain – an ex-naval officer called Spiers – persuaded the Sultan there to provide a letter of safe conduct for his vessel and crew around the nearby provinces of subordinate Rajas. Soon after, at Boona-Boona, where the Raja Bandar of Sulu came aboard the *Seaflower*, the Raja's party suddenly drew their daggers and made a treacherous attack. Forty or fifty Sulus were killed, and four of Spiers' crew.

Back in Sulu, the Sultan apologized, but the incident led Spiers to realize that the ruler had little jurisdiction over his district Rajas. Payments and presents had to be forthcoming if traders wished to engage in commerce and depart safely. It may have been that such extortion was perpetrated against Salty Sam, ultimately leading to his murder.

'The inhabitants are addicted to piracy' was the European view of the time, and the suppression of piracy became a rationale for all kinds of armed intervention by colonial leaders who were sometimes more intent on expansion than on enforcing the peace. Meanwhile, robbery and murder on the high seas continued to threaten European traders. *The Eastern Seas*, an 1830s account by Captain George Windsor Earl of his adventures around the archipelago, describes 'a most atrocious act of piracy'. A Java-based English merchant was bound for Samarang, in Java, carrying quite a bit of cash. A 'famous piratical chief' heard about this, launched a fleet of *prahus*, and

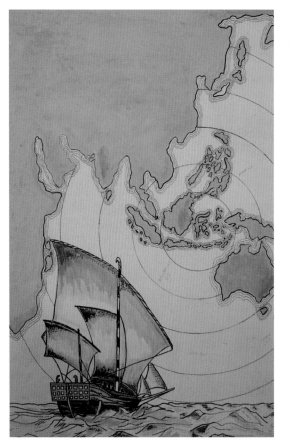

An early 'Malayan' prow – the type Salty Sam may have been travelling on in his final hours.

attacked the merchant's brig – whose crew comprised two English officers and thirty or so Javanese seamen. In the fighting the merchant was killed by a spear fired from a musket, and the pirates boarded the brig. The two officers fled, by jumping into the sea and swimming to a bamboo fishing platform. The pirates didn't bother with them any more, being too busy plundering the brig, but meanwhile the Englishmen were stuck up to their necks in water, and imagining the horrors of the deep. Soon after daylight, some Javanese fishermen turned up, but failed to rescue them. "First, tell us who are you, and where you come from," they demanded. Once convinced they were English, the fishermen took the two officers on board, treated them kindly, and delivered them to a European settlement at Indromayo.

"Had they belonged to one of the Dutch cruisers," wrote Earl, "their fate would probably have been different, for the fishermen are on bad terms with the officers of the government *prahus*."

Earl reckons the 'piratical chief' was the infamous Raja Raga, to his associates an idolized 'Robin Hood of the Sea'. Dutch and English alike had him in their sights. On one occasion his *prahu*, crewed by more than 150 pirates, had been entrusted to a favoured captain. This man fell in with a ship not far

Common modern vessel, the *pinisi*, known for its sturdiness, seaworthiness, and ease of maintenance.

from Makassar and opened fire in order to gain the glory of capture for his boss. To his dismay, a line of large gun ports opened in the side of the vessel and he found himself facing a British man-of-war that sent him and his crew straight to the bottom of the ocean.

"The pirates who infest the archipelago," wrote Earl, "consist wholly of the inhabitants of the free Mahommedan states in Sumatra, Lingin, Borneo, Magindano, and Sulu... The Europeans who are unfortunate enough to fall into their hands are generally murdered, while the natives who compose the crews of the captured vessels are sold for slaves.'

Salty Sam was lost some time in the months of September–October. The regularity of seaborne raids in the area was predictable, since in navigating their *prahus* many pirates relied on the prevailing winds. Each year warnings were issued by the Dutch and English to coastal towns and small craft on the approach of the 'pirate wind' in August, September and October that brought the Ilanun to the Strait of Malacca. These raiders had a thorough knowledge of the area, and could navigate using sun, moon, stars, and the directions of winds and currents. Many also carried compass and telescope. They had their own uninhabited islands that furnished them with food, water and firewood and where their *prahus* could be hauled onto a beach for repairs. Pirates had their own names for these islands so as to hide their whereabouts. But, thanks to the testimony of escaped captives, the Dutch knew where some at least were located: off the north-west coast of Borneo; south and north-east of Celebes (now Sulawesi); also small bays and coastal sites were used on Komodo and Flores. And Sumbawa, right by the Straits of Alas.

APRIL 24

Beautiful day, but no wind. We should be in Makassar tomorrow or the day after. It's Tessa's birthday. Nice, calm atmosphere on board. Not much to do. We played a few guessing games trying to figure out the lengths of some of the massive tankers that have been passing us in the distance. The answer is usually displayed on our ship's AIS (Automatic Identification System), but the one time a ship wasn't listed Dan got on the radio and asked. The tanker's captain was mystified. "God," I bet he was thinking, "it's time those sailors got a life."

Professor Lapian's book on underwater archaeology has been invaluable, and I spent the morning writing an outline of our plans for diving on the wreck of the *Rosalie*, if we ever find it. After outlining the construction, age and origin of the vessel herself, I list what I think we should be looking for:

- **Possible archaeolgical artefacts:** Ship's bell (brass), telescope (brass, leather), compass (brass) and wheel (wood and brass). Other remains might include lamps (possibly brass), hinges (brass), ropes and lines, iron anchor (archaeological sources indicate that these are surprisingly difficult to date), wooden hull, tools (hammers, chisels), figurehead, chains, copper nails, trunks and water containers, cutlery, plates (ceramic, pewter), jugs, galley equipment (glass bottles, bowls and storage jars, cooking pots, kettles and saucepans), and personal items such as buckles, combs, coins, shoes, inkpots, candlesticks.

- **Purchased by Captain Stephenson in Surabaya for carrying aboard to the Moluccas:** 55 canisters of sugar, 3484 bags of rice, a quantity of coal, 300 Kudyans nuts, 50 straw bags, 3 cases of chintz, 2 bales, 15 cases of Bengal chintz , 50 cases of gin, 12 boxes of cheroots, 1 piece of shirting, 2 bundles of twine, 2 pecols of rice, 1 empty water cask, 1 pecol, 37kg of old iron, 10 packets of copper nails, 10 water buckets, 674 measures of old rope, 93 cayangs, 1 pecol [and] 41 catties of rice, 54 canisters of sugar, 4 pipes of brandy, 23 cases containing 104.5 doz of brandy (4.5 doz broken) = 109 doz , 12.5 doz of Madeira, 12 doz of vinegar, 9 doz of claret and several old trunks.

- **Weapons on board were probably:** carronades, cannon, muskets and pistols plus ammunition. Carronades were introduced towards the end of the 18th century, and were a kind of large, anti-personnel mortar which, being small in proportion to the weight of the shot it fired, could be mounted high up. Probably 68-pounders weighing 1½ tons. The *Rosalie* probably had at least 8 gun ports, four each side.

Using modern charts and navigation equipment, we must first try to ascertain where the *Rosalie* would have most likely run aground. After inspecting the likely sites and evaluating depth, currents, and winds, we should begin to search for the wreck using systematic area dives, metal detector and possibly a magnetometer. If we find something it is essential to start by photographing the site extensively. At this point we should consider employing a marine/nautical archaeologist, and ensure that permits are in place before proceeding.

Next we should plan some inspection dives according to depth and conditions. If the ship is lying shallow enough for regular recovery dives we should situate auxiliary lighting around the wreck area, stake out a cord grid over what is readily visible, and probe the surrounding area with metal rods in search of wreckage concealed by sand. We could use the metal detector and magnetometer to pick up concentrations of iron, brass, and other metals and establish their locations, and use 'air-lifts' (suction tubes) or other excavation tools to remove superficial sand and dig to uncover metal objects and anything else still remaining. Delicate areas should be cleaned with brushes.

In the event that a highly important discovery is made, i.e. the ship in excellent condition, more advanced equipment could be employed, such as a mini submarine equipped with stroboscopic lights and cameras, closed circuit television, telephone booth, submersible decompression chamber, pulleys and buoy balloons. After recovery, waterlogged timbers could be immersed in a bath of polyethylene glycol. During a treatment of over six months this compound diffuses into the wood, bulks it, and prevents its disintegration. Theoretically, the hull of the *Rosalie* could then be reconstructed using original timbers.

APRIL 25

Happiness is a full spinnaker. At noon, Dan and I were having a chat in the saloon when Rolle approached us. "Let's fly a kite!" he said excitedly. And he wasn't talking about a little one. Anxious to save fuel and make the most of the very light winds we were experiencing, it was all hands on deck to peel off the biggest condom in the world and release a 40-metre, yellow-and-white-striped beauty. Spinnakers are technically known as MPSs (Multi-Purpose Sails) but Rolle calls them MPAs (Mostly Put Away) because people are frightened of them. If left out in the wrong conditions they can pull the mast over into the water, or even bring down the rigging.

"It's a beautiful thing," cried Rolle as he turned off the engine, echoing the thoughts of us all.

"Could it get any better?" was my own rhetorical question.

"Not much," was the response all round. Pete jumped into the tender to get some shots. It's only the second time I've seen the *Takapuna*'s spinnaker up, but we're going to practise the routine until it gets easy, because on our ongoing

Below and following pages: putting out the spinnaker.

voyage across the Indian Ocean one of our passages will be 3,000 miles – further than our fuel range. We have to make use of every scrap of wind.

Earlier in the day Sean, Dev and Tek were watching a couple of fast local power boats following our wake. Another one joined them, and I wondered if this was the moment I'd dreaded – pirates checking us out, deciding whether or not to attack. We observed them carefully through the binoculars for a while. They seemed organised and intent, and I was convinced they were on some kind of reconnoitering mission – but in the end we decided they were curious tuna fishermen, whose mother ship was just beyond the horizon on our starboard side. Nevertheless, we upped our piracy watches until further notice. I only hope we don't get attacked during our final leg, because Sean has just announced he has to return to the UK when we reach Bali. Perhaps it's too tame for him on board now, without all the aggro.

Our spinnaker experience did not last long. When Scotty noticed a waterspout, an intense vortex that looks like a tornado, coming our way we scrambled to drop the 'kite'. This occurred smoothly and expertly. I'm so proud of Dan and the way this young crew has pulled together after the loss of their captain. One spirit is all we ever needed.

APRIL 26, MAKASSAR

Makassar, Gateway to Eastern Indonesia, was a disappointment, and presented us with unexpected challenges. We arrived in the harbour late last night, after dodging a long line of squid-fishing boats that were lit up so brightly, they ruined our night-vision. Besides Dan at the helm, it took the concerted efforts of Kayt, Rolle and myself looking out on the bow, Ricky and Hengke sitting on top of the pilot house, and anyone else who could stay awake long enough, to identify the harbour entry beacons and see that our way ahead was clear. We dropped anchor around 2am. Later that morning, when Rolle looked out into the surrounding water, the first thing he saw was a large, swollen, dead pig. "What kind of shit-hole have you brought us to, Pamela?" he growled, worried about the effect of pollution on our generators, the impossibility of making drinking water with our reverse osmosis system, and the risk of catching something nasty in our sea strainer. We named the area the 'Bay of Dead Pigs'.

Opposite: Canal leading to Makassar harbour.

Right and below: Makassar urchins enjoy the harbour.

The customs guys came on board first thing. They looked at our weapons closet to make sure the seals were still intact, and checked that Ricky's drugs were properly labelled and documented. More importantly, they got to see where our booze is stored. They always like to meet Johnny Walker. They wrangled three bottles and some cigarettes out of us; that's just the way things happen in Indonesia.

Billy called and reminded me that when he was growing up Makassar was 'home of the hair-oil'. Lacy white doilies called anti-Makassars were draped over the backs of couches to protect them from men's grease slicks.

"I'll bring you back some of that oil," I told my husband, "if you promise not to use it."

In Makassar harbour the *pinisi* were out in force. This southern tip of Suluwesi is home to their crew, the sea-nomadic Bugis people. Many of them waved a greeting as we set off in the tender to find Professor Lapian. As we came into a landing point beside a busy market canal, a dozen naked boys were noisily leaping into the putrid water between us and the shore.

"What's wrong with their penises?" Tessa was aghast, eyeing the strips of tape bound around their genitals.

"They've just been circumcised," replied Ricky calmly. 'Sea water is recommended as a healing agent."

"Eughh!" Between that sight and the floating porker, I wasn't feeling too well.

The serene new Hotel Sahid was an extraordinary contrast to the overcrowded canal market we'd negotiated on foot and the begging children banging on the window of our car. We found the Professor busy with his workshop.

I couldn't wait to hear what he had discovered. "Well?" I said eagerly. "What's the news?"

"I'm sorry," he sighed.

"What, no luck?"

"I've checked the archives," he said, stirring his coffee, "but unfortunately they did not go back beyond 1850."

I was gutted. We had come all this way, and I had really hoped we might have some important findings here in Makassar. In particular I was keen to see the official report of the Regent of Bima, who was said to have received the survivors of the *Rosalie*. That document might provide us with more details about the incident, the names of the survivors, and perhaps even the Regent's own views on their story.

Seeing my disappointment, the Professor kindly offered to fly to Jakarta to search the archives there. This cheered me up considerably, because as an historian who speaks near-perfect Dutch and English as well as Indonesian, he is the ideal person to research those elusive Javanese files. I know he will come up with something. But he cannot leave just yet, so I will have to wait a week or so for this large piece of the puzzle. His precious parting gift was a copy of the Bugis maritime manuscript, the *Law of the Sea* written by the chief Amanna Gappa in the 1600s. It's in Indonesian, but I'm going to get it translated as soon as I can.

We visited Fort Rotterdam, a huge compound in the shape of a turtle, rebuilt by the Dutch in 1667 from an earlier bastion. It was beautifully preserved – the best in Indonesia – but its two museums – rich with traditional crafts, dress, tools and a few maritime objects, held nothing much for our quest. Our guide was a young Buginese man with a ponytail who solemnly told us his name was Meatball, then later confessed he was a Bugis prince.

"Prince Meatball!" I hailed him.

"Yes," he said modestly, "but I don't use it."

Left: with guide Prince Meatball at Fort Rotterdam, Makassar.

Below: Professor Lapian presents a copy of the Bugis maritime manuscript *Law of the Sea*.

"It's all so ... Joseph Conrad!" At the 'Gateway to Eastern Indonesia'.

We hurried back to the *Takapuna* to cut our losses and leave for Bali a day early. Rolle in particular was itching to get out, before our sea strainers got bunged up with dead animals, human waste and plastic bags. "Those swimming boys are going to die before they get a hard-on," he snorted. Then, remembering the fun they were having he added: "But at least they'll have smiles on their faces."

Sailing out of the harbour in the late afternoon sun, I caught a last glimpse of the *pinisi* marina. Prince Meatball told me the Buginese have a saying about sea voyages: "It's better to sink than to return." I suppose we have something in common, them and me: gypsy hearts, nomadic lives, and irrepressibly beckoned by the sea.

Chapter **14** Wreckdiving
Havoc

Above: Volcanic Mount Agung, north east Bali.

Opposite: The view from the Ritz Carlton Hotel, Jimbaran Bay, Bali.

Below: Working the winches.

APRIL 28, BALI

On our approach to Bali, we sailed past the starkly silhouetted volcano of Mount Agung, at the base of which sits the holy Hindu temple of Besakih. Staring nostalgically at the mountain's summit, I thought about the first time I came to this island, around thirty years ago. At that time I found it uplifting and peaceful, with a society that seemed to have found a miraculous balance between rice farming, spirituality, and the arts. I spent my first trip living with a Balinese family in a small village. Eschewing my jeans in favour of the sarong, a kebaya and a pointed coolie hat, I attended Balinese dance and music classes, sought out temple festivals and picked up some of the language.

It was very different then. Tourism was in its infancy, and there were none of the jarring sights that now greeted us. Our entry to the noisy Benoa Harbour was an obstacle course of giant inflatable bananas, jetskis, and bouncy passenger kites that threatened to shake off their clinging, shrieking riders. Back in the seventies, people enjoyed a more traditional lifestyle, and no one had even thought about bombing a bunch of twenty-year-olds bopping merrily at a noisy nightclub. But Bali is still an exceptionally beautiful island, with a unique culture that retains its particular brand of Hinduism – despite being situated in the midst of the biggest Muslim country in the world.

The *Selat* or Strait between Bali and the island of Nusa Penida is called Selat Badung, which in Indonesian means 'naughty'. We soon knew why. This is notoriously troublesome water, and for an hour or so we were rolling quite alarmingly. Hengke told me that, in the old days, rulers of the various coastal kingdoms of Bali decreed that if any boat – including Dutch, English

or Portuguese – ran aground or got stuck on the reef, then everything belonged to the nearest kingdom. As late as 1904, when a Chinese-owned ship, the *Sri Kumala*, was wrecked off Bali's south-east coast, the locals ransacked it. The Dutch demanded 3,000 silver dollars in compensation from the Raja of Badang. His refusal was used as one excuse for the Dutch invasion of Bali. In 1906, more than 4,000 Balinese nobility marched to their deaths (a style of honourable suicide known as *puputan*) in the face of Dutch opposition.

Everyone seems tired, not only from many sleepless hours on watch, but from the mental strain of yesterday evening's 'quiz night'. After dinner we'd divided into four teams, each of which concocted ten questions to ask the others. Answers were written down and passed to the next team for correction. I was on the 'Doctors' Team' (dubbed 'Overdose') with Ricky and Hengke. Scotty, Kayt and Rolle were the 'Muppets', Dan, Tessa and Pete were the 'Wakeboarders', while Sean, Dev and Tek were the 'Shawshank Redeemers'. Questions ranged from "Where is the G-Spot?" (my own question) and "What is a Prince Albert?" (Russ's question, emailed from England), to "What is the capital of Iceland?" (Rolle), and "Where was Napoleon exiled?" (Sean's question, but he had the wrong answer, and an argument started between him and everyone who knew it was Elba). My best one was "Give three meanings for the word 'clubbing'" (answer: 1. hitting someone with a blunt instrument; 2. attending a series of nightspots and 3. drifting downstream with your anchor out). Pete asked "Who has the biggest porn collection aboard *Takapuna*?" (Answer: Sean), while other "*I should know that!*" questions were: "Who wrote '*Of Mice and Men*?" and "Where will the next World Cup be held?" Ricky put the three Australian-born crew members to shame by asking "What is the capital of New Zealand?" They all got it wrong.

Hengke is happy. He won the sweep for the arrival time (12 noon) and raked in 600,000 Rupiah. I came last, which means I have to buy the first round in the bar this evening. Our stop in Bali is an opportunity to recharge, give everyone time off, and have some planning meetings. I am due to rendezvous with Pascal, a specialist wreck-finder; Deborah, our 'fixer'; and Dewi, a local researcher. Russ and Jim will also be turning up soon, for the rest of our voyage. Then there's the matter of repairs. The starboard staysail winch is leaking oil, the main winch needs attention, and Rolle needs to strip down the gearbox. Once we're ready, we'll set off in a north-easterly direction and begin to recreate Salty Sam's final journey.

This evening we all went out to a swish beachside restaurant called Ku De Ta. I suppose the extensive gate-security checks gave patrons a certain confidence, but they were also a reminder of the incidents that made them necessary. We ate a grand dinner, all at one big table. Demanding the raising of glasses, I offered a toast: "To Takapunians all. We survived Hurricane Larry, we survived Van Dieman's Gulf; we survived the Arafura Sea. We survived the Banda Sea, the Celebes Sea, and the Makassar Straits; and we survived the naughty Straits. Here's to us!" A *Takapuna* drink was promptly invented – Scotty's citrus-coconutty-rum lethalness. If anyone fancies a sweet, swift intoxication, mix equal parts of Cointreau, Bacardi Limone and Malibu Rum with a teaspoon each of cream and pineapple juice. Shake hard. Those who tried it crashed out, on mood-lit loungers by the surf-lined sea.

APRIL 29

Today I received a discouraging missive from Robert, who's also helping with our researches in Mauritius:

> I gather from the little info you passed on that you believe the ship was lost on a reef. In this case you can expect to find zero/very little wood on the site and certainly nothing resembling a Walt Disney wreck with the tattered sails still attached to the masts waving to and fro in the current under the sea. If the locals knew of the wreck (which seems to be the case) and if the ship could not be salvaged by the owners, she would normally have been broken up quite rapidly by a combination of sea action and looting (ships were often set on fire intentionally just to recover the nails and fittings). The only exception may be if she struck a reef and then sank in deeper water nearby which could permit some wood to be preserved…
>
> If your intention is to try to find the actual wreck you should keep in mind the following. If you are ever able to positively identify the location of the wreck site from records, AND you found a wreck at the very place identified by records, it would still be extremely unlikely that you would ever have conclusive proof that the ship really was the Rosalie.
>
> You could expect to find heavy metal fittings (anchors, maybe cannons if they were too heavy for the locals to steal), broken pottery and porcelain, and other miscellaneous ships fittings from masts, spars and hull which could help in ship nationality and period. In other words, some pieces may give you info on dating, countries the ship had visited, (ballast stones) some cargo information (broken glass, etc) which may eventually give enough circumstantial evidence for you to feel comfortable about establishing her identity. You may also find two or more wrecks in almost the same position to further confuse things. (I have been diving on wrecks in tropical waters for over 30 years, so the above comments are based on experience.)
> Robert

I hate it when people use the words 'needle in a haystack' but they're being bandied about a lot. Nevertheless, I believe that, with good research behind us, if we sail into the Straits of Alas and drop anchor close to the island of Carabatoo we'll be able to pick up essential information about tides, currents, shoals and so on. This should help us figure out where the *Rosalie* most likely ran aground. In my opinion the rest – diving to find the ship – should be easy, although no one else seems to think so.

Anne emailed me to say she has discovered Salty Sam's birth date: November 9th, 1775. Nice work! Consequently we also know he was baptized on 26th November at St Leonards Shoreditch, London, that his father was also called Samuel Stephenson, and his mother's name was Jane.

Geoff, our London genealogist, has researched Salty Sam's daughter's line. Mary Thornton Stephenson married Richard Henry Jones in the City of London on 23rd April 1825 at Dunstan in the East. He was born in Whitechapel in 1801/2, and was a West India merchant in 1851, a mercantile clerk in 1861 and 1871 and the chairman of an insurance company by 1881. In 1851, four sons of Mary and Richard were living at 11 Holford Square: Edward and Henry, who became clerks at the Bank of England, Charles, who was an apprentice engineer, and Frederick. Mary died in Clerkenwell in 1865. In 1871, Richard married again, to Eliza Mercy Manwaring, born in 1840/1. They had no children, but Eliza remarried after Richard died. She and her new husband took care of Jones' children (Salty Sam's grandchildren). But when Eliza died in 1913 she left nothing in her will to the children, which means that they can no longer be traced. The fact that their name is Jones makes it all the more difficult.

My last email of the day was from Russ:

> Hi Pamela
> How is the mood on the boat? Better I am sure. Any cheese left now that the gaoler has gone?

APRIL 30

Today I met up with my old friend, film-maker Lawrence Blair. A self-described 'psychoanthropologist', he strikes me as a neo-romantic pirate himself. We sat drinking tea beside a waterlily pond at the Ritz Carlton Hotel in Jimbaran Bay, while I told him the story of Salty Sam. He listened attentively, then offered to search for clues among the books accumulated during his own research into piracy in Indonesia. The man knows what he's talking about – for, as previously described, he's faced pirates himself.

Today Lawrence told me how one of his friends, a Frenchman, was pirated in exactly the area we're headed for, just off Sumbawa. The unfortunate man wrecked his catamaran on a reef, after which he was surrounded by a bunch of sea-robbers who took everything he had.

"They gave him his passport, which was rather generous." Frowning, he added, "It's dangerous, here, for private yachtsmen. In fact, there's an elite club for people who survived both being shipwrecked AND being 'rescued' by the bugis or *bajo* people."

"What?"

"Yes," he laughed, "in other words, their boats came to grief, following which they were saved by pirates – in exchange for everything they own."

Lawrence Blair, psychoanthropologist and neo-romantic pirate.

Bali boat boy, Benoa
harbour.

Lawrence knows of at least five people who belong to that tenuously fortunate
group. I was flabbergasted: the quintessential 'good news/bad news' scenario!
"To paraphrase Harpo Marx," I said, "I wouldn't want to belong to any club that
would require that particular member qualification from me."

"You know," said Lawrence, "there is a fair chance that Salty Sam fell victim
to Bugis pirates. They, of course, are the great romantic pirates of this region –
and the possible origin of the word 'bogey-man'.

"They terrified the first Western mariners who came here. They were
supernaturalists who went berserk when attacking people, and entered a trance
state that made them invulnerable to being shot or stabbed – which is fairly
inhibiting for a start. They sailed with the right brain rather than the left,
navigating though dreams and through subtle indications from nature such as
bird droppings, wave patterns, and which particular grasses were being washed
along on the surface of the sea – special skills which made them the world's
most sophisticated navigators at the time."

"What are they like today?" I asked.

"The full-on gypsies of our time," he replied sadly. "They're not doing
so well."

Lawrence also knew plenty about those particularly fierce Kalimantan
pirates called the Ilanun.

"They had circular atoll islands with inner lagoons," he said "and the circle
was thick mangrove swamp. They had amazing boats that were thirty feet long
and could be quickly disassembled. They could be pushed right up into the
mangroves – that were pulled apart with ropes – so if they were being chased,
they could disappear inside the trees." That explained their apparent
disappearance into thin air that had baffled European pursuers.

"They were ferocious, and would go around capturing slaves with hooks.
In the museum in Sarawak they have examples of their special 'slave-grabbing'
hooks. They used to sneak up on unsuspecting fishermen, prod them into the
water, then hook them on board their vessels. The victims would never see their
homes again."

"Some pirates," Lawrence continued, "were after your head to sell it to the
Dyak people, who needed a head in order to get married. One of the big trades

in pirates along coast of Borneo was in heads – because the Dyaks were running short. Pirates would take anybody's head and flog it to the Dyaks, because there you needed a couple to bring to your father in law."

"Well, it was only decent," I laughed.

"And they didn't mind what kind of head," he said. "You could even take a funny little pink head from London."

I asked him if he'd heard much about mutiny in that period. "It seems likely," he said, "that people would have their differences, especially in the tropics, without air conditioning. But I wonder, where would the mutineers have gone? White faces roaming round in Indonesia? You would have thought that if a whole pile of them who'd killed their captain went off somewhere there'd be records."

"But there were so many rogues in those days…"

"The local people would know who you were," he argued. "Tales would still exist. And those people have long memories because they don't have many books."

Lawrence lost an eye some years ago, a tragedy of course – but it gave him a genuine excuse to wear an eye patch – and look even more piratical. I ended our conversation with a howler. "I'm so glad to be able to run this by you," I said. "I desperately need a fresh pair of eyes."

"Well, I've got one," he replied with a half-smile, "…but even that one's not so fresh!"

Earlier this morning I met Dewi, our Balinese-based researcher. She's a Texan-born American, with a sharp, investigative edge, and I was very pleased to have her help. Her command of Indonesian is impressive.

"I grew up here," she explained. "An oil brat."

Dewi, Deborah and I began to pore over the various charts they'd accumulated. "Look at that," said Dewi suddenly. She pointed to a place on the east coast of Lombok marked 'Balli' and wondered aloud if that might be the 'Bally Hill' mentioned in the *Prince of Wales Island Gazette*. Our excitement grew when we realized that, in Salty Sam's time, Balli was the biggest centre in Lombok. Moreover, it is close to Pulau Kere, or Kere Batu, one of the main contenders for the island of Carabatoo. You would pass Balli when travelling

Below left: detective work with Dewi (left) and Deborah.

Below: searching for clues in old Dutch chart of the Alas Straits.

northwards to Bima, so it is conceivable that the episode of the 'falling in' of the *prahu* and the San Antonio could have occurred just near there.

"So that means," I cried, "we have not only found Bally Hill, but we have located the island of Carabatoo!" I drew a sweeping circle with my finger around Kere Batu, Bally Hill and Bima. "That's where the whole drama took place!"

The 19th-century sailing directions for the area provided more hints. They show the Straits to be worthy of great caution, and explain why a mariner would head for the main towns:

> *The streams in Alas strait are tidal, the flood setting North. The streams overrun the time of high and low water by about 3 hours, and may have a velocity of as much as 5 knots at times. At Balli the tides are described as regular, the flood coming from the southward and setting along shore at from 1 to 2 knots per hour… Stock and fresh water can be obtained at a reasonable rate at Balli, Piju, Alas and Lombok.*

So Sam may have been making for Pijut, just south of Kere Batu, for supplies, and possibly ran aground before he arrived! I am thrilled with today's detective teamwork. At last we have a sense of where this all took place. And just in time. Russ will be arriving on Friday and we must immediately sail to the Straits of Alas. We also need to narrow down the areas where we will dive to search for the wreck of the *Rosalie*.

Dewi will travel to Lombok tomorrow, carry out some research, and report back. She says the people there are notoriously tricky. I hope they will be friendly towards us, because their oral history could provide vital clues about whether or not there are tales of a ship being wrecked off the coast, and whether any foreigners settled there.

One other lead has been Heinrik Jessen; however, I heard from London that, when contacted, he denied being related to the earlier Jessens. Hmm, I wonder about that.

Discussing the wreck search with Pascal.

MAY 1

Today I met Pascal, a Frenchman living in Jakarta, who has been involved in finding wrecks and salvaging all over the world. Pascal has had considerable success in the treasure-hunting business. His most recent discovery is a cargo of Ming porcelain in Indonesian waters. From archives he has compiled a comprehensive register of every wreck found so far in Indonesia between 1400 and 1987. I flipped through it.

There was no *Rosalie* listed in the Straits of Alas area from the correct period, but I looked to see if any ship fitted her description, in case she'd been disguised. Among other contenders I found the Alice from Mauritius, lost off Sumba Island with 820 sovereigns saved. Pascal pointed out that people sometimes invented stories about where a ship was lost, to prevent others from finding it.

Pascal also mentioned the need for official permits at certain stages. We're fine, he thinks, to dive and photograph, but as soon as we do more, such as stake out grids with ropes to conduct a systematic search, then technically we're surveying – and that requires a special permit. If we bring in heavy machinery, we're definitely salvaging – and that's a whole other story.

"The problem," he said, "is to identify the ship – because a piece of wood is just a piece of wood, you know. If she was a three-masted ship the draught would be 3-4 metres; so if she went aground she could be in less than ten metres. If it's shallow, though, the local people would have stripped her of all her portable metal and cargo."

I wanted to know more about the potential problems we might have in identifying the ship without the (frankly unlikely) discovery of a nameplate on bell or hull. Wood, said Pascal, can be analyzed. Identifying the age by carbon 14 dating, and the species, one could know if such wood was used in Mauritius at the time the *Rosalie* was built. We assume that the *Rosalie* would have had a certain amount of iron and brass fixed to the structure, such as shackles, hinges and nails. These too could be period-dated.

As I'd learned from the First Sea Lord, copper sheathing was first used by the Royal Navy in 1761. Pascal told me that it was commonplace in the British merchant fleet by in the early 1800s; and from 1832 an alloy of copper and zinc was introduced, becoming the most common type of hull protection on merchant ships until the invention of anti-fouling paint in the early 20th century. Thus, if we found some copper on a ship that might be the *Rosalie*, one form of identification would be to analyze this, to see if its composition fitted the exact period.

We discussed the possibility of hiring a metal detector or possibly a magnetometer or some side scan sonars. The latter would be extremely expensive. In any case, Pascal pointed out that, being volcanic, the area had magnetic anomalies that might distort the readings.

"Then, how would you recommend going about this?" I asked.

He thought for a moment. "Go there and do a pre-survey. Talk with the local people if you like, but be careful. In some areas the police pay the fishermen to tell them when a foreigner is looking for a wreck. There was recently a big problem when some people didn't have the right permits and a German guy landed in jail."

Fortunately we have film permits, and we have the protection of the Ministry of Culture and Tourism and the Ministry of Foreign Affairs. And Pascal says he has connections with the Ministry of Maritime Affairs, which is vital.

"If you want to use electronic equipment, that is a sensitive issue," he warned.

"You'll need someone official on board to check what you're doing. But for you, why not take an easier first step. You're 'just looking around,' just 'doing a dive', you know. It's often the best way to find something anyway."

MAY 2

Dewi returned from her trip to Lombok. She'd looked round the city of Mataram, then travelled to the east coast. The Tourism people say that Pijut is still there, but it's now called Pijot. As we thought, it was the main trading port of Salty Sam's time. Dewi was still perplexed by the location of the island we'd identified as Carabatoo, i.e. Kere Batu. When asked, the local people would say, "Oh it's over there!" – but they could not show her on the map. The reason was, she discovered, that the small islands had undergone many name changes over the years. Our 'Carabatoo' in the past was named Pulau ('island') Kere Batu, but now it's called Gili Kere ('gili' means 'island' in the local Sasak language).

"I spoke to a man who is over a hundred years old," said Dewi. "Older than Santa Claus. He looks like a wrinkled walnut. No teeth, but his mind is very keen." She says the man, Amar Krimar, is a *dalang* or traditional story teller and shadow puppeteer. "To do what he does," she said, "you have to have a rich oral history in your head." He had remembered a story of a ship that sailed from the east, ran aground on Kere Batu and sank.

"When?" I asked excitedly.

"Nebulous time," replied Dewi "because he doesn't even remember how old he is. But he says it's still there – he was a fisherman – and there may have been more of the ship there before. He said what's left of it appears to be a metal hull."

My hopes sank. Back to the copper-sheathing issue. "What kind of metal?"

Dewi didn't know. But she had more news.

"This old man also said there was an anchor and ship lying in ten metres of water around there. Apparently you can see it from a fishing boat although, as tides shift, the visibility becomes poor."

I was elated by this information. I've been afraid that we'll find a wreck

Bugis stilt-houses in fishing village on Lombok shore.

that's lying too deep to access without submarine equipment.

"Everyone knows it's there," said Dewi, "and they still fish on top of it, but not on Wednesday or Thursday nights, because it's haunted. They hear voices."

"I can't wait to get there," I said, "and especially to meet the man who's older than Santa Claus."

"He did say," cautioned Dewi, "'If God is willing, I will still be alive to meet them.'"

"Not a moment to lose!" I'd always wanted to say that.

Thanks to Dewi we have many new leads. She also canvassed local opinion concerning what may have happened to Salty Sam.

"They all say, 'Oh, it was pirates' because that was an everyday occurrence. Of course, they don't want to take any blame either."

But the port of Pijot today is full of little *prahus*. "They said Bugis *prahus* don't come down here, and if they do they're pirates." Bugis people settled in the area and now live side by side with Sasak people. "You can tell who's who," Dewi said, "from the types of houses. The Sasak houses are on the ground, and the Bugis dwellings are all on stilts."

I was curious to find out more about the Raja who was either friend or foe to Salty Sam after he ran aground off Lombok, so Dewi educated me about the politics of the island in Sam's time. The Balinese entered Lombok from the Karangasem kingdom, ruling the island from 1724 to 1894. During this time the House of Karangasem ruling the island of Lombok there split into two rival factions, one based in Cakranegara, the other in nearby Mataram, whose Raja gained the upper hand by 1838.

This means that the Raja of Mataram was likely the 'ruler' in 1821. However, the 'Raja' mentioned in the Prince of Wales Island Gazette was more likely a local chieftain rather than the overseeing Raja, far away in Mataram on West Lombok. It is even more likely that the one actually in control of East Lombok or at least the coastal areas, was the Raja of Sumbawa Besar, whose great-great-grandson is now the Vice Governor of West Nusa Tenggara.

I received an invitation tonight to, of all things, a film premiere. It turned out to be a thoughtful offering about the plight of Sumatran elephants, who are being displaced and killed now that their jungle habitats are disappearing at a ferocious rate. After all my time on the high seas, it was truly a shock to see a red carpet.

MAY 3

Today is the start of an important, three-day Balinese festival called Galungan-Kuningan. Pete, Ricky, Tessa and I drove north to find some temple ceremonies, and were delighted to see so many people in their traditional dress carrying towers of temple offerings on their head. It was charming, if slightly alarming, to see a beautifully dressed family of five on one motorbike setting off to pray. We briefly attended one ceremony at Batubulan, then pushed on to Ubud.

"I used to live near here," I said, "in the middle of the rice fields."

"Rice fields?" laughed our diver. "There are no rice fields here now." It seems they've become a novelty hereabouts. Pity. I became very boring for the next four hours, telling everyone in the car 'how it was before'. I hate being a tourist here. Bali is too special to me. I am mourning the old days – no, I am mourning my youth.

Right: View of crater lake and volcano Gunung Batur, from Penelokan, northeast Bali.

Opposite: Balinese dancers and temple festival scenes.

MAY 4

Gill, a British friend of mine who lives in Bali, took me for an early-morning horse ride along Legian Beach. A far more experienced rider than I, she cantered on while I hung behind with one of the men from the stables whose task it was to be my nursemaid. Legian is a gorgeous, long, wide beach lined with rather nice hotels. In Bali, after one concrete monstrosity was built many years ago, a rule came into force that hotels cannot be built any higher than the palm trees, so what could have ended up as another Waikiki Beach has been avoided, thank goodness. I rode along happily for a while, past a few topless sunbathers and the odd body-surfer. I had thought my horse was quite an agreeable little mare, but I soon changed my mind. In shallow surf, right in the middle of the biggest clump of holiday-makers on the entire beach she decided to stop and have a torrential wee. Gallons and gallons of the stuff. The scattering holiday-makers looked at me in loathing – but what was I going to do? "Good morning," I said, politely, as if I hadn't noticed.

That's not the only antisocial act my beast committed. Right at the end of the ride she decided to give me a rodeo experience, during which I was thrown unceremoniously onto the beach. Fortunately I landed on soft sand.

"I know I should get back on," I said, dusting myself down, "but she's given me enough excitement for one day." My Los Angelean colleagues in the world of psychotherapy tell me that 'Equine Therapy' has become all the rage over there. I emailed back to say I'd just had a profound session on fear, rejection and humiliation. And it didn't cost 500 bucks an hour.

Dear Pamsy,

I have arrived in New York safe and well. Everything seems to be going along quite jollily until now. I just want to get the promotional work behind me now and get on with the task of playing America properly. I did the funniest radio show today with a studio full of rock 'n roll disc jockeys, we had a blast, doing phone-ins is such a good experience here, the people communicate so effortlessly, it makes it so easy. That's one of the things I like about life here, the desire to make your life easier.

I hope all is well with you wherever you are. Slice the mainbrace! Keep your eye on the yardarm or ye'll be keelhauled! You wouldn't like that, trust me.

Bill Bill xxxxx

MAY 5

Stepped rice fields, central Bali.

I went to visit Lawrence at his beach house, which looks like a film set of an eccentric explorer's pad. Wait – he IS an eccentric explorer. A puffer fish sat above his fridge beside the beak of a giant swordfish, while a glass-framed stick insect hung on one wall beside a batik-covered couch. He showed me a book, *The Pirate Wind* by Owen Rutter, containing some terrible tales of the sea robbers around this archipelago.

One gruesome tale concerned a barque called the *Regina*, owned by master mariner Captain James Ross. A rumour circulated that she was carrying great wealth in silver dollars, so a pirate fleet lay in wait for her and attacked. The captain was taken prisoner, and the pirates started plundering the ship. They were unable, however, to find the silver. The pirate chief promised to spare Ross's life if he told them where it was. He protested, truthfully enough, that there was no more than they'd already taken. The pirates refused to believe him. To try to make him talk they lashed Captain Ross's son to one of the ship's anchors and, when the captain still protested that there was no treasure, flung the anchor into the sea, drowning the boy before his father's eyes. They then began torturing Ross himself. They cut off his fingers joint by joint and mutilated him in several other ways, leaving him bleeding on his deck. After killing the officers and taking native crew as slaves, they set fire to the *Regina* and sailed away. Nice. I haven't allowed myself to think too much about the exact details of my great-great-grandfather's death, but however it happened, I bet it was nasty.

Another question: why would they have killed the woman aboard the *Rosalie*? I suppose if they did, that lends credibility to the mutiny story. As I've heard, most pirates would keep her, either for ransom (especially if she was Caucasian) or slavery. Dewi mentioned that in those days there were a number of half-Caucasian women in Surabaya and Jakarta. They were not accepted by full-blood locals, and regarded marriage to a European as a way out. A woman with a perceived claim to Sam's fortune, who was also a witness, might well have been done away with by mutineers. But in the case of piracy she'd be currency.

We have not yet decided whether to set sail tomorrow, or wait for Sunday partly because the tides for exiting Benoa Harbour can be very tricky. Russ and I would like to sail immediately to Surabaya, but we hear discouraging stories about piracy, and disparaging accounts of the harbour. We got a message from our former captain, who kindly warned us that we risked being boarded by thieves posing as maritime officials in fake uniforms. The modern face of piracy. My crew, especially Rolle, is dead against our going.

Then Tessa told us about a friend of hers who sailed to Surabaya on a large catamaran for repairs in a shipyard. He was barely inside the harbour when he was set upon by hordes of people in boats who boarded without permission before he could stop them. Two uniformed customs officers then turned up and instructed him to sail to a 'safer place' just up an inlet. But the water turned out to be too shallow, even for the catamaran. It ran aground as night was falling. The officials took off, saying they'd finished work at five. So the man was left to face the menace of robbers who turned up soon after and who spent the next six hours on board, stripping the boat of everything he owned. I think we'll give Surabaya a miss.

What we'll do instead is pick up the Salty Sam trail just north of Bali and travel east, following his wake towards Ambon. Just as he did, we'll dip into the Straits of Alas and head for the island of Carabatoo.

Russ arrived this evening and came straight to meet me, Dewi and Deborah at the Ku De Ta beachside restaurant. The four of us had a wonderfully furious and passionate argument about the problem at hand – murder or mutiny? Loved it.

"It's good to be back on board," said Russ much later this evening. "Ah, that empty seat!" He eyed the former captain's chair.

"In your cabin," I smiled, "you'll find a large plate of cheese. Don't eat it all at once."

MAY 6

Given all the piracy accounts in the area, evidence for a mutiny aboard the *Rosalie* now seems thin. Except, of course, it was the story I grew up with. Where did the lawyers who documented the fight over Salty Sam's estate receive that account of a mutiny? It reads as though they talked to a witness, the one who was 'confined below' and heard 'a scuffle and a splash as though someone had been thrown overboard'. But who was that person? Also, were the lawyers aware of the newspaper accounts I found? If so, why didn't they quote them? After all, much of the arguing was over whether or not there was proof of Salty Sam's death, and the *Prince of Wales Island Gazette* clearly states that the gunner and six Lascars saw the bodies of the Captain, his 'wife' and the officers floating past. You'd think the lawyers would have tracked down those seven men and got them to testify that Salty Sam was dead. Maybe Dewi is right: she has a hunch that the people on the cutter may have been the perpetrators.

Fortunately, Anne is continuing to dig on my behalf, and she doesn't mind casting aspersions on my long-dead relatives:

Dear Professor Lapian,
Pamela Stephenson has given me your e mail address as an expert on piracy and the spice trade. I queried whether you had come across many instances of mutiny in merchant vessels in your researches I presume that the Rosalie probably had a mainly Lascar crew with serang and tindals with possibly three or four European officers, gunner etc. I have not come across mutiny among Lascars to date, who seem

Balinese wood carving, Ubud.

Indonesian navy soldiers patrol the Malacca Straits in an effort to combat piracy after Indonesia scored the highest number of pirate attacks in an International Maritime Bureau survey.

peaceful sort of people fishing from the deck and living on a little rice and fish etc. On the other hand Stephenson had a law case which he lost against his chief officer in his former ship and seems to have put two ships on the rocks – Mauritius and Alas Straits. He may have been a difficult man. We found that before his last fatal voyage he spent almost six months lying off Sourabaya which may have led to frustration. Were the 50 cases of gin he loaded too great a temptation to disaffected officers? All the same mutiny was such a heinous crime and where could they hide? It would help to know if there are any instances in small ships around this period. It has not yet been established where the story of mutiny originated. It appears for the first time in the case put by lawyers for Council's opinion on the question of the release of Stephenson's funds from Java. The newspaper report from Prince of Wales Island Gazette is specific on it being a ship aground, the major part of the crew 'rescued' by Malay pirates to be taken to the Rajah of Bima, but murdered instead.

Russ, the crew and I had a meeting to decide our onward route, and to try and figure out why Salty Sam ended up sailing so far down the Straits of Alas, considering the fact that he was headed further north to Ambon. Our former captain once told me that, given the prevailing winds and time of year, he might have been tacking through the Straits of Alas in order to pick up winds south of Sumbawa that would pitch him back up northwards. Perhaps that was an established sailing route. Alternatively, he might have entered the Straits of Alas from the southern end, but most people I've consulted think this is unlikely.

Russ arrived with a book about the salvaging of a ship called the *Diana*, that was similar to the *Rosalie*. The *Diana* was a country traders' ship of around the same period and size. She carried three anchors – it never occurred to me that we could be looking for more than one. The author has given us a formula for estimating the weight of the *Rosalie's* anchors: one hundredweight per 20 tons of the ship's overall weight. That means each anchor should have been about fifteen hundredweight. Nice to know, but if I find an anchor, how on earth am I going to haul it up and get it on the scales?

Then there were the guns, without which no one in his right mind would cruise these waters. The *Diana* had eight cannon on each side, with thirty rounds of shot stored close to. Carronades were popular – they were relatively light, portable cannon. It would be nice if we could find the *Rosalie*'s armaments, but they might have been taken off by local people after she ran aground – or placed on the cutter, or even put aboard the *prahu* for transport to Bima.

It took 800 days to find the *Diana*. She was discovered lying at thirty metres by a team that had all the works: divers, sidescan sonars and so on. Her cargo was intact, but to get at it the team had to shift 200 tons of sand. Oh, God. I've noticed Russ is gloomy about that, too. Not only that, but I've just heard that the area we're headed for is known for dynamite fishing, and that local people use bottles of cyanide to flush out drowsy grouper from their hidey-holes so they can be scooped up for the live-fish market. With these illegal, environmentally disastrous activities going on, it sounds a dodgy place to go diving.

Chapter 15 The Island of
Carabatoo

MAY 7, LOMBOK STRAITS

We've finally left for the island of Lombok. We shall sail north of Bali and take up Salty Sam's eastward trail. In 1812, Major William Thorn found a very different population there than that of today: "The inhabitants of Lombok are chiefly emigrants from Bally (Bali) and Sumbawa. They retain many Hindoo customs, particularly those of burning their dead; and the widow also, as in India, immolates herself on the funeral pile of her husband." Today, native Lombok people are Sasaks who follow the Islamic faith.

It's not only human culture that is divided by the strait between Bali and Lombok. Sailing here, we are tracing the Wallace Line, delineated by Alfred Russell Wallace who explored the area in the mid 1800s. He found marked changes in terrestrial wildlife on either side of a divide he described as lying between Kalimantan and Sulawesi in the northern part of the archipelago, and between Bali and Lombok in the south. Almost pipping Darwin's 'survival of the fittest' to the post, his findings have been debated by modern biogeographers; but most agree on 'Wallacea' as a transition zone between Asian and Australian animal life.

After we pass the north coast of Lombok we'll sail south down the Straits of Alas, and head for the island of Carabatoo, now known as Kere. We're sailing extra carefully. I suspect Russ would love history to repeat itself, because that would make good television – but I have no intention of allowing the *Takapuna* to run aground.

Pascal and Dewi will join us in Lombok. We'll dive in the waters all around Kere to try to find the wreck of the *Rosalie*, and search on land for other clues.

In the true wake of Salty Sam – entering the Straits of Alas, with Batukarang in the distance.

MAY 8

At dawn, we reached the northern coast of Lombok. Now we are truly following the same course as Salty Sam, after he left Surabaya bound for Ambon in 1821. To starboard, three lofty volcanoes were sunlit by golden rays. From 6am I sat on the bow in a state of hyper-vigilance. Ahead were two narrow, flat islands: Gili Awang and Gili Sulat, while to port we could faintly discern the mauve silhouette of Sumbawa. Soon we'll be entering the Straits of Alas – the supposed scene of Salty Sam's demise.

Top: "Any shipwrecks round here?" Questioning Bos, the island-minder on Batukarang.

Below: Snorkelling on the anchor off Batukarang, Straits of Alas.

Between Awang and Sulat and the mainland of Lombok there is a narrow area of sea dotted with fishing boats. Three shipwrecks were marked here on the Max Sea chart. I wondered if Salty Sam might have entered this channel – either trying to escape bad weather, or being sucked in by a running tide or current. Once inside the strait, might he have gotten into difficulty? He certainly could not have tacked there, without the risk of running aground.

As Commander Rod Craig had told me in his London office on board HQS *Wellington*, many pirate attacks, then as now, are carried out near a point where approaching victims can be observed from the shore. Gazing at the north-east corner of Lombok, it occurred to me that this would be a perfect spot, considering the narrowness of the channel and the flatness of the island.

On the other hand, in this particular place I have a strange feeling, as if something was not right on board the *Rosalie* herself. Perhaps an argument? A problem with the ship? I need to use all my powers today, not just observation. I am sceptical about many so-called paranormal people, but I do find that when I manage to elude the anxiety and bustle of modern living, and listen to myself, I know things. Maybe it will all come to me today.

As we began to travel southwards down the Straits of Alas, I had an overwhelming urge to sail closer to Batukarang, a cluster of four small islands on the Lombok side. I remembered that if you invert the name 'Batukarang' (which means rocky coral) you get 'Karang Batu' – which sounds awfully like 'Carabatoo'. I asked Dan to change course, and as we got closer I could see that the islands were connected by coral reefs. I was so eager to see them close to, I couldn't wait for the tender to be launched, so when four fishermen came by in a small outrigger *prahu*, I asked them to ferry me to shore. They agreed, and I set off with my little gang of curious fishermen.

"Bye," grinned Russ. "*The Takapuna*'s mine now."

We landed on the nearest beach and walked a short way to a charming bamboo house, inhabited by Bos, whose job it is to mind the island for its owners. "Do you know about any shipwrecks around here?" I asked, "From a long time ago?"

"There's a big anchor out there," he said, pointing to where I'd just come from, "and there's a shipwreck close to the pearl farm. But people came here, in 1990, and took all the metal away."

"What kind of ship was it?" I asked. "What was left?"

"Metal," he repeated, tracing the shape of a hull with his hands. Rats. It may have been a modern ship, unless the *Rosalie* was copper-sheathed.

"Will you show me the anchor?" I asked. By now our tender was arriving. I donned snorkeling gear, and, not even bothering to change out of my jeans, ran after him into the water.

Sure enough, about 200 metres from the shore a large anchor was embedded in the sea floor, encrusted with coral. It measured around two and a half metres high and nearly two metres broad, with the flukes discernable despite their living decorations. It was really quite beautiful. Given the estimated size of the *Rosalie's* – probably three – anchors, this might fit the dimensions of one of her smaller ones. But the shank looked more modern, having a round knob on the top rather than a circle for a chain. We photographed it, then went to another island to inquire about the location of the ship itself.

"Do you know about a sunken ship near here?" we asked a growing crowd. They conferred for several minutes.

"There's one right near the pearl farm."

We set off eagerly to scout for it, throwing ourselves into the water beside a hut on stilts. A couple of surprised fishermen observed us from their platform. "Please explain we're not here to steal pearls!" I asked Hengke.

Visibility was poor, and without scuba gear we could see nothing. There were five of us in the water: Russ, Tessa, Scotty, Pete and I. We tried splitting up into teams to search more methodically, but that didn't work. I wished Pascal was with us.

"Ask them," I said to Hengke, pointing at the fishermen. "Do they know anything?" Hengke consulted with them, in what seemed like an interminably long conversation. Finally, he told us, "They say there's definitely a ship down there."

"Really?" I said. "But where exactly? Can they show us?"

"Oh they can show you all right. One of them has been trying to salvage the engine."

We returned to the *Takapuna* and continued down the Straits of Alas. Standing with me on the bow, Rolle said he'd heard that, because of the tides and bad currents here, ferries are occasionally turned over while crossing between Lombok and Sumbawa. That would fit with the old sailing directions that warned of strong currents. If even a vessel with an engine cannot withstand the ebb and flow, the threat to a wind-powered ship must be enormous.

This evening I found an email from Pascal:

I would suggest the following phases for your project and options for my collaboration to your venture:
Pre-survey: to try to identify the location of the wreckage. No need of sophisticated and expensive electronic tools, a fish finder would do. Maximum 5 divers to deploy around the supposed location. We need the basic diving equipment. A trustworthy Balinese should try to talk with the local fishermen etc… Few days search. Just be careful, my Indonesian friends from Bali warned me about the people from Lombok. They cannot be trusted at all! (It could have been the same for Salty Sam…)

At 4pm I glanced at the chart; we were further south than I thought and had missed Bally Hill. Pijot was off to starboard, but we were so far from the coast I could see very little. I felt frustrated, but the light would be gone in a couple of hours so we couldn't go back. The best course, I decided, was to continue south

Opposite: The fishing canoe that transported us from the *Takapuna* to Batukarang.

Pearl farm hut, near the location of the modern shipwreck, Straits of Alas.

to Kere Batu, as the place we'd decided must have been Carabatoo, anchor for the night, and start afresh tomorrow.

Dewi emailed to say she had met with the Vice Governor of West Nusa Tenggara, who is the great-great-grandson of the Raja of Sumbawa Besar. Her contact in Lombok, who is also a member of the royal family, told her that in 1821, the governance of this area was most likely under that same Raja. The Sultan of Bima of that time and the Raja of Sumbawa Besar were relatives. Their families originally came from Makassar and Bone in Sulawesi – where Bugis people come from!

I also received a definitive expert opinion from maritime experts at Hartlepool's museum, HMS *Trincomalee*, concerning what we should look for under the sea. The anchor is likely to be six feet long, with a wide chain. A metal capstan may still be attached, with wooden bars. The shape of the anchor would be typical, and there should have been at least two of them aboard. In addition, metal containers weren't used at that point, so all goods would have been stored in wooden barrels. I found a photograph by Australian expert Len Zell of copper sheathing at the wreck site of HMS *Pandora*, so at least I know what that might look like if I come across it.

Anne struck gold again today. She has traced the *San Antonio* – the brig that witnessed the events in the Straits of Alas, or at least heard the survivors' tale. This was a Portuguese ship that, on August 1821, delivered 10 chests of opium at Macao. Anne has also been researching the number of crew the *Rosalie* might have had. As a comparison, she found that the *Lord Castle*, tendered to the Bombay government in 1820 as a transport ship with the same tonnage, had only one officer, and a crew of 35 Lascars, 1 gunner and 4 seacunnies (steersmen). She was copper sheathed.

So far, in scouring the *Asiatic Journals* Anne has found no further mention of the *Rosalie*. She has, however, found more examples of piracy. On September 11, 1818 an American schooner off Japora was attacked by pirates. The crew escaped except one European. "The pirates took 20,000 dollars from the ship and supposedly murdered the European." In 1820 the brig Johnny was lost on the west coast of Sumatra. Her "crew and cargo were saved through the humane assistance of Rajah Analaboo. At last – a good Raja!"

A Mr Thornton was captured in the Java seas with the entire crew of Gen de Koek. The pirates burned the ship and demanded ransoms – a few chests of opium and 10,000 dollars. Thornton was eventually picked up by a coastal vessel, having been found clinging to a fish stake. Those ubiquitous fish traps have been hindering our progress lately, but if we get attacked, I hope there's one nearby.

MAY 9, KERE BATU, LABUHAN LUAR

The island of Carabatoo is a delightful place – far too nice for a murder.

Before going there, at 8am we set off in the tender for the nearest mainland town. We made this our first stop because Hengke said it was an important courtesy to call on the local chief. I drove the tender up to the stone landing of a fascinating village. Gaily painted fishing *prahus* were lined up beside a market thronged with people. The inhabitants were curious about us, but not unfriendly. Decorative horse-drawn buggies ferried people along the street, hawkers waved us over to inspect their vegetables and fruit, while teenagers banged on makeshift metal drums balanced on a cart already loaded down with gigantic loudspeakers.

Lined up in rows in an open pavilion was a horribly grim spectacle. Nearly two hundred dead and rotting sharks lay there, arranged in species on the

concrete floor. There were many types, including (not my favourite) several tiger sharks. The stench was unbearable.

"What do they do with them? asked Russ.

"Probably cut their fins off to sell them to the Chinese," I said, "and they're lucky they didn't get their fins cut off while they were still swimming – which is what some Thai fishermen do." Of course this sight begged a question none of us wanted to answer about the marine environment we were about to dive in.

We went in search of the local chief. He was an unexpectedly young man, in jeans and black top. He did not want to talk to me, focusing only on the men, but aside from that annoyance I had a bad feeling about the meeting.

"May we go onto the island?" I asked.

"It's fine with me, but I need to check with my superiors," he replied in Indonesian, fast-dialling on his cell phone.

I didn't like the sound of that. I knew that technically we did not need his permission. Our Indonesian cruising permit was enough, and we had only asked him as a formality. Yet he was far from welcoming, and I sensed that we'd made a big mistake. I kept thinking about a yacht that recently got impounded in Jakarta for salvaging, and the crew thrown in jail. I heard they had all the permits in the world, but someone just didn't like them.

I wondered afterwards if that chief might have been a descendant of the Raja who offered hospitality to my great-great-grandfather – and possibly ordered his death. Perhaps Salty Sam was at my shoulder during that meeting, warning me to be careful.

This afternoon we landed on Kere Batu, or Carabatoo, for the very first time. It's tiny, and a perfect shape for an uninhabited tropical island. Its bay, with a yellow-sand beach and turquoise water, is flanked by a rocky promontory on one side and an enticing low-tide cave on the other. In fact, there were several caves in the island's exposed reef. Had Salty Sam hidden anything here, to keep it safe until he could return with another ship? We peered inside some of the caves but they seemed fairly shallow and devoid of hiding places.

We climbed above the beach to a flat, grassy table – a cover for flying insects that scattered as we approached. A fisherman's hut stood on the lee side of the island. Inside was a tiny cooking mound, and a frying pan that stank of old breakfast. Someone had evidently spent some time here, because nearby they had planted a bed of sweet potatoes.

We hurried back to the beach and began to snorkel. The water all around was shallow, and as the tide retreated, a long sand bar became visible. It would be easy to run aground here, especially at night. I was anxious to search the reef in earnest, but it seemed sensible to wait for our professional wreck finders. We returned to the boat in the mid afternoon, just in time to avoid being stranded by an extremely low tide. The *Takapuna* had been surrounded by ten to fifteen fishing boats, and Dev and Tek were fully occupied trying to keep local

Opposite: More scenes from Labuhan Luar.

Below: Salty Sam's hidden treasure? Checking shoreline caves on the 'Island of Carabatoo'.

181

Right: An accessible, shallow water beach on Kere Batu (the 'Island of Carabatoo'), probably where Salty Sam first landed.

Opposite: Treacherous reefs and shallow shoals surround the 'Island of Carabatoo'.

people from either boarding or bumping into our hull. Our trusty security officers have resorted to deploying 'persuaders', bamboo poles used to fend off an approaching craft. I don't like the feel of it.

Dewi, Pascal and another French diver called Fred arrived this evening. I'm relieved they're here, but we have no more room on board and local accommodation is undesirable. So Russ has given up his cabin to Dewi because she is a girl (he'll share with Pete), and Pascal and Fred will have to sleep on deck. *Dommage!*

At 10pm today we faced a piracy attempt. A small, motor-powered vessel with around eight menacing men cruised by our stern. A man in uniform asked to board, saying he wished to check our papers. Fortunately, Fred fiercely stood his ground and, flanked by Dev and Tek, managed to prevent them. "It's late," he said in good Indonesian, "and official business should be conducted in daylight hours. Besides, our papers have already been seen by the harbour master."

This was a piracy attempt of the contemporary variety. If we had not shown that we had a significant security presence it could have gone horribly wrong. We've heard plenty of stories about people in fake uniforms boarding boats and robbing them. Or even people in real uniforms, since I've been warned several times about officials moonlighting as pirates. I'm completely wigged, and can't wait to and get out of here.

> Dear Pamsy,
> I opened tonight in New York and it went down really well. All of my chums showed up. We had a good old gas after the show, it was really nice. Scarlett enjoyed it.
> Love Love Love,
> Ahab

MAY 10

As soon as it was light, Pascal, Fred, Ricky, Tessa, Pete and I prepared to return to Kere Batu. Even at this early hour the *Takapuna* was surrounded by fishing boats. It's weird how people just sit and stare at us. I always greet them warmly, but Kayt

Right: Fishing boats, somewhat ominously 'in attendance' in the Straits of Alas.

Opposite: The snorkelling group begins a preliminary search of the waters surrounding Kere Batu.

reported that she had woken in fright with the sight of a stranger's face at her porthole. As we began to pull away in the tender one of the men began to shout angrily at us.

"What's he saying?" I asked Dewi.

"Oh, something about Indonesian freedom."

"Freedom from whom? People like us?"

And here we were, lots of us pulling away from the boat, and leaving it far less protected. I summoned a few more crew to man the deck, then reluctantly left for Kere.

There we began searching the waters of the surrounding reef for any sign of the *Rosalie*. They were shallow, and the coral was trashed. It looked like someone had been dynamiting here, which is not good for our quest. Except for a few orange starfish, below the surface there was little visible life.

Pascal instructed us to form a line stretching away from the island, so we could comb the water systematically. He was frankly sceptical that we'd find anything. He prefers to search where local information has identified that there is definitely a wreck. But it seemed important to at least rule out the possibility that some piece of the *Rosalie* was lying here. It now seems far more likely that she slipped into deeper waters, and possibly drifted further away in the racing tides. This is actually good news, because it increases the likelihood that there'll be something left unsalvaged by the locals and, hopefully, preserved by sand. Now, on Pascal's recommendation, we are trying to locate a metal detector. Unfortunately, every supplier in our part of the world is closed at the moment, and sending one from the UK would take too long.

Late morning, when we returned to the boat, two Tourism Department officials, Ainul and his translator Yayak, came on board. They were accompanied by five other local officials, including the harbour master and the Chief of Police. They had heard from Dewi about the intrusion last night, for which we received an apology but no real explanation.

Sitting round the pilot-house table with these uniformed men I felt afraid – yet I knew I had to rely on them for information and protection, and to expedite our approvals and clearances. After a difficult internal debate, I decided they had to know what was in my heart. So, with Yayak translating, I took a gamble and told the whole

story of Salty Sam. I took my time, for I knew that most people love a good story in cultures where oral history is valued. As I revealed each twist and turn I could see that they were more and more engaged. At the end, most of the men I had feared were looking at me with great kindness. "We are ready to help you," said one.

At that I burst into tears. His words were so unexpected. They left soon after, each with a warm shake of the hand, and instructed me to follow them ashore within the hour. They also mentioned that there was another shipwreck nearby, with a large anchor, that might be the *Rosalie*.

When we arrived at the port, we found smart, air-conditioned vehicles waiting for us. Ready to lead us on some kind of tour was the Head of the District – an official whose position is similar to that of mayor. They drove us to a town a couple of miles inland, explaining that we were now where the old Pijot was situated. The town by the harbour we thought was Pijot was actually Labuhan Luar (*labuhan* means 'harbour'). "The beach was once right here," explained one.

Then we were led into a piece of jungle, humming with mosquitoes. "Where are they taking us?" I asked our guide, a little nervously.

"To see a well," replied Yayak.

It turned out to be a sacred artesian bore that lay on the site of the old Raja's palace. Not just any old Raja, though – but the Raja who met my great-great-grandfather! Nothing else was left of the building, but I was excited. Salty Sam was here! He was entertained by this local ruler, who promised to lend him a *prahu*. Whether his host was friend or foe, my great-great-grandfather came to this very spot.

We were introduced to two men and some youths who were said to be descendants of the Raja, but they were not at all forthcoming about their ancestor. Even though I'd played down the possible treachery of the Raja in my telling of the story this morning, I wondered if someone had tipped them off about this. It was weird to be standing there with them, all of us progeny of men who'd met briefly so many generations ago.

"Would you like to see the grave over there?" asked Ainul. "No one knows whose it is, except that it belongs to a foreigner."

It was said to be the only foreign grave anywhere near here, and dated back centuries. We walked over to an ill-kept pile of stones with a couple of carved urns at the head. The men worked briefly to clear the encroaching vegetation, while I pondered several scenarios.

"According to your customs," I said, "what would happen if you found bodies floating out there in the sea?"

"We'd fish them out," was the reply, "and bury them before the sun went down, in accordance with Muslim custom." Their answer made me wonder if perhaps this was Salty Sam's resting place. Well, it's not out of the question.

I stared at the grave. Could this village really be where Sam ended up, whether dead or alive?

Opposite above: Negotiating with Indonesian officials, Straits of Alas.

Opposite below: In Pijut jungle with some living descendants of the Raja who offered Salty Sam 'seeming hospitality' and transport to the port of Bima.

Salty Sam's grave? Over 100 years ago, an unknown foreigner was buried here.

Above: Older than Santa Claus – the 100-year-old man, Lombok.

Opposite: Noisy neighbours disrupt our session with Bugis paranormal, Labuhan Luar, Lombok.

We heard that another foreigner had settled here centuries ago and married a local woman of Chinese descent. This man was wealthy and helped to build a mosque and many other aspects of the village. I wonder if he was either Sam or a crew member from the Rosalie.

Back where our cars were waiting, a crowd had gathered. We are definitely the main attraction hereabouts. One of the onlookers turned out to be yet another descendant of the Raja. He was Kahmaruddin, born in 1928, and he told us of a foreigner who married in the village and likewise had many descendants. While some are scattered across Lombok, others still remain here in the village.

I finally got to meet the man who is older than Santa Claus. Having obligingly stayed alive for our visit, understandably he did not think anything else should be required of him during our meeting, so whatever history he held within his walnut-seeming head will doubtless die with him. Rather, he was intent on crushing his betel nut with a knife and chewing it voraciously, until his mouth and gums were stained scarlet. I had to look away at the moment when he conveyed a large dollop of unsightly, dripping red pulp into his puckered mouth. That sure must be good dope.

Our last appointment was in the living room of a house on stilts – a Bugis residence – at the backside of the port. We climbed up a ladder, and removed our shoes. Children played noisily below, and again, our presence caused a stir. We were met by a thick-set man with oddly-focused eyes. Perhaps astigmatism? Or was he stoned? He invited us to sit on his ornate new vinyl-and-wood couch. He was a 'paranormal', as they are called here, named Puang Abashim.

In preparation for meeting with us he had fasted and meditated all night to commune, not with a spirit or soul, but directly with the sea. That was his specialty, he explained. He cannot be helpful when it comes to events on land, because he is exclusively a maritime soothsayer.

I asked Puang Abashim what had happened to Salty Sam. He replied that he had received a message at three this morning to say that the Rosalie had turned into the Alas Strait, although she had not been destined here. He said she had sustained damage, and was taking on water, so she headed to Pijot for repairs. There, she ran aground on the east side of the island. All the crew survived, and a local leader called Keke (grandfather) Samin helped the crew and sheltered them on Pulau Meringke (then known as Batu Kera) for three nights. He gave them a 7-metre sampan, but it was not large enough to make it to Bima. Beyond that, he had no further details. Blimey. It all made so much sense.

We raced over to Pulau Maringki, a larger island next to Kere Batu, in the hope of finding someone to corroborate this story of the crew sheltering here for three nights, under the protection of Keke Sámin. We found a pretty fishing port, with gaily painted boats lined up parallel to each other along a broad stretch of beach, but no one we met could recall such a story from oral history. We continue to be baffled by what the local people reported of the various island name-changes. We have now been told that Pulau Meringke has previously been known as Kali Abu and Batu Kera. More and more confusing.

An audience with Puang
Abashim, a maritime
soothsayer, who
communicates directly
with the sea.

While we were on Meringke, hordes of children followed us wherever we went, and Russ persuaded Dewi to teach them to shout 'Murder or Mutiny!' I imagine the next group of English-speaking foreigners who turn up will get quite a surprise.

So our queries today created more questions than answers. The idea that the *Rosalie* may have come here for repairs, though, was highly plausible. Even more theories arose as the day wore on, such as that her cargo had been dangerous. A fax Russ received from the UK late this evening informed us that a cargo of rice was rare, because if any leakage dampened the rice, it could expand and split the hull. Likewise sugar was rarely carried, due to its flammability. The *Rosalie* was carrying both, as evidenced from the accounts of goods it took on board before leaving Surabaya. Then again, maybe Sam did simply jump ship and start a new life. This is a beautiful place, after all, with lovely women.

Before darkness fell, we took a quick tender ride to inspect the supposed location of the wreck mentioned today by the officials. The water was dark and rough – not my favorite kind of dive site. Nearby was a large clump of wave-battered rocks on which a few hardy souls were fishing, all wearing construction helmets. Now that's a hard-core way to catch your dinner.

We returned to find that Tessa and Dewi had created a diorama on the pilot house table. Using an old bedsheet, colour pencils, shells, and anything else they could find, they reproduced the Straits of Alas on which sailed Dewi's cardboard *Rosalie*, cutter and *prahu*. Russ and I then reconstructed the scene to try to come up with new insights. In particular we are baffled by exactly what role was played by the brig San Antonio that was said to have 'fallen in' with the prow near Bally Hill. But nothing really emerged from this exercise, except that we both gleaned a greater sense of the geography and chronology of the story.

After we left the table Dan and Rolle vented their frustration by reproducing the scene in a preferred form:

"They sailed to the island..." said Rolle.

"...stayed a minute or two..." said Dan.

"...then went straight back to Bali and had a few beers."

MAY 11

Dewi went into the port early with Pete and Russ to hire a dive boat. She negotiated for a boat, crew, their food, water and cigarettes for two million Rupiah a day. The money here gives us all a laugh, as in, "Would you put down a million to charter a fishing boat?" The chosen vessel was called *Bintang Mas* or 'Gold Star', owned by Haji Umar. We also engaged a diver from the main town of Mataram.

Diorama with cardboard sailing vessels, created by Tessa and Dewi, to help recreate the supposed final drama of Salty Sam.

The men on the *Bintang* boat said they could take us to the wreck we looked for by the rocks last night, the one described by the officials who came aboard yesterday. So Scotty, Russ, Dan, Tessa and I followed them in the tender. After twenty minutes we had passed the rocks, and it became apparent that they were taking us a lot further on. We became concerned about our fuel level, but eventually we arrived at a small harbour called Labuhan Haji, so named because this is the departure point for Lombok people joining the Haj pilgrimage. Our Mataram dive guide led us into murky, seaweed-laden water, on a wild goose chase. He clearly has no idea how to locate this wreck – if it even exists. Meanwhile, back at Kere Batu, Pascal and a group of Takapunian snorkellers were continuing to search the shallows. Neither group found anything.

We have heard about yet another wreck – a Dutch or Portuguese ship, they say – somewhere near Tanjung Ringgit ('Money Harbour'), which is south from here, just round the point. It is said to be a dangerous marine environment. So what else is new hereabouts? The Japanese were based in this area during the Second World War. They used natural caves as their clandestine observation bases, and after the war ammunition was dumped off the point. We have heard that

Above and opposite below: Our dive support vessel, the *Bintang* ('Gold Star') boat.

Opposite above: The end of an exhausting day's dive search, off Labuhan Haji, Lombok.

quite a bit remains there in the sea, and that the local people salvage the metal. They even cut up the live munitions to make fishing bombs.

According to the *Bintang* men there is a large anchor, north of Labuhan Haji, lying in 17 metres of water. It has, they say, a round hole at the top that 'you can put your head though'. Sounds promising. Of course, these straits are littered with shipwrecks – and no wonder. Between the shoals, sand bars, dangerous reefs and hidden coral heads, even we have been lucky to pass by without incident. So far, that is.

Deborah has placed an ad in the *Jakarta Post* and another local newspaper called *Kompas*, in the hope that someone in Indonesia who reads them may know something about Salty Sam: we placed one in the London *Telegraph* a week ago, but so far we've only had crank replies.

This evening an entertainment group came aboard at my request. I thought it was time we looked more like tourists. Eight men sat in a circle and played traditional music called *cilokak* while an attractive female dancer, dressed in a *kebaya*, sarong and, surprisingly, a men's hat called an *udang*, tried to make everyone gyrate with her – even the women. Russ, Dev and Tessa were brave enough to give it a go, but it was Hengke who surprised us with his sensual moves – and got the biggest applause.

After the show, a couple of the *Bintang* men boarded us unexpectedly and without invitation. Because they are known to us, everyone's guard was down. The ostensible reason for the visit was to engage in more financial negotiations with Dewi, a continuous hassle for her. But I was pleased that our crew quickly picked up on a slightly menacing atmosphere and formed a human barrier

between the men and the hatch that leads below decks. I've given instructions that these men cannot come on board again.

> Dear Pamela,
> A thought suddenly occurred to me that someone might have suppressed the newspaper report because of its reference to a 'wife'.
> I hope all is going well off Kere Batu.
> Yours Anne

Well, the Stephensons do generally pride themselves on being a very religious, morally upstanding lot. I can see them wanting to avoid a scandal, especially in those days. Or was there a general attempt to protect Ann Stephenson from the distressing news that she had a counterpart in Indonesia? Did they sacrifice getting the money to maintain propriety?

> Dear Pam,
> I got your e-mail today, but it was incomplete, I only got three words or so. I hope everything is rolling along singing a shanty. The shows are going well and the audiences are responding well. I did the John Stewart show last night and we had a good laugh together. He is so easy to get along with. It's the hottest show in the country. I feel very lucky, which is always a good sign.
> Try to stay afloat, and remember, never use both feet when testing the depth of the water,
> Love Love Love xxxx
> Bill Bill

Chapter **16** Finding the *Rosalie*

MAY 12, KERE BATU, STRAITS OF ALAS

I have waited many months to write the following words: we may have located the *Rosalie*.

The *Bintang* men brought another diver along today, a local man who knew what he was doing. We all returned to the site we searched yesterday, and anchored beside a white buoy that was bobbing in the water. Apparently the local diver had gone down this morning and attached this buoy to a wooden wreck. Pascal donned scuba gear and followed him to check it out, with Tessa filming, and found something very promising. Several beams of dark wood are lying at about 75 feet, considerably further from the shore than we were looking yesterday with the Mataram diver. Pascal is encouraged, so I am too because he is very conservative.

"It's definitely a wreck," he announced on his return. "An old ship. And the locals say they have taken quite a bit of porcelain away from the location."

"But why would it be here," I asked, "if she ran aground off Kere, a good mile or so away?"

The answer was obvious to Tessa and Pascal, who had experienced terrifyingly strong currents, and had only managed to descend by dragging themselves down on the rope attached to the buoy. Given these conditions, it would make sense for the *Rosalie* to have been swept down here after she ran aground and end up in this sandy catchment. The trouble is, those particular qualities make diving here very difficult – not to say dangerous. Nevertheless, I was cautiously excited, and waited impatiently for a safe time to descend and see the wreck for myself.

Around 1pm the tide seemed to be changing. The currents were reduced to just under two knots, although that is still strong for divers. Russ wanted to take a scooter down, but I decided I'd prefer the rope method used this morning by Pascal and Tessa.

"But we'll stick together, right?" I agreed with the rest of the team – Russ, Tessa, and Pascal.

We began to descend. Russ and Pascal, on scooters, were ahead, while Tessa and I used all our strength to pull ourselves against the current. I was below Tessa, who was filming my descent. Visibility was poor. At around 20 metres, I felt the rope go slack. Ten feet later, I was facing an empty loop: the wreck to which it had supposedly been attached was nowhere to be seen. So the boys took off in search of the wreck – thus breaking our agreement to stick together.

I hate being in such murky water and when it comes to diving rules, I'm a safety geek. I took a slate and wrote 'FUCKING STAY TOGETHER!' in readiness for their return. Tessa and I hung around for a while, but after a few more minutes, we abandoned our search, and surfaced with some considerable difficulty.

The dive had turned out to be reckless and wreckless. And now that we have lost the location of the wreck, someone better than us will have to try to find it again. Unfortunately we did not take a GPS fixing on the buoy, which was a big mistake. We fixed the location of our own anchor instead, and asked the *Bintang* men to relocate the wreck as soon as possible and put another buoy on it.

Meanwhile, Russ, who had been impressed with the reports of our audience with the paranormal man, suggested we bring him to the island of Kere Batu to see if it inspired him to divine anything else. So we planned to go ashore there late in the day, to light a bonfire, and hold some kind of mini-séance. Russ is into all that hocus pocus.

Ibu Habrani and her 'psychic' family in the Straits of Alas.

But when sunset came we realized that the tide was far too low for the tender to land, and, in any case, Dewi announced that the psychic had insisted we receive him on board at 5pm. She had been informed that a total of six people would accompany him, including the tourism officials, Ainul and Yayak. This seemed a bit strange, particularly when 5pm came and went, and no psychic. Then we received a phone call that he and his entourage were at prayers (of course – today is the Muslim holy day) and they would come at 6pm instead.

Some minutes after the appointed time, our tender turned up with a strange family aboard. They were beautifully dressed in correct mosque attire, the woman, Ibu Habrani, and her small girl in *jilbab* headscarves, her husband and a teenager in black velvet *peche* hats, and a young boy, whose name was Sayyid Muhammad Yusuf, in a skullcap. Ainul and Yayak were in jeans.

"Where's the paranormal?" I asked them, lifting the little girl on board, smoothing down her pink frilly dress, and settling her in a deckchair.

"The whole family is psychic," I was told, "especially the children." I glanced quickly at the girl, Syarifa Jann, who was no more than four years old.

But it was the boy who interested me. Solemn and composed, he sat down at the pilot-house table with his family, saying nothing. The adults completely deferred to him. He was the first to be introduced to me, and the others whispered among themselves behind his back as he readied himself for his work.

"You may ask him anything about your grandfather," said Yayak. "He will tell you the whole story."

Evidently Yayak had dreamed that he must find a boy, and when he asked in the village about a psychic he was taken to young Yusuf, who immediately expressed a desire to come aboard the *Takapuna* and help us.

"What's his background?" I asked.

The boy, explained his mother, was born from a 13-month pregnancy. "He had the face of a monkey when he was born," she said. When I sought an explanation, Yayak said he was ugly, and covered with hair. Mother and son were both ill for the first three years of his life, following which he became well and his face returned to normal. From then on he had visions, which he described as 'waking dreams', in which he could see 'everything', past and present. Hundreds of snakes began visiting his house on Thursdays and Fridays, drawing crowds of spectators.

Right now, the seven-year-old's eyes were downcast. Yayak asked him if he was ready, and he nodded.

"What can you tell me," I began, "about my great-great-grandfather?"

The boy was silent for a moment. When he finally spoke, his voice was raspy and halting, yet he spoke with impressive certainty.

"He had a good journey."

A long pause followed. I had asked an open question, which was not the correct form. "You must ask very specific questions," explained Yayak.

"Was there any problem with his ship?" I asked.

"No," he replied. That seemed strange.

I tried another tack. "Did he die near Kere Batu?"

"No," replied Yusuf. "He died in the area of Tanjung Ringgit."

The nearby 'Money Harbour'. "How did he die?" I asked. "Was he murdered?"

"No. He died of old age," replied the boy, "at 80 years of age. He liked it here. He lived with Lombok people and was buried here."

That surprised me. If the boy was right, then perhaps Salty Sam did run away from his old life, and disappeared on Lombok.

"Did he have family here?"

"No. He stayed with one man on Lombok." Now a new, 'gay lover' theory was emerging.

"Did he have children here?"

"No."

In answer to my questions over the next hour, Yusuf solemnly related that Sam was 'hiding' here, that he had little money, kept his own name, was not Muslim, and worked as a fisherman.

"What happened to his ship?" I finally asked.

"His friends took it." My eyes widened. Was the boy about to tell of a mutiny?

"Where did they take it?"

"To the place that they came from," he replied. "He had no family in England. He did not remember his history in England. He loved it here more. No one else from the ship stayed here."

Seven year-old Sayyid Muhammad Yusuf, the 'paranormal' boy with 'knowledge' of Salty Sam.

"Can I go down again without getting narked?" Consulting the dive computer.

I was confused, desperately trying to make sense of all of this. Was it possible that Sam sustained a head injury with attendant long-term amnesia? What exactly was going on here? The boy had a gift, but he was inaccurate about most of the details.

"How does the boy manage to see things?" I finally asked Yayak. He conferred with Yusuf. "Like a dream," was the reply.

"And how does this gift help him?" I asked, pressing some rupiah into Yusuf's hand, 'for his education'.

"It gives me more from God," the boy said, passing the cash to his father.

As the group departed, Yayak asked me to give Yusuf some water. I grabbed a bottle and passed it to him. Seated in the tender with head bowed, he clutched it and began to mutter. "He is blessing it," said Yayak. "Now you must sprinkle it on yourself three times a day. Then you will receive the answers you seek."

I decided to comply.

By nightfall the *Bintang* men had still not relocated the wreck. This is most frustrating. Given that we are paying a daily rate for the boat, they could keep their search going for some time, with the excuse that conditions are difficult. Indeed they are difficult, but there are windows of low current if you watch for them.

After dinner, Dewi came to me, very agitated, to say she is concerned about our safety. She's got a bad feeling, prompted by this guy in an orange T-shirt who has a habit of turning up wherever we go. They say he's from the army. He wormed his way into a role as middleman in our deal with the *Bintang* boat, he hired the divers we need tomorrow, and he's always coming up with a new and patently bogus 'extra expense', such as 'money to clean the boat'. The latest ploy was a yarn about his divers being afraid of ghosts on the dive site and the apparent necessity of hiring an exorcist to 'cleanse' it. We now suspect he may be one of the men from the 'pirate' boat that tried to board us on our second night here. Dewi's advice is that we should finish up our work and get out of here as soon as we possibly can.

That made me scared. It's my worst nightmare to get on the wrong side of Indonesian officialdom, and to make matters worse, the tourism representatives Ainul and Yayak, who have so far acted as our protectors and go-betweens with the locals, have mysteriously disappeared. I told the crew about Orange Tee and asked Dan to upgrade our security protocol tonight. Jim advised us to lower our deck lights so we could see better, but to be prepared to flood the boat with light if someone menacing approaches. We put flares at the ready, and prepared our MRAD to warn off any would-be intruders with a noisy command. Our weapons are still locked away in a cupboard bearing the official Indonesian seal – but I'll get them out if I have to.

MAY 13

We had planned an early dive to try to inspect this wreck that might well be the *Rosalie*. We would weigh anchor in Labuhan Luar at 6am, then the *Bintang* boat was to meet us at Labuhan Haji an hour later, having already relocated the wreck so we could dive right away. But at 7am there was no sign of our local guides. Worse, the buoys they had promised to attach to the wreck yesterday were nowhere to be seen, and we could not start without them. Then Dewi got a message from the *Bintang* boat to say they'd had engine trouble and were still half an hour away. Frustrated, I went ashore to search for any locals who might know something about this wreck, which is just offshore from their village.

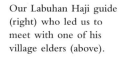

Our Labuhan Haji guide (right) who led us to meet with one of his village elders (above).

The beach where we landed was bustling at this hour. "Are there any old people around?" Dewi inquired of a man who looked at least seventy.

"I'll take you to one," he replied.

"How old does he think *he* is?" I asked Dewi sarcastically. I was in a bad mood because of the delay this morning.

"Oh, he's probably only forty," smiled Dewi. "People here age faster."

We followed this geriatric forty-year-old to a little concrete block home with cement floors. After being invited inside we were asked to sit down in a tiny reception room with a well-worn couch set by a small wooden coffee table. Ricky was instructed to open the curtains behind him, presumably so more people could watch what was going on through the back windows. As many villagers as possible crowded into the room, the porch and the adjacent room behind us.

We sat there for quite a while. "The old man is bathing," explained Dewi, "and he's not so well."

"I wouldn't want to disturb a sick man," I said, starting to get up, "especially while he's bathing."

"He's bathing because of you." She eyed me meaningfully, forcing me to sit down again.

After we'd been there, on show, for another twenty-five minutes, an 88-year-old man emerged from a back room. I asked him if he knew about any ships running aground near here before he was born. But he didn't. Nor did he know of any foreigners settling hereabouts, and he seemed particularly reticent when it came to discussing the Raja. I didn't push him, for he clearly couldn't help us, and besides, our turning up at his house had caused a regular spectacle. He could have charged admission.

While we were ashore, we learned to our surprise that this tiny place had a harbour master, and that he and the village chief were displeased about something we had omitted to do. We sent Hengke to sort it out, and he reported back that, even though this was an insignificant port in our eyes, we needed to clear in and out of it just like the larger places. Moreover, he said, the people here in Labuhan Haji were upset that we had turned up here with a boat and crew we had hired from Labuhan Luar. "We are locals," they complained. "We know these waters. You should have hired us."

Worse, they threatened to send a gang of fishermen out to chase the *Bintang* boat away if it came any nearer.

As we sped anxiously back to the *Takapuna*, the occupants of a grey paramilitary motor-canoe waved us over.

"There's something wrong with your papers," frowned one man, which sounded ominous. Perhaps my worst fear of being thrown in jail here is about to come true. I considered instructing Dan to up anchor and make a run for it. But managed to control that urge, in the hope of seeing what I was now convinced might be the wreck of the *Rosalie*.

By 8.30am we were back on the *Takapuna*. The *Bintang* boat had arrived and the buoys, which had indeed been placed the night before, were now revealed as the tide ebbed. Russ was eager to attempt a dive. Unfortunately, the speed of the current now made the site a divers' deathtrap, and no one except him wanted to enter the water until conditions improved. Then Russ came up with a plan. Pascal and Scotty would go ahead and secure a line from the *Takapuna* to the wreck so the rest of us could avoid having to fight our way down on the buoy line. Pascal and Scotty peered nervously at the racing tide, but bravely prepared to make an attempt. Russ's idea was that, along with him, Tessa and I would wait for a tug on the rope signalling that the line had been attached, then follow it on our descent. We would use the scooters, he said, to force our way through the current.

Dan hopped into the water with a scooter to test Russ's hypothesis. "I'm on full speed now and finning as well," he shouted, "and I'm still going backwards."

"There's no way," I told Russ. "It's not safe. Let's wait until there's less current."

But Russ is a man who likes to get going. You could see his frustration mounting. He is also a man who inspires others to do his bidding, even against their own better judgement. Pascal and Scotty got in the water. "Are you sure

Dan and Scotty cling to *Takapuna*'s anchor chain, after an aborted attempt to force their way down through the current.

Opposite: Excavating near the sunken ship's spars, and (bottom) returning just in time to avoid the most lethal tides.

you are comfortable attempting this?" I asked each in turn. Frankly, I was less than comfortable with the situation myself.

"Well," said Pascal, "we can try it."

Four and a half minutes later I saw him being swept downstream into the further regions of the Straits of Alas, waving for help. I leapt into the tender, almost catching Russ's 'safety line' in the propeller as I spurted backwards in panic, before roaring off to rescue him.

"This sort of thing will not happen again," I said curtly as I peeled off my wetsuit. "From now on our dives will be properly planned by people who know what they're doing." I was furious, and needless to say no one dived for the rest of the morning.

Russ is a brilliantly creative man, and it's definitely worth figuring out how best to work with him. I need to let him dream up his marvellous ideas unhindered, then insist on being the one to implement them. That way we can achieve them without getting anyone killed.

At 1.30pm, when the current died a bit, I was finally able to dive on the wreck for myself. With Kayt as my buddy, I scootered tandem behind her down the buoy line until the wreck came into partial view: a couple of long, parallel pieces of old, dark wood sticking out of the sand. At first I thought, "It's just a couple of tree trunks." But I soon changed my mind.

When we arrived on the sea floor, three divers we'd hired from the *Bintang* boat were already working on the site, attempting to remove sand to expose more of the wood. The environment was therefore clouded, and the poor visibility had been further diminished. But after poking around, and positioning myself up-current from the swirling sand, I could make out smooth edges and contoured lines indicating that here lay part of the spars of a large ship. I fanned away the sand from one piece and discovered that it was joined to another large piece of wood lying sideways on the sea bed. Excitedly I thought, "This must be part of the hull, or a bulkhead!" I tried to attract Russ's attention, but he was busy zooming round on his scooter. Boys! They love their vroom vrooms. I spent the rest of the dive trying to see through the clouds of sand stirred up by the *Bintang* men, and resolved to return later with a smaller party.

Relieved after rescuing Pascal.

I was so engrossed in my amateur excavation, it took Kayt to tap me on the back and indicate that it was time to surface. I began to swim towards the guide line, and was horrified when I realized that the current had increased its velocity in an instant. Of course, the scooters could not be used for our ascent, so we had to cling to the rope to avoid being swept up too fast. Visibility was awful. As I was trying to read my dive computer, the force of the current suddenly spun me away from the rope. Tessa bravely went after me, and it honestly took the last of our strength to return to the relative safety of the guide line while avoiding a too-rapid ascent.

If only we could work out these tides and currents we could get a lot more done with a lot less risk. But there's no tide-table available, and the currents seem erratic.

Late this afternoon, riding back to Labuhan Luar aboard the *Bintang* boat, I had a chance to talk to its crew. "Where are you all from?" I asked.

"We are from Sumbawa," one replied. "From the village of Alas."

"They are *bajo*," said Pascal. "Sea gypsies. They live on this boat, sometimes with their whole families."

"Weren't the *bajo* originally pirates?" I asked him excitedly.

"Oh, yes," he nodded. "Absolutely."

"And the man in the orange T-shirt." I pointed him out. "Is he also from Sumbawa?"

"No," they replied. "He is from Pijot. The chief's son."

In that instant, the whole drama of the last day or two fell into place. This was not about us. It was inter-island and inter-village stuff. It had been going on for centuries. I had read how these small places were run by petty chiefs who were hostile to each other. Sumbawan pirates had frequently raided these Lombok villages, so that, by the 1860s, most of the original inhabitants had moved inland. Often the Europeans had played off these factions, one against the other. Orange Tee was simply trying to cream off something he thought was his right. He was protecting the *bajo* from his own people in order to make a buck.

We hired a Labuhan Haji man to watch over our buoy all night (which went down well with the locals) and returned to Labuhan Luar for the night. I went below to check the news about Mount Merapi, a volcano in central Java that has just begun to erupt. When I re-emerged, Pascal informed me that some local people had come by in an outrigger with some artifacts they claimed were salvaged from the wreck we'd just been diving on. Russ had asked them for a price, but fortunately Pascal and Dewi had prevented him from buying anything. It could have been a trap. We don't want to be accused of taking something from the wreck, and besides, it is illegal to take anything outside the country that is more than one hundred years old. I looked at the photos they'd taken of one item: a honey-coloured, glazed ceramic water bottle with

STKAMP & Z & MOLY,
ROTTERDAM

written on the side and KPM on the bottom. Pascal thought it looked authentic, but we have no proof that it came from our wreck.

MAY 14

I woke up at 6.15am in the middle of a dream, and realized it was one I had also dreamed the previous night. In it, I was huddled beneath a large wicker fish basket, rather like the traps placed beneath the *bagang* or bamboo fishing platforms commonly seen within the shallow, protective waters of Indonesian harbours. The basket under which I lay was situated, it seemed, in the hold of a ship. I felt physically restrained but aware of my surroundings, and I awoke with a phrase in mind from the survivor's tale as recorded in the legal documents concerning Salty Sam's Will: 'confined below'.

We had planned to dive at 7am sharp. I had to get moving; yet my mind was arresting my body. Confined below. Confined below. It's almost a symbolic notion for unconscious processes, I thought. We know things deeply that our conscious mind has not grasped. Knowledge, the truth, as it were, confined below. I forced myself out of bed, and, thinking it was still dark, cursed myself for insisting on such an early descent. But when I opened my deadlight the sun was well and truly up. Perceptions from below decks can be distorted. At that moment, the answer came to me.

Items said to have been recovered by locals from the 'Rosalie' and (top left) driving the *Bintang* boat.

Previous pages: At the excavation site, with a local diver using a compression hose connected to the generator aboard the *Bintang* boat.

Right: A piece of singed wood from the wreck.

I went for my dive, descending onto the sea floor as part of a 'chick team' with Kayt and Tessa. We were working in fast-rotating teams, to expose as much of the wreck as possible within the limited minimum-current time. Ricky, Scotty and Pascal, who'd preceded us, had done a good job, so I could see even more of the wreck's geography. Still, only the very top section is visible. To think there may be an entire ship underneath, buried in sand over a couple of centuries of currents and silting! Using reversed scooters we did our best to blow away more sand. I paid particular attention to one area where I'd felt sure there was a join between a bulkhead and part of the hull. As I was feeling around, a small piece of wood broke off in my hand, and I brought it up to the surface. "That's charcoal!" exclaimed Rolle. True enough, the wood did appear to be charred. That led to more theorizing about the possibility of fire aboard or even spontaneous combustion, perhaps due to the sugar Sam was carrying. Pascal reminded us too that survivors often deliberately burned a ship that had foundered, to avoid leaving it to anyone else.

Pascal himself found an important item – a piece of iron that may turn out to have been one of the ship's shackles, covered in coral and barnacles. We will try to have both items tested. We also filmed every exposed part of the wreck and took measurements, so we have a fairly complete visual record to show the archaeologists. Have we actually found the *Rosalie*? Very possibly.

Chapter 17 The Tale of
Salty Sam

MAY 15, STRAITS OF ALAS

I'm not usually impressed by 'paranormals'. I believe most people can tap into their own psychic abilities if they're open to it – and I do it myself, especially with patients in my psychotherapy work. The boy I met two evenings ago was wrong about most of Salty Sam's details, but what he did for me was to act as a link between myself and my own secret knowledge. In focusing on his, for want of a better word, 'psychic energy', he tuned me in, as it were, to unravel the answer. Acting as a catalyst, he allowed me to make different connections than before.

It was so simple, and it had been there all along – although the details could not have been gleaned without travelling here to the Straits of Alas and having the many illuminating experiences of the past three months. The peripheral pieces of the jigsaw will continue to be found, but I believe I can now make out the broad picture. I went for my next dive, as part of the second three-man excavation team, nursing the secret knowledge that, no matter whether or not the large chunk of ship's spar I brought up from the deep belonged to the *Rosalie*, nevertheless I feel at peace. I know what happened, and I now understand why there were different stories. Tonight we'll light a bonfire on the sands of Carabatoo, and I'll tell my own story. My great-great-grandfather's story, the tale of Salty Sam.

"So let me tell you," I addressed our band of adventurers under the stars this evening, "the events that I now believe took place right here, on and around this very island, one hundred and eighty-five years ago.

"Why the two conflicting reports? Murder by pirates, or mutiny? The answer, I now believe, is that the two stories tell of the same event, from two different points of view. One truth lies in the perception of the 'witness' who gave an account that was recorded in the legal documents. My friends, that survivor's perception that mutiny occurred was accurate – but I now believe the mutiny did not occur on board the *Rosalie*. No, the mutiny occurred on board the *prahu* that was conveying Salty Sam and his entourage to the Port of Bima!

"The *Rosalie* indeed must have run aground. We've seen enough of the shoals, sand bars, other low-tide phenomena and fast-changing currents to know how easily that could have happened in these parts. She's lying

somewhere out there, probably where we've been diving, or else scattered throughout the Straits of Alas and beyond. Perhaps she was already damaged when she got down here, through water entering the hold and swelling the rice that in turn burst some of the timbers – or perhaps a fire broke out from spontaneous combustion of the sugar on board. Perhaps that's why Salty Sam ducked down here for repairs and provisions.

"Whatever the reason, somewhere near here my great-great-grandfather was forced to give the command "Abandon Ship!" In many ways, he and his crew were lucky. Here the water is warm, and this island was near. No one was going to die of hypothermia before he got onto dry land. They had time to ferry people and valuables onto Carabatoo in the ship's cutter and longboat. Salty Sam would have kept his money about him in his Captain's belt. His chests of opium would have been beside him, and any other valuables in a trunk carried by his most trustworthy crew members. They would have brought some provisions ashore here, but not too many; they knew Pijot was an established nearby port where European ships would receive friendly treatment and take on stores and fresh water.

"Sam had hoped to refloat the *Rosalie*, but after a while she began to sink rapidly, and be carried downstream in the racing currents. Fishermen came out from the Lombok mainland, but (just like us) Sam didn't trust them. He hid his valuables from them, and eventually took a small party in the longboat over to Pijot to suss out the situation there, sensibly leaving his goods in the hands of his officers.

"Once in Pijot, Sam was delighted to find he was among friends. Just as we've experienced here, the local Raja relied on good relationships with Europeans for trade. It could be tricky to do a deal, but they wanted European custom because we paid better prices for bullocks, vegetables, water, chickens – whatever the ships needed. Salty Sam probably presented the Raja with a gift – a chest of opium perhaps – and the Raja entertained them at his palace and made them feel welcome.

" 'What will you do now?' he asked the Captain.

" 'We must take passage on a ship back to Surabaya,' replied Sam. 'I have an agent there who will help me deal with this loss.'

" 'The nearest colonial Port is Bima,' said the Raja. 'Plenty of ships stop there on their way back to Java. You should head there. I will find you some transport.'

" 'We will need a pretty large *prahu*,' said Salty Sam. 'There are thirty or so of us, as well as our belongings – although I would like some of my crew to sail our cutter to Bima. It's too small for all of us to travel in, but once we get to Bima it could be sold to offset the loss of the ship.'

"Next day, Sam returned to the island of Carabatoo to find the rest of his crew grumbling about what might happen now. Their food was nearly gone, and some of them had attacked the Captain's liquor supplies.

" 'Good news,' he said. 'I've been offered a vessel to get us to Bima and from there we can return to Surabaya.' Sam tried to soothe the brewing unrest over whether or not they would be paid.

" 'We don't want to go to Bima,' said some. 'Give us our pay and we'll make our own way' (to Batavia, India, Mauritius, or wherever each of them came from). The Captain reached into his trunk and pulled out some silver.

"When high tide came, they saw a large *prahu* sailing towards them. The crew of the *prahu* helped the *Rosalie* survivors aboard – all except the gunner and six Lascars who had been chosen to sail the cutter to Bima. On board the cutter they had loaded as many of the ship's weapons they had been able to carry off – just a few pistols and carronades. Salty Sam, his lady friend, and his officers boarded the *prahu*, while the rest of the Rosalie crew, helped by the crew of the *prahu*, loaded everything of value. There were now around sixty people on board: twenty or so from the Rosalie (some had disappeared after they got paid) while the *prahu*'s crew outnumbered them at forty odd. The decks were overcrowded, so the commander of the *prahu* ordered some of his own crew and most of Salty Sam's to go below for the duration of the journey. Some slept, some played cards, and some shared a few bottles of arak.

"But some members of the *prahu* crew, particularly those who had helped load Salty Sam's valuables, began to talk among themselves. Perhaps they were *bajo* people, sea gypsies from Sumbawa, or maybe Buginese who had just returned from a long fishing trip. In any case, they may have been people who did not have any particular loyalty towards the Raja on Lombok. There was often fighting between the peoples of the two islands separated by the narrow Straits of Alas. From time to time, *bajo* swooped across and raided the towns on the east coast of Lombok. Right now they enjoyed a reasonable peace with the people of Pijot, to whom they sold their fish and other goods in the marketplace – but scratch the surface, and tensions were there.

" 'Why are we bothering to take these people to Bima?' demanded one of the crew. 'They have money and opium. We outnumber them. We could slit their throats, take their goods, and be home in time for dinner with a nice prize each.'

" 'No,' replied other crew members, who were subjects of the Raja, and therefore feared him. The men began to argue, with the outsiders pitted against the Lombok crew.

"One of Salty Sam's crew members had noticed that trouble was brewing. On a pretext of being ill he managed to get himself on deck, where he approached Captain Stephenson.

" 'Captain,' he said, 'we may not be safe on board this vessel with this crew. The crew are not of one mind.'

" 'I've been thinking something similar,' said one of Sam's officers. 'After all, what's to stop them robbing us?'

" 'The Raja gave his word,' replied Sam, 'that nothing would happen to us. And besides, he relies on Europeans for trade.' Nevertheless, Salty Sam's ears had pricked up, and he kept a careful eye on the *prahu*'s captain.

"The *Rosalie*'s crew was exhausted from the events of the past few days, and many fell into a deep asleep. As they headed northwards up the

Straits of Alas towards Bima, Salty Sam was silent and brooding, trying to figure out his next course of action. He had lost the *Rosalie*, but he still had 80,000 Dutch florins deposited with his Surabayan agents, so he was by no means a pauper. Nevertheless, some of the cargo was uninsured, so there would be substantial losses. He must sort out his affairs as soon as possible. Meanwhile his lady friend was crying; she had been afraid on Carabatoo, and was uncomfortable on board the *prahu*. The sooner they reached civilization the better. His officers were thankful to be alive, but irritable and worried about their futures. There would be no new ship for Captain Stephenson for some time, so they must now find employment on board another vessel.

"The force of the violence that befell Sam took him by surprise. Suddenly he was grabbed around the neck from behind by a man with a drawn *kris*, or dagger. His first mate leapt to pull the assailant off, and was stabbed from behind, falling to the deck in agony. Sam and his lady friend witnessed this in horror. Vainly they looked around for help; all would-be-protectors had been deftly restrained by the aggressors. Now the *prahu* commander attempted to intervene; he would face the wrath of the Raja for anything that went wrong. But at least half his crew had already taken matters into their own hands. Three arak-soaked sailors strode up to Salty Sam with their *krisses* drawn. With the first slash, Salty Sam's money belt went clanging to the ground, and even before it was snatched up it was spattered with blood from the throat of Salty Sam, his consort and the three other British officers.

Below decks, the *Rosalie* crew member who had first seen trouble coming was frozen with apprehension. After most of the *bajo* had disappeared up on deck, ominously locking the hold behind them, he had heard a scuffle, then shortly afterwards some splashes, as if several heavy items had been thrown overboard. Fearing the worst, the *Rosalie* crew lay fearfully for a few minutes, until the hold was flung open and they were dragged on deck. There they saw that fighting had broken out between the two local groups. There was no sign of anyone from the *Rosalie*. Several of the crew were stabbed and flung overboard; others managed to break free and threw themselves over of their own accord.

All was not lost, however, for the few that still lived. From the water they could see their own ship's cutter, that appeared at first to be on its way to save them. Unfortunately, their hopes dwindled as they watched it turn tail and flee when the *prahu* crew attempted to summon it. Unbeknown to the others, those aboard the cutter had witnessed with horror the bodies of Salty Sam, his consort and officers floating past. They were not going to risk becoming the next victims of people they now believed were pirates.

"Abandoned to their fate, most of the men in water drowned. But two lucky ones – including a mate and a seaman – somehow got ashore, perhaps picked up by a passing vessel, and eventually reached Sumanup on the north Java coast.

"Meanwhile, the gunner and six Lascars in the cutter eventually made it to Bima. There they were kindly received by the Resident, who put them on board a *prahu* bound for Surabaya. On the way back they stopped for provisions at Bally, where they came across a brig called the *San Antonio* and told the crew their story. The *San Antonio* then carried on to Prince of Wales Island, where dockside gossip ensured their piracy story made the local Gazette."

So was that a pirate murder? Or a mutiny? Certainly the people who perpetrated the crime could be considered pirates, committing murder and robbery at sea. But they were also divided, and mutinied, against the better judgement of their own Captain.

The story I heard in my family was correct. A mutiny did occur, but not on board the *Rosalie*. The mutiny story must have come from the survivors who reached Sumanup, the mate and seaman who had been 'confined below'- and from their point of view it was entirely accurate. They were the ones who provided the eyewitness account reported in the Asiatic Journal and Miscellany, the first article I found at the British Library that mentions 'murder'.

The other account, from the gunner and six Lascars who eventually made it to Bima, was accurate from another point of view, for what they witnessed appeared to be a pirate murder. They assumed the people who offered the Captain safe passage to Bima were simply scurrilous pirates in cahoots with the Raja, such a thing being common at the time. From their vantage point it was an out-and-out pirate ship that pretended to be friendly but whose crew murdered and robbed the survivors as soon as Pijot was behind them – and nearly managed to prey on the cutter too.

So the two stories are really one, told from the differing viewpoints of two groups of survivors. Murder or Mutiny? No – Murder AND Mutiny.

End Matter

EPILOGUE

MAY 16, STRAITS OF ALAS

I don't know what really happened. As Russ said to me recently, the answer will probably come to us by email one rainy day in London. Someone who reads this book or sees the television programme will know something and contact us. But for me, aboard the *Takapuna* tonight in the Straits of Alas, a mere flying-fish leap from the island of Carabatoo, there is finally some peace. I have learned that there is at least one plausible explanation for the discrepancy in the two stories of my ancestor's death, and hereafter for the first time in many months I shall rest well tonight. I have travelled the seas to find answers to a riddle – and I have certainly found some.

For now, there is nothing much more to be said – except perhaps that the truth takes many forms. Once again, I have been faced with the fact that there is no absolute truth; it rests in the mind of the beholder, and in this case there were several of those.

Yes, I can rest now. I am riding at anchor here in the Straits of Alas, having travelled here on my own sailboat to uncover a mystery that concerns my family. It was right to do this, to honour the memory of my great-great-grandfather. He suffered a violent death right here, and his bones lie – maybe on the seabed, or perhaps in the unmarked foreigner's grave on Pijot. It doesn't matter; at last I know what kind of man he was. His legacy to me is his adventurous spirit, his 'do or die' sensibility, his willingness to risk all for a prize, and his passion for the sea. I am blessed with his spirit. And I am proud to have found one answer to the mystery of Carabatoo: so that's what most likely happened to Salty Sam!

Do you know more?

MAY 17, BADUNG STRAITS

The very day after the above Epilogue was written I received an email from Professor Lapian that put into jeopardy everything I had previously believed:

> Dear Pamela,
> At last, two letters found! However, they make things more complicated.
> I have ordered photocopies and take them with me to Bali on Sunday.
>
> 1) Letter from the Resident of Sumenep (Madura) to the Resident in Surabaya, 15 Oct 1821, about Thomas Kelly, 2nd mate of the *Rosalie*, together with six other sailors. They reported that Capt Stevenson [sic] 'and a woman who was with him' were murdered while sailing on a Butonese ship (Buton is an island off Southeast Sulawesi) which he

boarded after the *Rosalie* was shipwrecked, but … said Kelly, the accident "did not happen in Strait Allas but on a reef at the island of Flores, an island called Ende".

2) Letter from the Resident of Banyuwangi to the Resident of Surabaya, 1 December 1821. Reporting that six sailors from the Rosalie have arrived and will proceed to Surabaya. They have travelled overland across Bali and had to leave behind three men who were ill.

Problem: Why did Kelly tell that it did not happen in Strait Alas, but in Flores? But why did he appear in Sumenep (Madura) instead of Bima which is nearer to Flores? Why did the other six sailors arrive at Banyuwangi which is also the obvious place to go when the shipwreck happened in Strait Alas? In 1821 Bali was still independent. not yet Dutch territory.

Hoping to find more in the next few days, best regards,

Adri Lapian

THE BOAT

The *Takapuna*, an Italian-built Valdetarro, is a 112-foot cutter-rigged sloop with a 26-foot beam, designed by Briton Laurent Giles. She is named after my birthplace in New Zealand. '*Takapuna*' is a Maori name that means 'high place by the water', and is associated with a legend about romantic longing.

The *Takapuna*'s mast is 130 feet high, and she has three sails: mainsail, staysail and Genoa. She draws only 9 feet, which proves to be very useful when sailing and mooring in shallow waters.

She has a large, enclosed pilot-house with two navigation stations, and a fore and aft deck. The aft deck leads to a swim platform, and a lazarette (a garage) where we store all our dive equipment. Below is a large saloon, plus a galley with a crew mess leading to the engine room. With five cabins forward and six aft, she has an unusually large interior volume for a sailing boat, and can sleep up to 16 people comfortably. Communication by telephone, email and fax is possible anywhere in the world due to a comprehensive satellite capability, and our navigational equipment is also state of the art.

The *Takapuna* can be solely reliant on either sail or motor, and she can also motorsail (combine both to make the best speed). In the engine room there is a 326-horsepower MTU engine, two John Deere Kilopack generators, plus one large and one auxiliary Village Marine water-maker.

She underwent a massive refit in 2003, and again in 2005. Her new paint job, teak decks, improved rigging and outstanding navigation stations (as well as attractive new décor) are a testament to the crew and yard workers in Brisbane, Australia.

Crew photo taken in Benoa harbour, Bali.
(From left to right) Standing: Dev, Tek, Pete, Hengke, Dan, Russ, Ricky (modelling coolie hat and eye patch),
Pamela, Scarlett (Pamela's youngest daughter who was visiting at the time), Tessa and Scotty;
Sitting: Jim, Kayt, Rolle;
Not shown: the Captain, Sue, Sean.

BOAT CREW

Pamela: Owner and Boss!

Dan: First mate/Captain

Scotty: Second mate/First mate

Rolle: Engineer

Kayt: Cook

Sue: Stewardess

Ricky: Doctor

Captain

Sean: Security officer

Dev: Gurkha security guard

Tek: Gurkha security guard

Tessa: Underwater videographer, stewardess and production secretary

Teguh: Local shore guide and interpreter

Hengke: Local marine guide and deck hand

TV CREW
Russ: Producer
Lucy: Production Manager
Pete: Cameraman
Robin: Cameraman
Jim: Cameraman

RESEARCHERS
Anne
Professor Lapian
Dewi
Geoff

LOCAL ADVISORS
Deborah
Lawrence
Des Alwi
Ainul
Ahyak
Mr Sam
Sumardi

WRECK FINDERS
Pascal
Fred

BIBLIOGRAPHY

Ball, Dorian	*The Diana Adventure* Malaysian Historical Salvors: Kuala Lumpur
Bass, George F. (Ed)	*A History of Seafaring Based on Underwater Archaeology* Thames and Hudson 1972
Blair, Lawrence & Lorne	*Ring of Fire: An Indonesian Odyssey* Park Street Press 1988
Broeze, F.J.A.	*The Merchant Fleet of Java 1820–1850 – A Preliminary Survey* Paper given to the Sixth International Conference on Asian History, Yogyakarta, August 1974. Revised version
Buckles, Guy	*Globetrotter Dive Guide Indonesia* New Holland 2002
Bulley, Anne	*Free Mariner – John Adolphus Pope in the East Indies 1786–1821* British Association for Cemeteries in South Asia (BACSA) 1992
Crawford, John	*History of the Indian Archipelago* Frank Cass 1967
Crawford, John	*Descriptive Dictionary of the Indian Islands and Adjacent Countries* (2nd edition) London 1856
Cresswell, J.C.M.	*Murder in Paradise* J.C.M. Cresswell Books 1998
Earl, G.W.	*The Eastern Sea* Oxford University Press 1971
Farrington, Anthony	*Trading Places – The East India Company and Asia 1600–1834* The British Library 2002
Farrington, Tony	*Sailing With Mohammed* New Holland (NZ) 2005
Forrest, Thomas	*A Voyage to New Guinea and The Moluccas 1774–1776* Oxford University Press 1969
Gappa, Amanna	*Hukum Pelayaran Dan Perdagangan* (translated by Prof. O.L. Tobing) Yayasan Kebudayaan Suluwesi Selatan Ujung Pandang 1977
Hanes, W. Travis & Sanello, Frank	*The Opium Wars – the Addiction of One Empire and the Corruption of Another* Robson 2003
Hanna, Willard A.	*Banda – A Journey Thorugh Indonesian's Fabled Isles of Fire and Spice* Yayasan Warisan dan Budaya Banda 1997
Hanna, Willard A.	*Indonesian Banda – Colonialism and its Aftermath in the Nutmeg Islands* Philadelphia, 1978
Hanna, Willard A. & Alwi, Des	*Turbulent Times Past in Ternate and Tidore* Yayasan Warisan dan Budaya (Banda Neira) 1990
Heuken, A.	*Historical Sites of Jakarta* Cipta Loka Caraka 1982
Horridge, Adrian	*The Prahu – Traditional Sailing Boat of Indonesia* Oxford University Press 1981
Keay, John	*The Honorable Company – A History Of The English East India Company* Harper Collins 1991
Keay, John	*The Spice Route – a History* John Murray 2005
Kemp, Dixon	*Manual of Yacht and Boat Sailing and Architecture* 11th edition, Cox, 1913
Kemp, P. (ed)	*The Oxford Companion to Ships and the Sea* Oxford University Press 1988

Leys, Simon — *The Wreck of the Batavia & Prosper* Black Inc., 2005

Lombard, Denys — *Regard Nouveau sur les "Pirates Malais" 1ère motié du XIXe s.*

Macknight, C.C. & Mukhlis — *A Bugis Manuscript About Praus*

Mann, Richard — *The British in Indonesia* Gateway Books 2004

McHugh, Evan — *Shipwrecks: Australia's Greatest Maritime Disasters* Penguin Austalia 2003

McKenna, Robert — *The Dictionary of Nautical Literacy* McGraw Hill 2001

Merrillees, Scott — *Batavia in Nineteenth Century Photographs* Curzon Press 2000

Milton, Giles — *Nathanial's Nutmeg* Hodder and Stoughton 1999

Muller, Kal — *Spice Islands: The Moluccas* Periplus 1990

Nieuwenhuys, Rob — *Mirror of the Indies* Periplus (HK) Ltd 1999

Parry, David (Intro) — *Exhibition of Antiquarian Maps & Prints of Indonesia* Yayasan Gedung Arsip Nasional RI 2003

Pringle, Robert — *Rajahs and Rebels – The Ibans of Sarawak Under Brooke Rule 1841–1941* Cornell University Press 1970

Ross, R.M. — *A Guide to Pompallier House* New Zealand Historical Places Trust 1970

Rubin, Alfred P. — *Piracy, Paramountcy and Protectorates* Penerbit Universiti Malaya Kuala Lumpur 1974

Runciman, Steven — *The White Rajahs – A History of Sarawak from 1841–1946* Cambridge University Press 1960

Rutter, Owen — *The Pirate Wind – Tales of the Sea-Robbers of Malaya* Hutchinson & Co., 1930

Seabrook, John — *Soldiers and Spice* In: The New Yorker August 13, 2001

Sherry, Norman — *Conrad's Eastern World* Cambridge University Press 1966

Stephenson, N.G. & A.B. — *Samuel Stephenson Pioneer Merchant of Russell 1804 – 1885* Auckland 1984

Stockdale, John J. — *Island of Java* Periplus Hong Kong 1995

Tarling, Nicholas — *Piracy and Politics in the Malay World – A Study of British Imperialism in Nineteenth Century South-East Asia* Cheshire 1963

Thorn, Major William — *The Conquest of Java: Nineteenth-century Java seen through the eyes of a soldier of the British Empire* Periplus 1993

Trocki, Carl A. — *Prince of Pirates – The Temenggongs and the Development of Johor and Singapore* Singapore University Press 1979

Turner, Jack — *Spice – The History of a Temptation* Harper Perennial 2005

Wallace, Alfred R. — *The Malay Archipelago* Periplus Editions (HK) Ltd 2000

Warren, James F. — *The Sulu Zone 1768–1898 – The Dynamics of External Trade, Slavery, and Ethnicity in the Transformation of a Southeast Asian Maritime State* Singapore University Press 1981

Winchester, Simon — *Krakatoa: The Day the World Exploded* Penguin 2003

Wurtzburg, C.E. — *Raffles of the Eastern Isles* Singapore Oxford University Press 1984

Young, Charles F.T. — *The Fouling and Corrosion of Iron Ships: Their Causes and Means of Prevention, with Mode of Application to the Existing Iron-Clads* The London Drawing Association, London 1867

INDEX

The abbreviation PS is used to represent Pamela Stephenson as in:
Stephenson, Neville [PS father] 18–19, 21

PICTURE CREDITS

The Orion Publishing Group has made every effort to correctly credit all the photographs used in this book, and shall, if notified, make any amendments in future editions.

Peter Allibone: 66, 68a, 68b, 69a, 69b, 83, 86, 87b, 91, 97, 98, 99 (all), 100 (both), 101, 106a, 106b, 106e, 108b, 112b, 115, 117a, 122a, 122b, 126, 134a 141b 142–143, 147, 150b, 166, 177c, 178, 180a, 184, 189, 190, 192, 193; **Tessa Bickford**: 70, 71, 87a, 102, 104, 120c, 117b, 117c, 118a, 118b, 119, 129, 134a, 134b, 135, 139, 145 (both), 148, 151, 152, 155a, 157 (both), 158, 162, 163a, 163b, 163d, 163e, 163f, 170, 171, 174, 175, 177b, 180c, 181, 182, 183, 224–225, 226, 239; **Richard Butler**: 55b, 81, 105, 137, 172c, 191, 198, 201, 202 (both), 203. 204, 205a, 206 (all), 212, 213, 214, 218–219, 228–229; **Bettman/Corbis**: 22, 32; Michael S. **Yamashita/Corbis**: 51; **Reuters/Corbis**: 167; **Long Way Round**: 27, 33a, 33b, 34, 38a, 38b, 44, 46, 48, 55a, 56, 58, 59, 62, 64, 65 (all), 67, 76, 84a, 84b, 85, 94, 105, 110a, 124, 125 (both), 131b, 131c, 132, 138, 147b, 150a, 155b, 173c, 185 (both), 186a, 188, 197 (both), 205b, 208–9, 210; **Dr Teariki Puni**: 41, 92 (both), 93a, 96, 97a, 106e, 108c, 121, 127, 128b, 131a, 141a, 144 (both), 147a, 150b, 156, 163c, 165, 171a, 199; **Susan Rann**: 80, 93b, 105, 106c, 106d, 108a, 110b, 112a, 116, 120a, 120b, 128a, 177a, 180b; **Pamela Stephenson**: 17, 19, 20, 21a, 21b, 25, 60, 73, 130, 160, 173a, 186b, 187; **W&N Archive**: 10–11, 12–13, 28, 43, 52

ACKNOWLEDGMENTS

To start with, my late father and my cousin Brett Stephenson were responsible for a solid piece of research compiled in their booklet about Salty Sam's son entitled *Samuel Stephenson: Pioneer Merchant of Russell*. This sets out my family's 19th century history in New Zealand, and a brief version of Salty Sam's story as I previously understood it. Secondly, I don't know what mischievous spirit engineered the quirk of fate by which I met Trudy Adam, who also had an ancestor aboard the *Rosalie*, but I shall be eternally grateful to my late friend for the Big Question Mark – and for granting me an interview during her last, difficult weeks on earth – with the kind assistance of her daughter Fiona.

Russ Malkin made it possible for me to fund and record the expedition, and I am very thankful to him for his energy, enthusiasm and expertise. Lucy managed the project with extraordinary efficiency and zeal, while Lisa, Robin, Ollie and others from the Long Way Round office infused the project with similar gusto and hard work. My representatives John Webber, Robert Kirby and Alan Edwards provided crucial contacts, advice and guidance. I am likewise very grateful to the people at Sky Television, and also EMI; and to the Australian Broadcasting Commission (in particular Marena Manzoufas) for their touching belief in me and support for the entire venture.

In my research efforts, my thanks are especially due to Anne Bulley for her marvellous insights, findings and tireless endeavours on our behalf. Many other researchers and historians informed my journey, and I am particularly grateful to Penny Brooke, Dr Alistair Cook, Tony Farrington and others at the British Library; to Admiral Sir Alan West; to Commander Rod Craig and Priya Sohanpaul at the Honourable Company of Master Mariners; to Captain Chris Page, Iain McKenzie and Jenny Waight at the Naval Historical Branch of the Ministry of Defence; David Colquhoun and his staff at the Alexander Turnbull Library (National Library of New Zealand); to Obay Sobari; to Marleene Boyd and Pam Smith at the National Maritime Museum, Auckland; to Rose Young at the Auckland War Museum; Bruce Ralston at the Auckland Museum; to Cees Von Burgh and Anita Scheltinga at the Royal Library in The Hague; to Jan W. H. Werner at the University Library in The Hague; to maritime experts from HMS *Trincomalee* at Hartlepool; as well as to Leila Lak, Giles Milton, and expert cartographer W. V. Stormbroek. In Indonesia, Professor Adrian Lapian, Lawrence Blair, Debe Campbell, Deborah Carbonetti and Glen Crandall all made outstanding contributions to our body of knowledge.

When it came to actually setting sail, my fantastic band of fellow-adventurers bravely faced all the challenging demands of derring do – *Takapuna*'s sailing crew, security team and TV crew. I will never forget their dedication, and they are to be especially commended for agreeing to undergo such hardships under the scrutiny of the TV cameras. I am particularly grateful to the *Takapuna*'s former captain for simply being himself and allowing our on-board drama to unfold the way it did.

Experts and helpers in various fields played key roles in the success of this expedition, including administrators and instructors at the TAFE Queensland Institute, Don Wilson and the Queensland Fire and Rescue Department; Annette Burke, Mayor of Palmerston; Ted Egan, the Administrator of the Northern Territory and Ms Nerys Evans; Teresa Robson, Government House Darwin; as well as Dr Tim Huxley, Des Alwi, Paul Hicks, Pascal Kainic, Chris

Sargeant, Jim Foster, Troy Clarry, Mark Hughes and Len Zell. Thanks to all who have taken photos, including Tessa Bickford (who took the cover shot), Richard Butler, Jim Foster, Russ Malkin, Dr Teariki Puni, Pete Allibone, Susan Rann and Debe Campbell.

A great many Indonesian people helped us as guides, advisors, pilots, shipping agents, and protectors. I am thankful to Ainul and Yayak from the Tourism Department in Lombok, to Made and our driver in Bali, to Teguh, Hengke, Sumardi, Mr Sam, Hans and Helena. I would like to express my appreciation towards the people of Cairns, Darwin, Java, Kupang, Banda, Ambon, Ternate, Manado, Makassar, Bali, and Lombok (especially the residents of Labuhan Luar, Pijot, and Labuhan Haji) for their hospitality, assistance, and for allowing us to record them. In addition, I would like to thank Gill and David at the Ritz Carlton Hotel in Bali for their many kindnesses.

Dr Teariki Puni provided an inspirational level of support – even when I myself was flagging – for which I thank him from the bottom of my heart. Likewise, I appreciate my cousin Alistair for his unconditional help and understanding. I also received help from many other family members, incuding Deborah Townend and Brenda Jenkins. Paul and Martine at Candacraig; Steve, Natalie, Christiana and Melissa at Tickety-Boo, and Sheree and Christina at Premier Business Management, all remained my unfailing back-ups during my travels. Above all, Sharon and Dennis Dugan most generously provided a haven for my youngest daughter while I was away.

When it came to completing this book, I am immensely grateful to my marvellously insightful guide Michael Dover and editor Sue Webb. My very special thanks to Senior Editor Robin Douglas-Withers who tirelessly co-ordinated the terrific efforts of Art Director David Rowley and his in-house team, in particular Justin Hunt and Tony Chung; to designer Rob Hackett and others at Two Associates; to map-creator Nick Robertson – and indeed to the entire Orion team. Dr Dennis Sugrue kindly read the manuscript.

Finally, I continue to be utterly humbled by the way my husband and children have so lovingly supported my nutty adventures, sometimes even against their own needs, preferences and judgment. I'll make it up to you all one day; I promise.

First published in Great Britain in 2006 by Weidenfeld & Nicolson
10 9 8 7 6 5 4 3 2 1

ISBN-13: 9-780-29784-443-3
ISBN-10: 0-29784-443-1

Senior Editor: Robin Douglas-Withers
Editor: Sue Webb
Design Director: David Rowley
Design: Rob Hackett, Two Associates
Design assistance: Justin Hunt and Tony Chung
Maps: Nick Robertson

Repro by DL Interactive UK
Printed and bound in Spain by Cayfosa-Quebecor

Weidenfeld & Nicolson
The Orion Publishing Group Limited
Orion House
5 Upper Saint Martin's Lane
London WC2H 9EA